Mometrix TEST PREPARATION

MTTC

Business Management Marketing and Technology (98) Test

Secrets Study Guide

This product was developed by Mometrix Test Preparation. It was not developed in connection with Pearson Education, Inc., nor was it reviewed, approved or endorsed by these agencies.

DEAR FUTURE EXAM SUCCESS STORY

First of all, **THANK YOU** for purchasing Mometrix study materials!

Second, congratulations! You are one of the few determined test-takers who are committed to doing whatever it takes to excel on your exam. **You have come to the right place.** We developed these study materials with one goal in mind: to deliver you the information you need in a format that's concise and easy to use.

In addition to optimizing your guide for the content of the test, we've outlined our recommended steps for breaking down the preparation process into small, attainable goals so you can make sure you stay on track.

We've also analyzed the entire test-taking process, identifying the most common pitfalls and showing how you can overcome them and be ready for any curveball the test throws you.

Standardized testing is one of the biggest obstacles on your road to success, which only increases the importance of doing well in the high-pressure, high-stakes environment of test day. Your results on this test could have a significant impact on your future, and this guide provides the information and practical advice to help you achieve your full potential on test day.

Your success is our success

We would love to hear from you! If you would like to share the story of your exam success or if you have any questions or comments in regard to our products, please contact us at **800-673-8175** or **support@mometrix.com**.

Thanks again for your business and we wish you continued success!

Sincerely,
The Mometrix Test Preparation Team

Need more help? Check out our flashcards at:
http://MometrixFlashcards.com/MTTC

Copyright © 2026 by Mometrix Media LLC. All rights reserved.
Written and edited by the Mometrix Exam Secrets Test Prep Team
Printed in the United States of America

TABLE OF CONTENTS

Introduction

Thank you for purchasing this resource! You have made the choice to prepare yourself for a test that could have a huge impact on your future, and this guide is designed to help you be fully ready for test day. Obviously, it's important to have a solid understanding of the test material, but you also need to be prepared for the unique environment and stressors of the test, so that you can perform to the best of your abilities.

For this purpose, the first section that appears in this guide is the **Secret Keys**. We've devoted countless hours to meticulously researching what works and what doesn't, and we've boiled down our findings to the five most impactful steps you can take to improve your performance on the test. We start at the beginning with study planning and move through the preparation process, all the way to the testing strategies that will help you get the most out of what you know when you're finally sitting in front of the test.

We recommend that you start preparing for your test as far in advance as possible. However, if you've bought this guide as a last-minute study resource and only have a few days before your test, we recommend that you skip over the first two Secret Keys since they address a long-term study plan.

If you struggle with **test anxiety**, we strongly encourage you to check out our recommendations for how you can overcome it. Test anxiety is a formidable foe, but it can be beaten, and we want to make sure you have the tools you need to defeat it.

Copyright © Mometrix Media. You have been licensed one copy of this document for personal use only. Any other reproduction or redistribution is strictly prohibited. All rights reserved.
This content is provided for test preparation purposes only and does not imply an endorsement by Mometrix of any particular political, scientific, or religious point of view.

Secret Key #1 – Plan Big, Study Small

There's a lot riding on your performance. If you want to ace this test, you're going to need to keep your skills sharp and the material fresh in your mind. You need a plan that lets you review everything you need to know while still fitting in your schedule. We'll break this strategy down into three categories.

Information Organization

Start with the information you already have: the official test outline. From this, you can make a complete list of all the concepts you need to cover before the test. Organize these concepts into groups that can be studied together, and create a list of any related vocabulary you need to learn so you can brush up on any difficult terms. You'll want to keep this vocabulary list handy once you actually start studying since you may need to add to it along the way.

Time Management

Once you have your set of study concepts, decide how to spread them out over the time you have left before the test. Break your study plan into small, clear goals so you have a manageable task for each day and know exactly what you're doing. Then just focus on one small step at a time. When you manage your time this way, you don't need to spend hours at a time studying. Studying a small block of content for a short period each day helps you retain information better and avoid stressing over how much you have left to do. You can relax knowing that you have a plan to cover everything in time. In order for this strategy to be effective though, you have to start studying early and stick to your schedule. Avoid the exhaustion and futility that comes from last-minute cramming!

Study Environment

The environment you study in has a big impact on your learning. Studying in a coffee shop, while probably more enjoyable, is not likely to be as fruitful as studying in a quiet room. It's important to keep distractions to a minimum. You're only planning to study for a short block of time, so make the most of it. Don't pause to check your phone or get up to find a snack. It's also important to **avoid multitasking**. Research has consistently shown that multitasking will make your studying dramatically less effective. Your study area should also be comfortable and well-lit so you don't have the distraction of straining your eyes or sitting on an uncomfortable chair.

The time of day you study is also important. You want to be rested and alert. Don't wait until just before bedtime. Study when you'll be most likely to comprehend and remember. Even better, if you know what time of day your test will be, set that time aside for study. That way your brain will be used to working on that subject at that specific time and you'll have a better chance of recalling information.

Finally, it can be helpful to team up with others who are studying for the same test. Your actual studying should be done in as isolated an environment as possible, but the work of organizing the information and setting up the study plan can be divided up. In between study sessions, you can discuss with your teammates the concepts that you're all studying and quiz each other on the details. Just be sure that your teammates are as serious about the test as you are. If you find that your study time is being replaced with social time, you might need to find a new team.

Copyright © Mometrix Media. You have been licensed one copy of this document for personal use only. Any other reproduction or redistribution is strictly prohibited. All rights reserved.
This content is provided for test preparation purposes only and does not imply an endorsement by Mometrix of any particular political, scientific, or religious point of view.

Secret Key #2 – Make Your Studying Count

You're devoting a lot of time and effort to preparing for this test, so you want to be absolutely certain it will pay off. This means doing more than just reading the content and hoping you can remember it on test day. It's important to make every minute of study count. There are two main areas you can focus on to make your studying count.

Retention

It doesn't matter how much time you study if you can't remember the material. You need to make sure you are retaining the concepts. To check your retention of the information you're learning, try recalling it at later times with minimal prompting. Try carrying around flashcards and glance at one or two from time to time or ask a friend who's also studying for the test to quiz you.

To enhance your retention, look for ways to put the information into practice so that you can apply it rather than simply recalling it. If you're using the information in practical ways, it will be much easier to remember. Similarly, it helps to solidify a concept in your mind if you're not only reading it to yourself but also explaining it to someone else. Ask a friend to let you teach them about a concept you're a little shaky on (or speak aloud to an imaginary audience if necessary). As you try to summarize, define, give examples, and answer your friend's questions, you'll understand the concepts better and they will stay with you longer. Finally, step back for a big picture view and ask yourself how each piece of information fits with the whole subject. When you link the different concepts together and see them working together as a whole, it's easier to remember the individual components.

Finally, practice showing your work on any multi-step problems, even if you're just studying. Writing out each step you take to solve a problem will help solidify the process in your mind, and you'll be more likely to remember it during the test.

Modality

Modality simply refers to the means or method by which you study. Choosing a study modality that fits your own individual learning style is crucial. No two people learn best in exactly the same way, so it's important to know your strengths and use them to your advantage.

For example, if you learn best by visualization, focus on visualizing a concept in your mind and draw an image or a diagram. Try color-coding your notes, illustrating them, or creating symbols that will trigger your mind to recall a learned concept. If you learn best by hearing or discussing information, find a study partner who learns the same way or read aloud to yourself. Think about how to put the information in your own words. Imagine that you are giving a lecture on the topic and record yourself so you can listen to it later.

For any learning style, flashcards can be helpful. Organize the information so you can take advantage of spare moments to review. Underline key words or phrases. Use different colors for different categories. Mnemonic devices (such as creating a short list in which every item starts with the same letter) can also help with retention. Find what works best for you and use it to store the information in your mind most effectively and easily.

Copyright © Mometrix Media. You have been licensed one copy of this document for personal use only. Any other reproduction or redistribution is strictly prohibited. All rights reserved.
This content is provided for test preparation purposes only and does not imply an endorsement by Mometrix of any particular political, scientific, or religious point of view.

Secret Key #3 – Practice the Right Way

Your success on test day depends not only on how many hours you put into preparing, but also on whether you prepared the right way. It's good to check along the way to see if your studying is paying off. One of the most effective ways to do this is by taking practice tests to evaluate your progress. Practice tests are useful because they show exactly where you need to improve. Every time you take a practice test, pay special attention to these three groups of questions:

- The questions you got wrong
- The questions you had to guess on, even if you guessed right
- The questions you found difficult or slow to work through

This will show you exactly what your weak areas are, and where you need to devote more study time. Ask yourself why each of these questions gave you trouble. Was it because you didn't understand the material? Was it because you didn't remember the vocabulary? Do you need more repetitions on this type of question to build speed and confidence? Dig into those questions and figure out how you can strengthen your weak areas as you go back to review the material.

Additionally, many practice tests have a section explaining the answer choices. It can be tempting to read the explanation and think that you now have a good understanding of the concept. However, an explanation likely only covers part of the question's broader context. Even if the explanation makes perfect sense, **go back and investigate** every concept related to the question until you're positive you have a thorough understanding.

As you go along, keep in mind that the practice test is just that: practice. Memorizing these questions and answers will not be very helpful on the actual test because it is unlikely to have any of the same exact questions. If you only know the right answers to the sample questions, you won't be prepared for the real thing. **Study the concepts** until you understand them fully, and then you'll be able to answer any question that shows up on the test.

It's important to wait on the practice tests until you're ready. If you take a test on your first day of study, you may be overwhelmed by the amount of material covered and how much you need to learn. Work up to it gradually.

On test day, you'll need to be prepared for answering questions, managing your time, and using the test-taking strategies you've learned. It's a lot to balance, like a mental marathon that will have a big impact on your future. Like training for a marathon, you'll need to start slowly and work your way up. When test day arrives, you'll be ready.

Start with the strategies you've read in the first two Secret Keys—plan your course and study in the way that works best for you. If you have time, consider using multiple study resources to get different approaches to the same concepts. It can be helpful to see difficult concepts from more than one angle. Then find a good source for practice tests. Many times, the test website will suggest potential study resources or provide sample tests.

Copyright © Mometrix Media. You have been licensed one copy of this document for personal use only. Any other reproduction or redistribution is strictly prohibited. All rights reserved.
This content is provided for test preparation purposes only and does not imply an endorsement by Mometrix of any particular political, scientific, or religious point of view.

Practice Test Strategy

If you're able to find at least three practice tests, we recommend this strategy:

Untimed and Open-Book Practice

Take the first test with no time constraints and with your notes and study guide handy. Take your time and focus on applying the strategies you've learned.

Timed and Open-Book Practice

Take the second practice test open-book as well, but set a timer and practice pacing yourself to finish in time.

Timed and Closed-Book Practice

Take any other practice tests as if it were test day. Set a timer and put away your study materials. Sit at a table or desk in a quiet room, imagine yourself at the testing center, and answer questions as quickly and accurately as possible.

Keep repeating timed and closed-book tests on a regular basis until you run out of practice tests or it's time for the actual test. Your mind will be ready for the schedule and stress of test day, and you'll be able to focus on recalling the material you've learned.

Copyright © Mometrix Media. You have been licensed one copy of this document for personal use only. Any other reproduction or redistribution is strictly prohibited. All rights reserved.
This content is provided for test preparation purposes only and does not imply an endorsement by Mometrix of any particular political, scientific, or religious point of view.

Secret Key #4 – Pace Yourself

Once you're fully prepared for the material on the test, your biggest challenge on test day will be managing your time. Just knowing that the clock is ticking can make you panic even if you have plenty of time left. Work on pacing yourself so you can build confidence against the time constraints of the exam. Pacing is a difficult skill to master, especially in a high-pressure environment, so **practice is vital**.

Set time expectations for your pace based on how much time is available. For example, if a section has 60 questions and the time limit is 30 minutes, you know you have to average 30 seconds or less per question in order to answer them all. Although 30 seconds is the hard limit, set 25 seconds per question as your goal, so you reserve extra time to spend on harder questions. When you budget extra time for the harder questions, you no longer have any reason to stress when those questions take longer to answer.

Don't let this time expectation distract you from working through the test at a calm, steady pace, but keep it in mind so you don't spend too much time on any one question. Recognize that taking extra time on one question you don't understand may keep you from answering two that you do understand later in the test. If your time limit for a question is up and you're still not sure of the answer, mark it and move on, and come back to it later if the time and the test format allow. If the testing format doesn't allow you to return to earlier questions, just make an educated guess; then put it out of your mind and move on.

On the easier questions, be careful not to rush. It may seem wise to hurry through them so you have more time for the challenging ones, but it's not worth missing one if you know the concept and just didn't take the time to read the question fully. Work efficiently but make sure you understand the question and have looked at all of the answer choices, since more than one may seem right at first.

Even if you're paying attention to the time, you may find yourself a little behind at some point. You should speed up to get back on track, but do so wisely. Don't panic; just take a few seconds less on each question until you're caught up. Don't guess without thinking, but do look through the answer choices and eliminate any you know are wrong. If you can get down to two choices, it is often worthwhile to guess from those. Once you've chosen an answer, move on and don't dwell on any that you skipped or had to hurry through. If a question was taking too long, chances are it was one of the harder ones, so you weren't as likely to get it right anyway.

On the other hand, if you find yourself getting ahead of schedule, it may be beneficial to slow down a little. The more quickly you work, the more likely you are to make a careless mistake that will affect your score. You've budgeted time for each question, so don't be afraid to spend that time. Practice an efficient but careful pace to get the most out of the time you have.

Copyright © Mometrix Media. You have been licensed one copy of this document for personal use only. Any other reproduction or redistribution is strictly prohibited. All rights reserved.
This content is provided for test preparation purposes only and does not imply an endorsement by Mometrix of any particular political, scientific, or religious point of view.

Secret Key #5 – Have a Plan for Guessing

When you're taking the test, you may find yourself stuck on a question. Some of the answer choices seem better than others, but you don't see the one answer choice that is obviously correct. What do you do?

The scenario described above is very common, yet most test takers have not effectively prepared for it. Developing and practicing a plan for guessing may be one of the single most effective uses of your time as you get ready for the exam.

In developing your plan for guessing, there are three questions to address:

- When should you start the guessing process?
- How should you narrow down the choices?
- Which answer should you choose?

When to Start the Guessing Process

Unless your plan for guessing is to select C every time (which, despite its merits, is not what we recommend), you need to leave yourself enough time to apply your answer elimination strategies. Since you have a limited amount of time for each question, that means that if you're going to give yourself the best shot at guessing correctly, you have to decide quickly whether or not you will guess.

Of course, the best-case scenario is that you don't have to guess at all, so first, see if you can answer the question based on your knowledge of the subject and basic reasoning skills. Focus on the key words in the question and try to jog your memory of related topics. Give yourself a chance to bring the knowledge to mind, but once you realize that you don't have (or you can't access) the knowledge you need to answer the question, it's time to start the guessing process.

It's almost always better to start the guessing process too early than too late. It only takes a few seconds to remember something and answer the question from knowledge. Carefully eliminating wrong answer choices takes longer. Plus, going through the process of eliminating answer choices can actually help jog your memory.

Summary: Start the guessing process as soon as you decide that you can't answer the question based on your knowledge.

Copyright © Mometrix Media. You have been licensed one copy of this document for personal use only. Any other reproduction or redistribution is strictly prohibited. All rights reserved.
This content is provided for test preparation purposes only and does not imply an endorsement by Mometrix of any particular political, scientific, or religious point of view.

How to Narrow Down the Choices

The next chapter in this book (**Test-Taking Strategies**) includes a wide range of strategies for how to approach questions and how to look for answer choices to eliminate. You will definitely want to read those carefully, practice them, and figure out which ones work best for you. Here though, we're going to address a mindset rather than a particular strategy.

Your odds of guessing an answer correctly depend on how many options you are choosing from.

Number of options left	5	4	3	2	1
Odds of guessing correctly	20%	25%	33%	50%	100%

You can see from this chart just how valuable it is to be able to eliminate incorrect answers and make an educated guess, but there are two things that many test takers do that cause them to miss out on the benefits of guessing:

- Accidentally eliminating the correct answer
- Selecting an answer based on an impression

We'll look at the first one here, and the second one in the next section.

To avoid accidentally eliminating the correct answer, we recommend a thought exercise called **the $5 challenge**. In this challenge, you only eliminate an answer choice from contention if you are willing to bet $5 on it being wrong. Why $5? Five dollars is a small but not insignificant amount of money. It's an amount you could afford to lose but wouldn't want to throw away. And while losing $5 once might not hurt too much, doing it twenty times will set you back $100. In the same way, each small decision you make—eliminating a choice here, guessing on a question there—won't by itself impact your score very much, but when you put them all together, they can make a big difference. By holding each answer choice elimination decision to a higher standard, you can reduce the risk of accidentally eliminating the correct answer.

The $5 challenge can also be applied in a positive sense: If you are willing to bet $5 that an answer choice *is* correct, go ahead and mark it as correct.

Summary: Only eliminate an answer choice if you are willing to bet $5 that it is wrong.

Copyright © Mometrix Media. You have been licensed one copy of this document for personal use only. Any other reproduction or redistribution is strictly prohibited. All rights reserved.
This content is provided for test preparation purposes only and does not imply an endorsement by Mometrix of any particular political, scientific, or religious point of view.

Which Answer to Choose

You're taking the test. You've run into a hard question and decided you'll have to guess. You've eliminated all the answer choices you're willing to bet $5 on. Now you have to pick an answer. Why do we even need to talk about this? Why can't you just pick whichever one you feel like when the time comes?

The answer to these questions is that if you don't come into the test with a plan, you'll rely on your impression to select an answer choice, and if you do that, you risk falling into a trap. The test writers know that everyone who takes their test will be guessing on some of the questions, so they intentionally write wrong answer choices to seem plausible. You still have to pick an answer though, and if the wrong answer choices are designed to look right, how can you ever be sure that you're not falling for their trap? The best solution we've found to this dilemma is to take the decision out of your hands entirely. Here is the process we recommend:

Once you've eliminated any choices that you are confident (willing to bet $5) are wrong, select the first remaining choice as your answer.

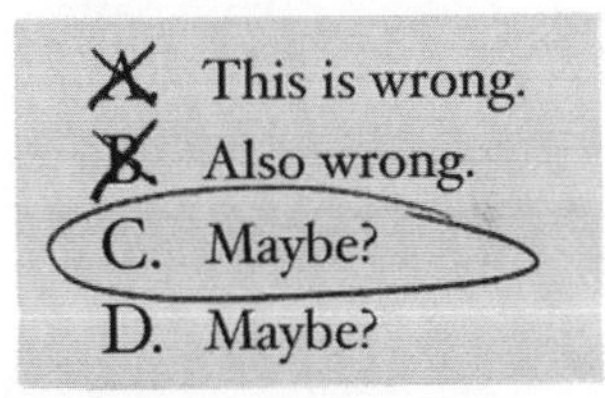

Whether you choose to select the first remaining choice, the second, or the last, the important thing is that you use some preselected standard. Using this approach guarantees that you will not be enticed into selecting an answer choice that looks right, because you are not basing your decision on how the answer choices look.

This is not meant to make you question your knowledge. Instead, it is to help you recognize the difference between your knowledge and your impressions. There's a huge difference between thinking an answer is right because of what you know, and thinking an answer is right because it looks or sounds like it should be right.

Summary: To ensure that your selection is appropriately random, make a predetermined selection from among all answer choices you have not eliminated.

Copyright © Mometrix Media. You have been licensed one copy of this document for personal use only. Any other reproduction or redistribution is strictly prohibited. All rights reserved.
This content is provided for test preparation purposes only and does not imply an endorsement by Mometrix of any particular political, scientific, or religious point of view.

Test-Taking Strategies

This section contains a list of test-taking strategies that you may find helpful as you work through the test. By taking what you know and applying logical thought, you can maximize your chances of answering any question correctly!

It is very important to realize that every question is different and every person is different: no single strategy will work on every question, and no single strategy will work for every person. That's why we've included all of them here, so you can try them out and determine which ones work best for different types of questions and which ones work best for you.

Question Strategies

Read Carefully

Read the question and the answer choices carefully. Don't miss the question because you misread the terms. You have plenty of time to read each question thoroughly and make sure you understand what is being asked. Yet a happy medium must be attained, so don't waste too much time. You must read carefully and efficiently.

Contextual Clues

Look for contextual clues. If the question includes a word you are not familiar with, look at the immediate context for some indication of what the word might mean. Contextual clues can often give you all the information you need to decipher the meaning of an unfamiliar word. Even if you can't determine the meaning, you may be able to narrow down the possibilities enough to make a solid guess at the answer to the question.

Prefixes

If you're having trouble with a word in the question or answer choices, try dissecting it. Take advantage of every clue that the word might include. Prefixes can be a huge help. Usually, they allow you to determine a basic meaning. *Pre-* means before, *post-* means after, *pro-* is positive, *de-* is negative. From prefixes, you can get an idea of the general meaning of the word and try to put it into context.

Hedge Words

Watch out for critical hedge words, such as *likely, may, can, often, almost, mostly, usually, generally, rarely*, and *sometimes*. Question writers insert these hedge phrases to cover every possibility. Often an answer choice will be wrong simply because it leaves no room for exception. Be on guard for answer choices that have definitive words such as *exactly* and *always*.

Switchback Words

Stay alert for *switchbacks*. These are the words and phrases frequently used to alert you to shifts in thought. The most common switchback words are *but, although*, and *however*. Others include *nevertheless, on the other hand, even though, while, in spite of, despite*, and *regardless of*. Switchback words are important to catch because they can change the direction of the question or an answer choice.

Copyright © Mometrix Media. You have been licensed one copy of this document for personal use only. Any other reproduction or redistribution is strictly prohibited. All rights reserved.
This content is provided for test preparation purposes only and does not imply an endorsement by Mometrix of any particular political, scientific, or religious point of view.

✓ Face Value

When in doubt, use common sense. Accept the situation in the problem at face value. Don't read too much into it. These problems will not require you to make wild assumptions. If you have to go beyond creativity and warp time or space in order to have an answer choice fit the question, then you should move on and consider the other answer choices. These are normal problems rooted in reality. The applicable relationship or explanation may not be readily apparent, but it is there for you to figure out. Use your common sense to interpret anything that isn't clear.

Answer Choice Strategies

✓ Answer Selection

The most thorough way to pick an answer choice is to identify and eliminate wrong answers until only one is left, then confirm it is the correct answer. Sometimes an answer choice may immediately seem right, but be careful. The test writers will usually put more than one reasonable answer choice on each question, so take a second to read all of them and make sure that the other choices are not equally obvious. As long as you have time left, it is better to read every answer choice than to pick the first one that looks right without checking the others.

✓ Answer Choice Families

An answer choice family consists of two (in rare cases, three) answer choices that are very similar in construction and cannot all be true at the same time. If you see two answer choices that are direct opposites or parallels, one of them is usually the correct answer. For instance, if one answer choice says that quantity *x* increases and another either says that quantity *x* decreases (opposite) or says that quantity *y* increases (parallel), then those answer choices would fall into the same family. An answer choice that doesn't match the construction of the answer choice family is more likely to be incorrect. Most questions will not have answer choice families, but when they do appear, you should be prepared to recognize them.

✓ Eliminate Answers

Eliminate answer choices as soon as you realize they are wrong, but make sure you consider all possibilities. If you are eliminating answer choices and realize that the last one you are left with is also wrong, don't panic. Start over and consider each choice again. There may be something you missed the first time that you will realize on the second pass.

✓ Avoid Fact Traps

Don't be distracted by an answer choice that is factually true but doesn't answer the question. You are looking for the choice that answers the question. Stay focused on what the question is asking for so you don't accidentally pick an answer that is true but incorrect. Always go back to the question and make sure the answer choice you've selected actually answers the question and is not merely a true statement.

✓ Extreme Statements

In general, you should avoid answers that put forth extreme actions as standard practice or proclaim controversial ideas as established fact. An answer choice that states the "process should be used in certain situations, if…" is much more likely to be correct than one that states the "process should be discontinued completely." The first is a calm rational statement and doesn't even make a definitive, uncompromising stance, using a hedge word *if* to provide wiggle room, whereas the second choice is far more extreme.

Copyright © Mometrix Media. You have been licensed one copy of this document for personal use only. Any other reproduction or redistribution is strictly prohibited. All rights reserved.
This content is provided for test preparation purposes only and does not imply an endorsement by Mometrix of any particular political, scientific, or religious point of view.

⊘ Benchmark

As you read through the answer choices and you come across one that seems to answer the question well, mentally select that answer choice. This is not your final answer, but it's the one that will help you evaluate the other answer choices. The one that you selected is your benchmark or standard for judging each of the other answer choices. Every other answer choice must be compared to your benchmark. That choice is correct until proven otherwise by another answer choice beating it. If you find a better answer, then that one becomes your new benchmark. Once you've decided that no other choice answers the question as well as your benchmark, you have your final answer.

⊘ Predict the Answer

Before you even start looking at the answer choices, it is often best to try to predict the answer. When you come up with the answer on your own, it is easier to avoid distractions and traps because you will know exactly what to look for. The right answer choice is unlikely to be word-for-word what you came up with, but it should be a close match. Even if you are confident that you have the right answer, you should still take the time to read each option before moving on.

General Strategies

⊘ Tough Questions

If you are stumped on a problem or it appears too hard or too difficult, don't waste time. Move on! Remember though, if you can quickly check for obviously incorrect answer choices, your chances of guessing correctly are greatly improved. Before you completely give up, at least try to knock out a couple of possible answers. Eliminate what you can and then guess at the remaining answer choices before moving on.

⊘ Check Your Work

Since you will probably not know every term listed and the answer to every question, it is important that you get credit for the ones that you do know. Don't miss any questions through careless mistakes. If at all possible, try to take a second to look back over your answer selection and make sure you've selected the correct answer choice and haven't made a costly careless mistake (such as marking an answer choice that you didn't mean to mark). This quick double check should more than pay for itself in caught mistakes for the time it costs.

⊘ Pace Yourself

It's easy to be overwhelmed when you're looking at a page full of questions; your mind is confused and full of random thoughts, and the clock is ticking down faster than you would like. Calm down and maintain the pace that you have set for yourself. Especially as you get down to the last few minutes of the test, don't let the small numbers on the clock make you panic. As long as you are on track by monitoring your pace, you are guaranteed to have time for each question.

⊘ Don't Rush

It is very easy to make errors when you are in a hurry. Maintaining a fast pace in answering questions is pointless if it makes you miss questions that you would have gotten right otherwise. Test writers like to include distracting information and wrong answers that seem right. Taking a little extra time to avoid careless mistakes can make all the difference in your test score. Find a pace that allows you to be confident in the answers that you select.

Copyright © Mometrix Media. You have been licensed one copy of this document for personal use only. Any other reproduction or redistribution is strictly prohibited. All rights reserved.
This content is provided for test preparation purposes only and does not imply an endorsement by Mometrix of any particular political, scientific, or religious point of view.

⊘ KEEP MOVING

Panicking will not help you pass the test, so do your best to stay calm and keep moving. Taking deep breaths and going through the answer elimination steps you practiced can help to break through a stress barrier and keep your pace.

Final Notes

The combination of a solid foundation of content knowledge and the confidence that comes from practicing your plan for applying that knowledge is the key to maximizing your performance on test day. As your foundation of content knowledge is built up and strengthened, you'll find that the strategies included in this chapter become more and more effective in helping you quickly sift through the distractions and traps of the test to isolate the correct answer.

Now that you're preparing to move forward into the test content chapters of this book, be sure to keep your goal in mind. As you read, think about how you will be able to apply this information on the test. If you've already seen sample questions for the test and you have an idea of the question format and style, try to come up with questions of your own that you can answer based on what you're reading. This will give you valuable practice applying your knowledge in the same ways you can expect to on test day.

Good luck and good studying!

Copyright © Mometrix Media. You have been licensed one copy of this document for personal use only. Any other reproduction or redistribution is strictly prohibited. All rights reserved.
This content is provided for test preparation purposes only and does not imply an endorsement by Mometrix of any particular political, scientific, or religious point of view.

Copyright © Mometrix Media. You have been licensed one copy of this document for personal use only. Any other reproduction or redistribution is strictly prohibited. All rights reserved.
This content is provided for test preparation purposes only and does not imply an endorsement by Mometrix of any particular political, scientific, or religious point of view.

Business

Business Law and Ethics

Ethical Issues

Conflicts of Interest

A conflict of interest occurs when a person has two adversary interests, one of which might not be best for his or her business. An example is an employee of a general contractor who is making a decision on which of five bidding subcontractors to choose. If one of the subcontractors is his brother, he will have a conflict of interest because he might want to choose his brother, who might not be the best choice. He might choose his brother over someone better qualified. There are many instances of conflicts of interest in business. Oftentimes they are related to money. A person may accept gifts in exchange for a contract, for example. It is unethical to do something bad for the company because of personal interests. The employee should try to avoid this if possible. For instance, the person who works for the general contractor may ask someone else to make the decision so he doesn't have to choose between his brother and the company.

Privacy of Employees

There are a variety of ethical issues regarding the privacy of employees. Some of it stems from the monitoring of communications. Businesses can monitor employees' business calls, such as when a customer service agent is providing service to a customer, but it is murkier if employees are on personal calls. If employees are not supposed to be making personal calls at work, then employers may have the right to listen. Some people feel that it is not ethical, but then it is also not ethical for employees to spend time on personal matters when they should be working. Most companies monitor internet usage. Again, some people may worry about the ethical issues with privacy, but if it is on company time with company resources, the business could be liable for the employee's actions. A lot of companies perform background checks and drug testing, which is allowed, although there are guidelines in place that must be followed. They must be reasonable. Most companies fulfill ethical duties by getting consent before performing the checks. It is very important for employers to keep records about the employees confidential.

Compensation

Wages should be fair. It is important that one employee not make more or less for the wrong reasons. For instance, it is ethical for a company to pay more to an employee with more experience, but it is not ethical to pay more to a man than a woman solely because of gender. Still, this often happens, as does pay disparity among races, religions, and other categories. Sometimes advocates call out companies in which the top people make an exorbitant amount of money and the lower employees do very poorly. Ethical issues arise when people do not make a living wage. It is important to ensure pay disparity among workers is not occurring for the wrong reasons.

Insider Trading

Illegal insider trading occurs when someone makes a trade while having "insider" information that makes it unfair to other investors. This can occur when a corporate officer discovers something significant about a company and makes a trade because of that information. For instance, an employee may learn of a big problem about to occur and get rid of the stock before the price plummets. Insider trading can also be committed by employee friends, family, and acquaintances; government employees; law or banking employees who deal with a company; or just anyone who manages to obtain the illegal information. It is unethical because it makes it unfair to investors who

Copyright © Mometrix Media. You have been licensed one copy of this document for personal use only. Any other reproduction or redistribution is strictly prohibited. All rights reserved.
This content is provided for test preparation purposes only and does not imply an endorsement by Mometrix of any particular political, scientific, or religious point of view.

have to trade without this information. Insider trading is taken very seriously by the US Securities and Exchange Commission and has serious consequences.

BUSINESS' SOCIAL RESPONSIBILITY

Businesses have a social responsibility to their customers, employees, investors, and society in general. To their employees they should have fair labor practices. Employees should be treated fairly and without discrimination. Those companies that deal with international business have a responsibility to make sure laborers involved in their business are also treated fairly. They also have a responsibility to investors to try to build their money (in socially acceptable ways). To customers they should be fair, putting out quality products without deception. Business practices and tactics should be fair and not deceptive—they should not badmouth a competitor, for instance. There are different ways to be socially responsible to society as a whole. Businesses should have practices that do not harm the environment or animals or create unsafe waste. Many companies also give to charity. Some use fair trade products or sustainably grown and processed products. When companies show socially responsible practices, people take notice and may give them more business. Corporate social responsibility is the business' responsibility to both make money and act in a socially responsible way. This can include economic responsibility, legal responsibility, ethical responsibility and philanthropic responsibility.

CRIMINAL AND CIVIL LAW

Criminal law involves someone accused of a crime. The individual broke a law and did something detrimental to society. Although it might involve a victim, that victim does not have to be the one to bring the case to life; the government (in the form of prosecution) will. There doesn't have to be a victim such as if someone was caught driving under the influence but did not hurt anyone. If the person is found guilty, he may have to pay money, could be sentenced to prison, or (in rare cases) executed. A civil case is a dispute between two parties. They are brought by one party against another because of a failure of a legal duty. The plaintiff may ask for compensation or for the party to fulfill the duty, but the defendant cannot be sentenced to prison or death. They both can occur in local or federal courts. Lawyers can be used for both, but are guaranteed for criminal defendants. Because of the seriousness of criminal law, defendants are presumed innocent and the state must prove the charges beyond a reasonable doubt. It is less difficult to prove guilt in civil cases.

CASE, ADMINISTRATIVE, STATUTORY, CONSTITUTIONAL, AND TORT LAW

Criminal law deals with crimes that are committed. **Case law** refers to the verdicts of courts that can now be used in new court cases to help plead cases and define the law. **Statutory law** refers to codes and statutes the legislative bodies have enacted. **Administrative law** refers to the procedures that administrative agencies create. It is very technical. Different agencies have different procedures and these must be fulfilled before a lawsuit can be brought. **Constitutional law** refers to how the United States Constitution is interpreted and implemented. **Tort law** refers to civil claims that one party brings against another. A plaintiff claims that a defendant harmed him in a way that constitutes a legal liability. Some attorneys specialize in one type of law while others practice a broader range.

LAWSUITS

A **lawsuit** occurs when one party brings a case against another party in a court of law. This is also known as a civil action. The plaintiff makes the complaint that the other party (defendant) did something for which they are legally liable. Unlike criminal cases, a person's freedom is not in jeopardy—there is no prison sentence. The person may not have broken a law to have a lawsuit brought against him (or her). It can also involve negligence. The plaintiff may ask for compensatory damages, which compensate the plaintiff for the money he may have lost, as well as pain and

Copyright © Mometrix Media. You have been licensed one copy of this document for personal use only. Any other reproduction or redistribution is strictly prohibited. All rights reserved.
This content is provided for test preparation purposes only and does not imply an endorsement by Mometrix of any particular political, scientific, or religious point of view.

suffering. There might also be punitive damages, which is like a punishment for being malicious, reckless, or grossly negligent. One person files the suit, followed by discovery, any pre-trial motions, and oftentimes discussions of settlement. If it doesn't get settled, then it will go to a trial and the judgment. Finally, one party can appeal. Sometimes, parties will come together to make a lawsuit as a group, which can appear much stronger because of the amount of people. This is called a class action lawsuit.

Court Systems

There are many different court systems in the United States, including a federal court system and state courts. State court systems consist of many different tiers. State trial courts may consist of county courts, circuit courts, and city or municipal courts, among others. Trial courts may have limited jurisdiction, hearing lower criminal charges, cases involving juveniles, traffic issues, and some civil cases. More serious cases, such as those with more serious crimes or higher stakes civil cases, may go to a court of general jurisdiction. These may include circuit courts, superior courts, or courts of common pleas. There are specialized courts in many states. These include courts such as family courts and juvenile courts. States usually also have a supreme court where cases that have worked their way up the lower courts can be heard. Federal courts are generally divided into circuits and districts, with at least one per state. Many federal lawsuits are heard in those. The highest court is the US Supreme Court, which shapes many laws. It hears a small number of very important cases.

Due Process, Liability, Damages, Burden of Proof, and Negligence

Due process refers to a person's right to have the state respect his legal rights. It is about providing fairness to those involved in legal matters such as by providing a notice of rights. Liability refers to a party's legal responsibility for behaviors, actions, or inactions. If someone does not meet his (or her) duty, he could have a lawsuit brought against him. Damages refer to the money that may be given to the plaintiff from the defendant during a lawsuit. The plaintiff with a civil lawsuit has the responsibility of providing the burden of proof, which means he must bring a "preponderance of evidence" or a "weight of evidence" to show that he has enough facts to win the case. In criminal cases, the burden of proof refers to a prosecutor needing to show that the defendant is guilty "beyond a reasonable doubt." Negligence is when a party does not show a reasonable amount of care. Though negligence can be accidental, a reasonable person would have acted differently. One can be liable for this.

Laws and Regulations That Affect Business

There are a wide variety of laws and regulations that affect businesses. Business or **corporate law** refers to the laws surrounding how corporations are formed, dissolved, and run. **Labor laws** deal with many aspects of the relationship between employer and employee such as working conditions, wages, and discrimination. **Tax law** deals with the taxes that businesses owe. **Contract laws** govern the contracts that many businesses enter into on a regular basis. **Property law** governs how property is owned, commonly seen in business. **Antitrust law** strives to keep a competitive marketplace by not allowing mergers that would form monopolies and other antitrust activities. The **Uniform Commercial Code (UCC)** helps make transactions easier between states by helping make uniformity in commercial laws. Companies are also subject to accounting and financial management laws, as well as laws regarding their insurance and credit.

FTC

Formed in 1914, the **Federal Trade Commission (FTC)** protects consumers by stopping businesses from performing deceptive, unfair, and anticompetitive practices. It strives to stop fraud and other types of deception and keep competition fair by stopping anticompetitive mergers. It is a

Copyright © Mometrix Media. You have been licensed one copy of this document for personal use only. Any other reproduction or redistribution is strictly prohibited. All rights reserved.
This content is provided for test preparation purposes only and does not imply an endorsement by Mometrix of any particular political, scientific, or religious point of view.

federal agency that has competition jurisdiction and consumer protection jurisdiction. It helps make policies and shares information with the legislature and government agencies. When wrongdoing is suspected, the FTC will investigate and, at times, sue to stop it. They accept complaints about businesses regarding many matters including identity theft, deceptive advertising, and data security. They pass the information along to law enforcement agencies when appropriate. They also work to prevent mergers that would create anticompetitive organizations such as monopolies. They have had a large impact on the marketplace.

SEC

The United States **Securities and Exchange Commission (SEC)** plays a large role in protecting investors, maintaining the integrity of the market, and aiding in the forming of capital. It works to keep a fair market without unfair practices that would be detrimental to investors. It makes, investigates, and enforces requirements of fair disclosure of information so that one party does not have insider information that would compromise the market's fairness. Companies are required to disclose information on a regular basis so that investors can make informed decisions. It also investigates evidence of fraud. If the SEC finds a violation such as insider trading, a company purposely providing false information, or accounting fraud, it will bring a civil enforcement action against the party. It is led by five commissioners who are appointed by the president. Its main functions include making sure that federal securities laws are enforced; making rules; making sure brokers, securities firms, ratings agencies and investment advisors are inspected; watching private regulatory organizations; and working with authorities to coordinate United States securities regulations.

Sarbanes-Oxley Act and Bankruptcy Reform Act of 2005

Two acts that played a large part in business were the Sarbanes-Oxley Act and the Bankruptcy Reform Act of 2005. The **Sarbanes-Oxley Act** was signed by President George W. Bush in 2002 and increased corporate responsibility and financial disclosure while fighting accounting and corporate fraud. It included new or improved standards for management firms, public accounting firms, and United States public company boards. It also led to the creation of the **Public Company Accounting Oversight Board (PCAOB)**, which oversees auditing professionals. It was created in an effort to prevent corporate scandals at a time when such scandals were becoming common. It also made some types of misconduct crimes. The **Bankruptcy Reform Act of 2005** was created to lower Bankruptcy Code filings. Parties filing for bankruptcy would now need to get financial counseling first. In addition, they would have to undergo a "means test" to see if they qualified. Filers had to wait eight years before using Chapter 7 bankruptcy again. In addition, it created a limit of $125,000 for homestead exemptions if the property was acquired within three years and a weakened automatic stay for multiple filers. This made it more difficult for people to file for Chapter 7 bankruptcy.

Consumer Protection Laws

There are a number of consumer protection laws that safeguard individuals from unscrupulous business practices. Many of these laws are related to food safety and sanitation. Food must be handled, stored, and prepared in certain ways to prevent health hazards. For instance, meat must be stored at certain temperatures and can only stay out for a certain amount of time. The Food and Drug Administration (FDA), Department of Agriculture (USDA) and Food Safety and Inspection Service (FSIS) all play a part in administering these laws. There are also laws about credit and warranties. For instance, the Federal Warranty Law covers written and implied warranties. There are a number of laws about credit that the Federal Trade Commission enforces such as the Truth in Lending Act (TILA), Fair Credit Reporting Act (FCRA), and Fair Debt Collection Practices Act (FDCPA). Additionally, unfair trade practices, such as misrepresentation and fraud, are banned.

Copyright © Mometrix Media. You have been licensed one copy of this document for personal use only. Any other reproduction or redistribution is strictly prohibited. All rights reserved.
This content is provided for test preparation purposes only and does not imply an endorsement by Mometrix of any particular political, scientific, or religious point of view.

Many states have enacted laws against these, and consumers can complain to the appropriate consumer protection agency.

Agencies Related to Consumer Protection

The Federal Trade Commission is a national agency that protects consumers by taking complaints about unfair practices and stopping forbidden acts such as anticompetitive mergers. There are a wide variety of state, regional, and local agencies that provide the same services on a more local basis. These are often in the attorney general's office. They accept complaints, investigate claims, and take action as necessary. Another agency that provides consumer services is the **Better Business Bureau (BBB)**. The BBB keeps records on companies and list complaints. When people make a complaint, the BBB will contact the company and try to get it resolved. Businesses that have a good record with the BBB can use it to their advantage. Many consumers look up companies on the BBB website before doing business, thus many companies strive to keep good records. Sometimes consumers have a choice of several agencies from which to choose when making complaints.

Product Testing and Safety

Laws

The Consumer Product Safety Act (1972) and the subsequent Consumer Product Safety Improvement Act address safety in toys, chemicals in products, and more. The government tests products, makes safety standards, and bans products it deems unsafe. There are numerous product labeling laws as well. The Fair Packaging and Labeling Act (FPLA) requires commodity producers to label the name of the product, the identity and source of the manufacturer, the distributor or packer, and the net quantity. It strives to help consumers understand what they are getting. There are laws that specifically regard food standards, like federal grading of meat products. As a result of the Federal Food, Drug, and Cosmetic Act, the US Food and Drug Administration (FDA) requires testing on drugs to ensure their safety and efficacy. They also monitor food and food additives for safety. Many agencies and laws help ensure product safety.

Federal Agencies

Part of the US Department of Health and Human Services, the Food and Drug Administration plays a large part in protecting consumers by overseeing the safety of food, drugs, and medical devices. They require extensive testing on drugs to ensure both efficacy and safety. They regulate food and labeling and give guidelines for the conditions in which food is prepared. They inform the public on related issues. The US Department of Agriculture (USDA) creates and executes policies in the fields of agriculture, farming, food, and forestry. They help rural communities, assist with conservation efforts, make rules regarding food and nutrition, make rules and standards for products labeled organic, and play many other roles. They have had a large impact throughout the years.

Government Agencies and Laws Concerning Environmental Protection

The **Environmental Protection Agency (EPA)** strives to safeguard the environment. Its roles include reducing the environmental impact of business practices; providing information; creating regulations and national standards based on laws from Congress; giving grants to non-profit organizations, state environmental programs, and schools; and performing research into environmental concerns. The EPA was formed in 1970, and its main headquarters is in Washington, D.C. It has many programs based on specific issues such as fuel economy, air quality, and oil pollution, among others. There are a wide variety of laws to protect the environment in the United States such as the Clean Air Act, Clean Water Act, and Endangered Species Act. The EPA administers these and many more. Many of these also relate to business. The laws in other countries vary

Copyright © Mometrix Media. You have been licensed one copy of this document for personal use only. Any other reproduction or redistribution is strictly prohibited. All rights reserved.
This content is provided for test preparation purposes only and does not imply an endorsement by Mometrix of any particular political, scientific, or religious point of view.

greatly, and many countries do not have the same environmental protections. Many international business agreements address these concerns.

Business Accounting

Assets

An asset is something that has or produces value and is owned. There are different types of assets. A fixed asset is a tangible asset that is generally used to generate profit and will not be turned into cash within the year. These may be known as property, plant, and equipment assets and can include land, computer equipment, furniture, cars, buildings, and equipment used to build products. A variable asset may be transformed to cash sooner and will include the inventory of the actual product. It can also include accounts receivable, the money customers owe for delivered items. An intangible asset is not tangible—it's not physical. It includes recognition of the brand name as well as intellectual property like logos, trademarks, and patents. Though they aren't physical, intangible assets can be of high value.

Liquidity, Equity, Depreciation, and Cash Flow

Liquidity refers to how easily an asset can be bought or sold on the market at the same price. It also refers to being able to make an asset become cash easily and quickly. **Equity** in a business shows what the owner has contributed in addition to the retained earnings. Basically, it's the ownership minus the debts. **Depreciation** refers to how things lose value as time goes on. **Cash flow** refers to the actual cash that is going in and out of a business such as revenues or expenses due to business activities.

Generally Accepted Accounting Principles (GAAP)

Generally accepted accounting principles (GAAP) provide a set of standards for how accounting figures and statements such as income statements, balance sheets, and cash flow statements are prepared. It is a set of rules that directs how these forms are prepared so that investors understand what they are getting when they receive the statements. It covers economic activity measurement, timing disclosures, and details on how financial statements are prepared and presented. It directs what financial information should be reported and makes it easier for investors to understand and compare companies. GAAP is required of many regulated companies by the US Securities and Exchange Commission (SEC) (many small businesses are excluded). The Financial Accounting Standards Board (FASB) issues GAAP through pronouncements.

Cash and Accrual Accounting

The two major types of accounting systems are cash and accrual accounting. In **cash accounting**, the transactions are counted when the money is actually received or the expenses are paid out, regardless of when an item was ordered or delivered. Alternatively, in the **accrual method**, the transactions are counted when the orders are made or delivered, even if no cash has actually exchanged hands. For instance, if a furniture company sold and delivered a bed in January, but it was paid for in February, then the accrual method would record it in January and the cash method would show it in February. This affects where it is recorded for tax purposes. Most small businesses and individuals use the cash method but larger businesses may use the accrual method. The cash method is advantageous because it gives the company a better idea of cash on hand but may not show the correct profits, especially if a big sale has been made but not paid for. The accrual method shows the right profitability but may not give a good view of actual cash flow.

Copyright © Mometrix Media. You have been licensed one copy of this document for personal use only. Any other reproduction or redistribution is strictly prohibited. All rights reserved.
This content is provided for test preparation purposes only and does not imply an endorsement by Mometrix of any particular political, scientific, or religious point of view.

Fundamental Accounting Equation

The fundamental accounting equation states that **assets = liabilities + owners' equity**. It is used in double entry accounting and shown in the balance sheet, in which all assets can be added up as the equivalent of the liabilities and shareholder equality. When there is a purchase or sale, both sides will be affected equally. When a company buys an asset such as $100 in office supplies, then it will delete $100 of assets such as $100 of cash or it will be funded with shareholder equity or liabilities. This might be done by borrowing the money. When everything equals as it should, it is considered "balanced."

Accounting Cycle

The accounting cycle describes the steps taken in the accounting process. It is often shown as a circular diagram, thus the term "cycle." The first step is to attain all the source documents that are associated with financial transactions, including receipts, checks, and bank statements. Next, these transactions are analyzed to see how the accounts will be affected. The third step is to place entries into the journals for these transactions in a double-entry system. Next, the transactions are posted by moving them from the journals to the ledgers. An unadjusted trial balance is prepared showing the company's accounts. Next, the company will make adjusting entries as necessary. Account balances will go to where they should be. They will next prepare a trial balance with the adjustments in them. The company can then prepare financial statements such as the income statement. Closing entries are made as the balances of accounts that are temporary go to owner's equity. Finally, there is an after-closing trial balance.

Double-Entry Bookkeeping, Credits, and Debits

With **double-entry bookkeeping**, two columns are used. All of the debits are placed on the left while the credits go on the right. Debts are recorded in the debit column as debits; these make assets and expense accounts go up and income, liability, and equity accounts go down. Likewise, credits make liability, income, and equity accounts go up and asset and expense accounts go down. Essentially, money leaving an account is a debit and money entering the account is a credit.The debits and credits always need to equal each other. When one changes, there should be another change to account for that. For instance, if a $10,000 car is bought with cash, then there should be a $10,000 car shown as an asset and a decrease in cash by $10,000. Therefore everything stays equal. It uses the fundamental accounting equation (assets = liabilities + owners' equity) as a basis.

Ledgers and Journals

Both ledgers and journals are quite important to the accounting cycle. Although they contain much of the same information, they are used differently. When a transaction occurs, it is first put into a **journal**. Transactions are put in based on when they occur. Journals can be for something specific, such as sales or purchases, or transactions may go into the general journal for less routine transactions like a bad debt or depreciation. The company will have a record of the transactions to refer to in the future. Later, the information is transferred to the ledger. The frequency of this varies. The **ledger** contains different accounts like asset accounts, revenue accounts, expense accounts, liability accounts, and equity accounts. The two types of ledgers include the general ledger and subsidiary (sub) ledgers. The ledgers are very important because documents such as income statements and balance sheets are produced from them. The exact use of journals and ledgers may be different in a computerized system.

Trial Balance

A trial balance is a document showing the ending balances of ledger accounts. It is done on a certain date as the company is preparing to create financial documents. On the top is the title, entity, and

Copyright © Mometrix Media. You have been licensed one copy of this document for personal use only. Any other reproduction or redistribution is strictly prohibited. All rights reserved.
This content is provided for test preparation purposes only and does not imply an endorsement by Mometrix of any particular political, scientific, or religious point of view.

accounting period. Then the account titles are listed. Then there is a list of the debits (assets and expenses) on the left and a list of the credits (liabilities, income, and equity) on the right. The sum of the credits and debits are at the bottom. If everything is correct, these numbers should match, although they can still be inaccurate even if they do match. This can happen if incorrect entries were put into both the debit and credit sections at the same time, or if something was omitted altogether. Still, if they do not match, there is definitely a problem, and the company has a chance to investigate and fix it before creating the financial documents. If the company prepared the financial documents and then noticed the error, then the accountants would have to redo the documents, a much more arduous and time-consuming process. Accountants use the trial balance when making the financial documents.

Manual and Computerized Accounting Methods

Businesses can choose between manual and computerized accounting methods, and each has its advantages and disadvantages. In a manual system, people do the calculations on paper by hand; in a computerized system, they input them into a computer system. The actual formulas, calculations, and numbers are the same.

Computerized systems are far quicker. The user simply enters the numbers and can have calculations and reports generated in an instant. It is very convenient. They can change numbers to see potential outcomes. This can minimize accidents one may make when calculating by hand. The business has to pay for the computer system, of course, but the money saved in labor hours might more than make up for this. Data can be easily backed up. Disadvantages are that there could be a computer malfunction that causes a loss of data. There could also be a security breach in which the information is leaked to the wrong person or hackers get in. If the data is entered incorrectly, even by a single digit, everything can be inaccurate. Most large businesses use a computerized system.

Income Statements

One of the most important financial documents is the **income statement**, which shows company profitability for a period of time. It contains many elements including revenues, gains, expenses, and losses. It lists revenues from primary activities (also known as operating revenues) such as sales revenues, service revenues, and revenues from secondary activities such as if a business earns interest or money from a source other than selling. It also lists gains such as long-term asset sales or lawsuits from something other than the primary activity. The income statement also shows expenses in primary activities, such as those used during normal operation, and expenses from secondary activities like interest. Losses from other sources should also be listed. This can occur if the company loses money on the sale of a long-term asset or suffers a lawsuit outside of normal transactions. The income statement will display the net profit or loss for the period of time it covers.

Balance Sheets

A **balance sheet** is one of the major financial documents, showcasing a moment in time. Essentially, it is a snapshot showing the financial situation of the company. It showcases assets, liabilities, and ownership equity, with the assumption that assets = liabilities + equity. It lists **assets**, which are things that have value, in the order of their liquidity. These may include things such as cash, accounts receivable, inventory, plant and equipment, investment property, and more. After that, it lists **liabilities** such as accounts payable, promissory notes, corporate bonds, deferred tax liabilities, and more. Next it shows **equity**, which is the net worth of the company's capital. It is the difference between assets and liabilities. The two forms of balance sheets are the report form and the account form. The balance sheet is very important for every business.

Copyright © Mometrix Media. You have been licensed one copy of this document for personal use only. Any other reproduction or redistribution is strictly prohibited. All rights reserved.
This content is provided for test preparation purposes only and does not imply an endorsement by Mometrix of any particular political, scientific, or religious point of view.

STATEMENT OF RETAINED EARNINGS

The **statement of retained earnings** is a very important financial document, required when income statements and comparative balance sheets are given. It showcases how a business' retained earnings change over a period of time. **Retained earnings** are defined as a business' accumulated net income minus the dividends that were given to stockholders. The information it contains is sourced from the income statement; subsequently, the information from the statement of retained earnings is used for the balance sheet.

At the beginning is the starting balance. Factors like profits and dividend payments are added and subtracted to get the final retained earning balance. The general equation is **starting retained earnings + net income – stockholder dividends = final retained earnings**. Sometimes the statement gets into more detail by showing various types of retained earnings.

CASH FLOW STATEMENT

A **cash flow statement** is a major accounting document that outlines the influx and outflow of cash from a company. It is important because it shows what a company's cash position is, which can be different from its income if there are accounts that have not paid. It can show if the company is managing cash wisely or having difficulty with it.

A cash flow statement covers cash gained and used in operating activities, investing activities, financing activities, and supplemental information. **Operating activities** convert the business' net income to cash basis with the balance changes in the current liability and current assets accounts. **Investing activities** include balance changes of long-term assets like buildings and equipment. **Financing activities** includes balance changes in stockholders' equity and long-term liability accounts like preferred stock. Supplemental information shows interest, income taxes, and major non-cash exchanges. It will list each of these and show the increase or decrease in cash from each. At the end, it will show the net increase in cash from all, the cash at the beginning of the month, and finally the cash at the end of the month.

FINANCIAL RATIOS

Liquidity ratios measure if a company can meet its obligations in the short term. The more liquid assets it has compared to short-term liabilities, the more liquid it will be. The **current ratio** is equal to the current assets divided by the current liabilities. The **quick ratio** formula is $\text{quick ratio} = (\text{cash} + \text{accounts receivable} + \text{marketable or short term securities}) \div (\text{current liabilities})$. This is a tougher test for liquidity. The **cash ratio** formula is $\text{cash} = (\text{cash} + \text{marketable or short term securities}) \div \text{current liabilities}$. The higher these ratios are, the more liquid the firm is and the more likely it can reach its short-term debts. The **debt to equity ratio** shows the company's financial leverage. It is equal to $\text{total liabilities} \div \text{shareholders equity}$. If it is high, a lot of debt has been used to finance growth. The **return on equity (ROE) ratio** is a percentage with the equation $\text{ROE} = \text{net income} \div \text{shareholder's equity}$. It shows profitability. **Activity ratios** show how balance sheet accounts can be transformed into sales or cash. It shows a firm's efficiency. Two popular ones are the **inventory turnover ratio** and **total assets turnover ratio**.

PAYROLL RECORDS

Payroll records must include a variety of components. It will contain identifying information such as the employee's name, social security number, address, birth date (for employees under 19), gender, and occupation. It may also contain the hiring letter, a pay authorization, the employee's W-4 form, payroll deduction forms, direct deposit forms, time sheets, records of attendance, W-2 forms, and all other forms related to payment. It will have the details of the compensation such as

Copyright © Mometrix Media. You have been licensed one copy of this document for personal use only. Any other reproduction or redistribution is strictly prohibited. All rights reserved.
This content is provided for test preparation purposes only and does not imply an endorsement by Mometrix of any particular political, scientific, or religious point of view.

the wage base, pay rate per hour (if applicable), hours worked, dates, and more. It will also show deductions from the wages, such as taxes like income taxes, as well as contributions to retirement accounts or deductions for social security, healthcare expenses, and more. Many items are taken out of the pay before the employee receives them so the employee does not have to do so regularly.

Payroll Accounting Procedures

Companies follow specific payroll accounting procedures to ensure accurate compensation and reporting. First, a company must have a way to compute the amount of time an employee works. Sometimes this is set to a schedule, whereas other times an hourly employee works different hours every day. A time card or an electronic time clock may be used to keep track of this. Sometimes, employees keep their own records or are salaried and receive the same amount no matter how many hours they work. The pay must then be computed for each person. This may be a set amount based on a salary, or be the number of hours worked multiplied by the hourly rate. It may be more complicated and include other things such as investment account distributions, bonuses, or reimbursements. They must have a system to account for special time such as when the employee is taking paid leave. The company must compute and submit all applicable taxes such as income taxes on behalf of the employee and payroll taxes. They must make other deductions such as healthcare premiums. Once this is worked out, the company will distribute the money. This is often done by check or direct deposit.

Periodic and Perpetual Inventory Systems

Two major types of inventory systems are periodic and perpetual inventory systems. In **perpetual inventory systems**, the inventory changes and cost of goods sold are updated in real time as the item is sold. Other inventory changes, such as returns, are also recorded immediately. In a **periodic system**, a purchases account record is changed when the purchase is made, but the cost of goods sold and inventory doesn't change until the accounting period closes.

Perpetual inventory systems are very popular, especially with the increase in technology point-of-sale systems. They allow businesses to always know what inventory they have and restock as necessary. They provide much more useful and updated information. The disadvantage is that it can cost a lot of money initially to put in the technology for a perpetual inventory system. Some small businesses do not have the money or ability to do this.

Inventory Costing

Inventory costing is the process of assigning a cost to a particular item. There are various methods a company can use. With the **first in, first out (FIFO) method**, the oldest cost is assigned to the first item sold, then the next oldest cost to the next item sold, and so on. For instance, if five shirts were bought wholesale for $10, and then next five were bought for $12, then the first five sold would have the $10 cost and the next five would have the $12 cost, even if they weren't the ones actually bought for those amounts. This is very common because it is a good approximation of the real world. The **last in, first out (LIFO) method** is the opposite, and the most recent cost is assigned to the first items sold. In this case it would be $12 for the first five shirts sold and then $10 for next five shirts. This is used less often.

The average cost and specific identification methods are two inventory costing methods. The **average cost method** keeps a running average of inventory and assigns the item sold the current average. For instance, if a company buys five shirts for $10 and five for $12, then the next shirt sold would be assigned the cost of $11. This is good when a company has non-perishable items that are not sold sequentially. It can be steadier and more reliable as long as there is not a great change in the costs of the items. The **specific identification method** assigns the cost of a product with the

Copyright © Mometrix Media. You have been licensed one copy of this document for personal use only. Any other reproduction or redistribution is strictly prohibited. All rights reserved.
This content is provided for test preparation purposes only and does not imply an endorsement by Mometrix of any particular political, scientific, or religious point of view.

actual cost paid for that specific product. These are used for low-volume, high-dollar producers. For instance, a company that sells high-end cars might use this system so they know exactly how much they made on a car. It is not good for companies with a lot of very similar items.

Depreciation

Depreciation is the concept that assets such as equipment, machinery, and cars have a useful life and will only be usable for a certain amount of time and therefore depreciate (or lose value) as time goes on. This is used in accounting. There might be a residual value to the asset, or a value at the end. For instance, imagine a company buys a truck for $110,000 and expects it to have a 10-year useful life. At the end of the 10 years, they expect to be able to sell it for $10,000. They may use the **straight line method of depreciation** in which they simply average the depreciation across the years. For every year, they will show a depreciation expense of $10,000. Businesses can use this as an income tax deduction as long as it meets all the criteria.

Costs

Direct costs are the costs that go directly into making a product. For instance, if a company is manufacturing pens, then the cost of the ink would be a direct cost. An **indirect cost** is incurred to the company as a whole and is necessary but not directly tied into that one product. For instance, the office supplies used in the marketing department would be an indirect cost. They are not used directly in making the pens, but they are still important to the function of the marketing department that helps to promote the pen. **Fixed costs** are costs that stay the same. For instance, the cost of a salaried employee would be a fixed cost because it is always the same. No matter how many pens are made, it stays the same. **Variable costs** can change, however. For instance, if the pen making machine uses more electricity when it makes more pens, then this would be a variable cost. Companies work to minimize these costs while maximizing efficiency.

Cost Accounting

Cost accounting is useful for managers to help make decisions while planning and controlling. It looks at the costs of different items such as products and projects. To accomplish this, both the input costs of production and the fixed costs are considered. Once input and output are measured, these can be compared to see how the item is performing financially. This can help managers make a decision on whether to continue with the project or product and ways they can improve it. It analyzes many things such as cost-volume-profit connections, activity-based costing, and cost behavior. It helps managers decide how much to charge for certain processes or services because they will know how much it cost.

Management Accounting

Management accounting refers to the evaluation of information for the purpose of managers. It can include the identification, measurement, evaluation, interpretation, and communication of information. Its main goal is to help managers make decisions about the business. This is different than **financial accounting**, which is done to give information to outside parties. In management accounting, management accounts are created that have financial information suitable for managers. Managers use these to make short-term decisions. Elements that may be included in these reports include sales reports numbers, cash available, order amount, sales revenue, inventory reports, accounts payable and receivable accounts, trend charts, and more. Managers can get an idea of how projects will progress, understand how business choices will affect the business financially, oversee finances, and more.

Copyright © Mometrix Media. You have been licensed one copy of this document for personal use only. Any other reproduction or redistribution is strictly prohibited. All rights reserved.
This content is provided for test preparation purposes only and does not imply an endorsement by Mometrix of any particular political, scientific, or religious point of view.

Evaluating an Organization's Financial Performance

A **cost-volume-profit analysis (CVP)** is part of managerial economics and looks at how alterations in the cost (fixed and variable) and sales volume change the profit of a company. A **break-even analysis** calculates when the expenses of a company are covered and there is a profit. The general equation for this is breakeven point = fixed costs ÷ (selling price of a unit − variable costs). The **return on investment (ROI)** shows an investment's efficiency. It is calculated with the following equation: ROI = (gain derived from investment − cost of the investment) ÷ cost of the investment. The answer is a percentage. A company can use this to compare different projects. Managers might not want to continue a project that has a negative ROI. Likewise, when comparing two projects, they would look for the one with the higher ROI. It is a simple but powerful equation. Companies will often use multiple strategies to evaluate financial performance.

Insurance

Insurance Policy

An insurance policy is a legal agreement between the insured and the insurer in which the insurance company agrees to reimburse the insured for a certain level of loss according to policy. In exchange for premium payments, the insurance company will reimburse a percentage of the insured's loss under specified circumstances. Insurance companies use actuarial data to estimate the potential risk of loss for an insured population. It is easier to predict losses for a group of policyholders than an individual, and accurately estimating the size and number of insured losses is how insurance companies make money.

Underwriting

Through underwriting, insurance companies decide whom they will insure and at what rates. Through the underwriting process, insurance companies put together rate-classification schedules; premiums rise when the chance of loss is greater. Underwriters try to avoid adverse selection by preventing high-risk clients from getting coverage. It can be difficult for underwriters to figure out what the best classifying criteria is for potential purchasers.

Risk and Risk Avoidance

In terms of insurance, risk is the uncertainty of economic loss. When a financial interest such as health, home, car, or business is lost or damaged, financial loss occurs. Anticipating and protecting against potential risks will protect you financially. Risk avoidance, loss prevention and control, risk assumption, and insurance can help prepare for risk.

Risk avoidance is simply steering clear of situations that involve an increased level of danger. Some risk, however, is necessary. For example, if you avoid driving, your chances of being injured or killed in a car accident are reduced, but the inconvenience of not being able to drive may cause stress which can impact health. It is important to evaluate if avoiding the risk is potentially less harmful than taking the risk and its potential consequences.

Loss Prevention and Loss Control

Loss prevention lowers the likelihood that a loss will occur. For example, driving a car during good weather versus during a blizzard reduces the likelihood of being in a car accident. Loss control reduces the impact of a loss when it occurs. For example, wearing a seatbelt or having a car with airbags reduces the chance of injury or death in an accident. Both loss prevention and loss control are important to risk management programs and allow insurance companies to handle risk reasonably.

Copyright © Mometrix Media. You have been licensed one copy of this document for personal use only. Any other reproduction or redistribution is strictly prohibited. All rights reserved.
This content is provided for test preparation purposes only and does not imply an endorsement by Mometrix of any particular political, scientific, or religious point of view.

Life Insurance

Life insurance is a type of coverage people buy that pays out upon a person's death. Whole life insurance is also an investment. When the person passes away, a fixed amount is paid out. This builds cash value each year and can be borrowed against. Term life insurance does not have an investment component. People will buy it for a certain amount of time and pay a monthly premium. This can be very inexpensive for someone who is young.

There are many life insurance terms. A beneficiary is the person who receives the money upon the insured person's death. A rider changes provisions or clauses of the insurance policy. Annuities give a regular income. Most of the time these are for life. Actuarial tables show the chances that someone will pass away before their birthday, used by life insurance companies when developing plans and pricing. Those shopping for life insurance should familiarize themselves with all the concepts prior to choosing.

There are important financial benefits of life insurance including financial protection for dependents, creditor protection, tax benefits, and savings. The most important benefit is providing for dependents upon your death. Creditor protection is important because creditors cannot claim cash benefits even if the deceased has outstanding debts and bills if the life insurance policy is set up to pay a beneficiary directly instead of through the estate. Life insurance payouts made to dependents aren't usually subject to state or federal income taxes, and sometimes dependents do not have to pay estate taxes if specific requirements are met. Finally, some life insurance policies can be used as savings vehicles.

When buying life insurance, be honest about your medical history; insurance companies can and do check into medical backgrounds. You may be asked to take a medical exam before the insurance policy will be approved. Before taking an exam, do not drink alcohol or caffeine, smoke, or chew tobacco in the hours before the exam. Also, avoid strenuous exercise for twenty-four hours prior to the exam, which may be done in your home or office by a paramedical professional who may take blood, urine, and saliva samples to test for HIV, cholesterol, diabetes, and other health issues. If you are purchasing a large policy or are more than forty, an EKG or X-rays may be required as well as a treadmill test.

Factors That Affect the Decision Whether to Carry Life Insurance

First, an individual should consider who is counting on his income. A single person who lives alone and does not support anyone else might not need life insurance, whereas a father who is the sole support for three young children would need it much more. When the person is the breadwinner in the family or has dependents that count on him, he (or she) is much more likely to need the life insurance. If someone else would be able to get a job and provide the income, the need would be reduced. The person should consider how long others will depend on the income. Someone with very young children would need it more than someone with older children who are self-sufficient. The needs of the people depending on the income also matter. For instance, if one of the children has a disability and will incur expensive long-term medical bills, life insurance is more important. A person should also consider long term savings. Someone who has a lot of savings that can be used to support dependents will need less life insurance than someone who relies on every paycheck.

Multiple-of-Earnings Method

The **multiple-of-earnings method** multiplies the gross annual earnings by a certain number to estimate how much insurance coverage is needed. Though a simple method, it is not entirely accurate and only gives a rough approximation of life insurance needs. The needs analysis method looks at financial resources and obligations of the insured party and their dependents, and is far

Copyright © Mometrix Media. You have been licensed one copy of this document for personal use only. Any other reproduction or redistribution is strictly prohibited. All rights reserved.
This content is provided for test preparation purposes only and does not imply an endorsement by Mometrix of any particular political, scientific, or religious point of view.

more precise and detailed. The needs analysis method determines a family's total economic need and what financial resources will be available after the insured party's death, and subtracts these resources from the financial need to determine how much life insurance is required.

NEEDS ANALYSIS METHOD

The **needs analysis method** takes into account five different components for assessing a family's total economic needs. The first is how much income the dependents will need in order to live comfortably. Looking at a family's current monthly budget for housing, utilities, food, clothing, medical/dental needs, property taxes, insurance, recreation/travel, and savings is helpful. Special needs of a dependent that is chronically ill or disabled, is attending college or has another special circumstance is the second component to consider. The third component involves extra expenses such as funeral costs or childcare costs if a surviving spouse reenters the workforce. Liquidity is important so that payouts from the policy can be used to pay bills. Finally, it is important to figure out how much would be needed to pay outstanding bills in order to leave a family debt-free.

Financial resources not related to a life insurance policy include money from savings, investments, and Social Security survivor's benefits. Another resource may be payouts from the deceased employer's group life insurance or earned income from a surviving spouse and children. Additionally, many families have real estate, jewelry, stocks, bonds, and other assets that could be sold. It is important to put together a complete list of these resources and their values and update this list frequently.

TERM LIFE INSURANCE

Term life insurance is the simplest kind of insurance because a certain amount of insurance is purchased to cover a set period of protection. If the purchaser dies during that time period, the beneficiaries will receive everything specified in the policy. Term life insurance can be purchased for different time periods and premiums can be paid quarterly, semiannually, or annually. The two types of term insurance are a straight term policy and a decreasing term policy. A straight term policy covers a set number of years; the amount of life insurance coverage stays the same. A decreasing term policy keeps the premium the same throughout the coverage period but the amount of protection decreases over the life of the policy. This is done because the possibility of death increases with age.

The biggest advantage of term life insurance is lower initial premiums than other types of insurance, especially for younger people. Term life insurance is an affordable way to get a greater degree of protection for a specific period of time. The biggest disadvantage to term life insurance is that it only offers temporary coverage; once the policy term expires, the policy has to be renewed. Future underwriting factors can make it a challenge to qualify for insurance, but some term life policies offset this with a renewability provision which gives the policy holder the opportunity to renew without proof of insurability. There may also be a convertibility provision which allows the policy holder to convert term insurance policy to a comparable whole life policy in the future.

WHOLE LIFE INSURANCE

Whole life insurance provides ongoing insurance coverage for the insured's entire life. It also offers cash value, which is a small return on the investment. This cash value is obtained from investment earnings from premiums that have been paid. Savings rates on whole life policies are usually capped at a certain rate. The longer the policy is kept active, the greater the cash value.

Some of the advantages to whole life insurance are that individuals save regularly with periodic payments and there are tax breaks for these earnings. Premium payments can be budgeted over a

Copyright © Mometrix Media. You have been licensed one copy of this document for personal use only. Any other reproduction or redistribution is strictly prohibited. All rights reserved.
This content is provided for test preparation purposes only and does not imply an endorsement by Mometrix of any particular political, scientific, or religious point of view.

long time, making them more affordable and eliminating the possibility of being denied life insurance at a later point in time. Premium payments contribute toward the insured's estate regardless of lifespan. However, whole life insurance does not provide yields as high as other investment types and offers less death insurance per premium dollar than term life insurance.

With a **continuous premium whole life policy**, also called straight life, a level premium is paid every year until death or a nonforfeiture right is claimed. The younger the purchaser, the lower the premium will be. Although premiums are reduced by purchasing a policy at a younger age, the longer coverage period can mean a higher overall payment. Continuous premium insurance provides the highest amount of permanent death protection plus the lowest amount of savings per premium dollar, so it is a good choice for permanent life insurance.

A limited payment whole life policy provides coverage over the course of the insured's entire life, but the premium payment is for a specified period. If there are age provisions (e.g. paid up to age fifty-five or sixty-five), premiums are paid up until that age. Some insurance companies try to persuade consumers that they will save money because they do not have to pay premiums over a lifetime. However, this is not entirely true: First, the purpose of whole life insurance is permanent protection against financial loss in the event of death. It is not meant to be a savings account. Second, if the goal of the life insurance is permanent coverage, a person should buy continuous premium whole life instead of the limited payment policy.

A **single premium whole life policy** is purchased with a one-time cash payment at the beginning of the contract with coverage for life. Its investment components are attractive to those who want a tax-sheltered investment vehicle. Any policy interest and investment earnings are tax deferred, but there is a 10 percent early withdrawal penalty. Also, there is a capital gains tax if cash withdrawals or loans are taken against the single premium whole life policy before age 59 ½.

Insurance Company Ownership Structures Affect Premiums

Depending on how a life insurance company's ownership is structured, there can be considerable differences in insurance policy premiums. For all intents and purposes, the policy holders of a **mutual company** own the company. If mutual companies are managed well, policy holders receive income or periodic dividends that reduce their premiums. Shareholders of **stock companies** own the company but they may or may not own policies, and they directly receive any dividends paid. Because of the difference in ownership types, the policy premiums for stock companies should be lower than those issued by mutual companies.

Universal Life Insurance

Universal life insurance is a permanent cash value insurance that combines death benefits with a tax-sheltered savings/investment account that pays interest; this interest is usually paid at a competitive money market rate. Some of the premium pays administrative fees; the remainder is added to the cash value of the policy where it earns a return rate. Although this earnings rate varies with market yields, there is a guaranteed minimum rate. As long as there is enough in the savings part to cover death protection, the policy will remain in effect. If the cash value becomes very large, insurance coverage must be increased in order for the policy to keep its favorable tax treatment.

One advantage of universal life insurance is savings, because the policy is credited at the current rate of interest. Another advantage is flexibility, because the cost of death protection is covered with an annual premium. One disadvantage is that protection levels and premiums can change. A policy holder may have to pay higher premiums down the line if early premium payments were economized. Another disadvantage is fees and charges. The first premium has a front-end load or

Copyright © Mometrix Media. You have been licensed one copy of this document for personal use only. Any other reproduction or redistribution is strictly prohibited. All rights reserved.
This content is provided for test preparation purposes only and does not imply an endorsement by Mometrix of any particular political, scientific, or religious point of view.

commission, and there are fees for each annual premium, plus investment expenses and other charges.

Other Types of Life Insurance Besides Term, Whole, and Universal

Some other types of life insurance include variable, group, and special purpose. **Variable life insurance** means benefits are directly tied to the returns on investments made by the policy holder. Under **group life insurance** each eligible member of the group receives an insurance certificate for an overall, master policy for everyone in the group. **Special purpose insurance** can include credit life (life insurance sold along with installment loans), mortgage life (mortgage balance is paid off if the borrower dies), and industrial life insurance (policies with small face amounts, often less than $1,000).

Automobile Insurance

Automobile insurance covers drivers in the case of an occurrence that causes some sort of damage or harm. Many states force drivers to have insurance. There are many different types of policies with different coverage levels. Liability coverage provides benefits to damages suffered by other drivers. Collision coverage is for cars involved in an accident. People often have a deductible, or money they have to pay first. Premiums are the amount a driver pays monthly or regularly to maintain coverage. Comprehensive insurance also covers cars damaged without a collision such as from vandalism or weather-related events.

Personal Automobile Policy

A **personal automobile policy (PAP)** is a comprehensive insurance policy for automobile owners and is intended to be easily understood by a typical insurance purchaser. It has six parts, with the first four identifying the type of coverage provided: Liability coverage (Part A), medical payments coverage (Part B), uninsured motorists coverage (Part C), and coverage for damage to your vehicle (Part D). Part E explains the duties and responsibilities in the event of an accident, and Part F outlines the basic provisions of the policy, including policy coverage period and right of termination.

Liability Insurance

Liability insurance protects against financial burden in the event the insured is responsible for accidental injury or property loss to someone else. This insurance helps cover legal fees to in the event the insured is sued, although should the accident be determined to be the result of negligence caused by the insured's failure to act in a responsible manner, the insurance will not pay.

Property Insurance

Property insurance protects real and personal property against natural and manmade catastrophes such as tornadoes, fire, hail, theft, and vandalism. Property insurance lists both the property and the types of destructive acts (perils) that are covered. In order to receive property insurance, the owner needs to compile a comprehensive list of specific property to be insured. It may be necessary to include appraisals with this list. The more specific this list is, the easier it is to settle a claim. Second, a purchaser must decide on the types of perils property needs to be protected against.

Property insurance provides coverage against a wide variety of risks and includes fire insurance, earthquake insurance, home insurance, and flood insurance. **Open perils** is a type of property insurance that includes all causes except those exempted, whereas **named perils** lists the types of causes for the insurance. There are many plans with different premiums, coverage, deductibles, and exclusions. **Replacement insurance** will give benefits so people can replace the lost items,

Copyright © Mometrix Media. You have been licensed one copy of this document for personal use only. Any other reproduction or redistribution is strictly prohibited. All rights reserved.
This content is provided for test preparation purposes only and does not imply an endorsement by Mometrix of any particular political, scientific, or religious point of view.

whereas **actual cash value insurance** takes off for depreciation. People should evaluate the potential risk and costs of insurance when deciding on the plan that is right for them.

Insurance companies base their premiums on the amount of risk they perceive and the potential for losses. Limit potential hazards to lower premiums. Have good lighting around your property to minimize the likelihood of someone falling, and to ward off potential thieves. Make sure that electrical wiring, stairways, carpeting and flooring are in good shape to avoid accidents. Swimming pools need to be secured with fences and locks and should be covered or drained when not in use. Keep valuables in a safe deposit box and do not keep valuables or a lot of cash at home. Take photos of insured items and keep detailed records, including appraisals.

Supplemental Property Insurance

Not all types of damage are covered by homeowner's policies, so it is important to decide if you need any type of **supplemental coverage**. Some common types of supplemental coverage include flood insurance, earthquake insurance, and transportation insurance. In 1968, the federal government established a subsidized flood insurance program to work with private insurance to offer lower-cost flood insurance coverage in certain areas. Under this program, land-use controls are put in place to help reduce future flood losses. With earthquake insurance, a 15 percent deductible on the replacement cost of a home that is destroyed or damaged by an earthquake is required. Besides car insurance, an individual may want to insure vehicles such as motorcycles, boats, RVs, mobile homes, and personal watercrafts.

Home Insurance Costs

Home insurance costs can be affected by risk factors that pose a hazard such as trampolines, swimming pools, and even certain pets. The construction materials used on a home also affects insurance costs; brick and HardiPlank homes cost less to insure than those built of wood. The age and style of the house also are figured into the costs. Finally, the location of the home affects insurance costs. Insurance premiums for all homeowners will be higher if there are a large number of claims filed from in area (e.g. high-crime level areas).

Renter's Insurance

Even if the building being rented is insured, anything that you own in that building is not. **Renter's insurance** covers losses due to fire, lightning, explosion, windstorms, hail, theft, civil commotion, aircraft, vehicles, smoke, vandalism, falling objects, building collapse, and the weight of water and snow. A standard policy takes care of carpets, furniture, appliances, clothing, electronic equipment, and other personal items at their value at the time of loss. Renter's insurance premiums are dependent upon location, but are generally very affordable. You can also purchase replacement cost insurance, which pays to fully replace lost items with new ones.

Health Insurance

Health insurance is very important for individuals and families to help pay for medical expenses. People typically pay a monthly fee or premium for coverage. They may have to pay a deductible, or an amount of money before the insurance company pays. Sometimes there are out-of-pocket limits or the maximum amount the consumer has to pay. There are many sources of health insurance. Many people get an employer-sponsored plan from their place of work. Others may get a private plan in the marketplace. Some may receive it from the government through Medicare or Medicaid. Still others might find it from a different source. There are many different types of plans. A PPO is a **preferred provider plan**, which generally gives greater benefits if an individual sees someone "in network" as compared to "out of network." An HMO, a **health maintenance organization**, contracts physicians, hospitals, and other providers and gives benefits based on that. When

Copyright © Mometrix Media. You have been licensed one copy of this document for personal use only. Any other reproduction or redistribution is strictly prohibited. All rights reserved.
This content is provided for test preparation purposes only and does not imply an endorsement by Mometrix of any particular political, scientific, or religious point of view.

choosing health insurance, people should consider current and potential healthcare concerns, the dependents who also need coverage, the premium, the coverage the plans offer, deductibles, limits, exclusions, and more. Plans vary in all these aspects.

When choosing a healthcare plan, it is important to know what the plan will cost each month and co-pays for doctors outside the plan's network. Understanding out-of-pocket limits in the case of a major illness or injury is essential. Review doctors, hospitals, services, and other medical providers covered under the plan. Know the deductibles you have to pay before insurance kicks in to help cover the costs.

Private health insurance plans are offered to both individuals and groups. These plans are either traditional indemnity plans or managed care plans. With traditional indemnity plans, healthcare services are obtained from someone other than the insurer; the insurer reimburses a portion of payments when a claim is submitted, or they pay the health service provider directly. With managed care plans, certain organizations or individual providers are contracted to provide services for a monthly fee. These plans include HMOs, PPOs, EPOs, and similar plans. It is estimated that private health insurance pays for about 35 percent of medical expenses in the United States.

About 25 percent of the US population is covered under some type of government health insurance program. **Medicare**, administered by Social Security, is one of these programs and is paid for with social security taxes of covered workers and their employers. Medicare provides basic hospital insurance and supplementary medical insurance. Medicaid is a state-run public assistance program which provides health insurance benefits for those who are not able to afford health insurance. Worker's compensation insurance is another government health insurance plan that compensates workers who are injured on the job or become ill from work-related causes.

Disability Insurance

To estimate your disability needs, figure your take-home pay (disability benefits are usually tax-free so you'll only need to replace your take-home pay). Policies paid by employers are either partially or fully taxable. Figure out the monthly disability amount you will receive from Social Security, other government programs, company disability benefits, and group disability policy benefits and subtract your existing monthly disability benefits from it. This will give you an idea of the monthly disability benefits needed.

It is important to understand the definition of disability since policy standards differ. Ask if there are provisions for cost-of-living adjustments and guaranteed insurability options. Know both the probationary period (when the benefits kick in, usually seven to thirty days) and the waiting period (usually thirty days to one year). Determine whether the insurance is noncancelable or guarantee renewable. Finally, understand the amount and duration of benefit; group plans tend to pay a fixed gross income percentage but most individual disability income policies pay a flat monthly benefit.

Some ways to save on disability income insurance include reducing premiums by extending waiting periods, getting a policy that has benefits to age sixty-five instead of a lifetime, asking about premium discounts for prepaying, and requesting that recurring medical problems (e.g. back problems) be excluded. Get a number of price quotes since rates can vary, and check with your employer to see if disability insurance is offered as a benefit. Think about getting a small policy with a rider that allows you to buy more later on.

Long-Term Care Insurance

There are some important policy provisions to think about when purchasing long-term care insurance, including the type of care. Some policies only offer nursing home care and some only

Copyright © Mometrix Media. You have been licensed one copy of this document for personal use only. Any other reproduction or redistribution is strictly prohibited. All rights reserved.
This content is provided for test preparation purposes only and does not imply an endorsement by Mometrix of any particular political, scientific, or religious point of view.

offer home health care, while others also include assisted-living, adult daycare, alternative care, and community-care; respite care for the caregiver is also a possibility. Find out if preexisiting conditions are covered. Understand how much the policies will reimburse per day as well as for how long these benefits will be covered; some coverage is only for a year while others are for the insured's lifetime. Ask about the waiting period, which is usually between ninety and 100 days. Know the requirements for eligibility and what services are covered, including skilled, intermediate, and custodial care. Check to see that there is guaranteed renewability and be wary of those that have an optional renewability. Find out the premium levels and if there is inflation protection.

Long-term care is non-hospital medical and personal care for chronic medical conditions. Determine whether the cost of premiums outweighs the cost of a potential nursing home stay. If you have a family history of disabling diseases or if you are a male, your chances of needing long-term care increases. If you have family members who will provide care, this can reduce long-term care costs. Finally, since most assets have to be depleted before Medicaid will cover any costs, those who are older than sixty-five and have a net worth more than $100,000 and income more than $50,000 should consider purchasing long-term care.

Check long-term care policies to determine if they include Alzheimer's disease coverage as well as at least one year of home health or nursing home coverage, including intermediate custodial care. There should be a guarantee against nonrenewal or cancellation due to age or deteriorating physical or mental health, and you should have the right to return the policy within thirty days for a refund. Study the outline of coverage that explains the policy's benefits, limitations, and exclusions in great detail; this will also help comparison shop against other policies. Make sure there is not a requirement for policy holders to be hospitalized before they receive home healthcare or nursing home benefits, or a requirement that they have to receive a higher level of care first before they can receive lower care levels.

It is a good idea to buy long-term care insurance before you need it; if you are diagnosed with a serious illness, you will become uninsurable at that point. It is important to buy the coverage that you need, but not more coverage than you need. Make sure the policy has provisions for skilled, intermediate, custodial care, adult daycare centers, and assisted living facilities. If you have family caregivers or home health services, then you only need nursing home coverage. It's important to understand what the policy covers and when it pays benefits, as well as how the policy defines benefit eligibility, the amounts paid, benefit periods, and the services covered.

Investments

SECURITIES

Securities are financial assets that can be traded. These investments include many different types, such as stocks and bonds, and are not tangible items. **Bonds** and **banknotes** are two common types of debt securities. With **debt securities**, the investor is the lender. **Equity securities** are stocks in which the investor purchases a small portion of a company. Securities are advantageous because they can provide a great deal of return on an investor's money. A disadvantage is that they often involve risk. With some of them, an investor can lose everything. Securities range in both risk and return; in general the greater the risk, the greater the potential for a large return. Investors may get a certificate or an electronic form.

Copyright © Mometrix Media. You have been licensed one copy of this document for personal use only. Any other reproduction or redistribution is strictly prohibited. All rights reserved.
This content is provided for test preparation purposes only and does not imply an endorsement by Mometrix of any particular political, scientific, or religious point of view.

STOCKS

Stocks are a common form of investment in which investors purchase a very small amount of a company. The returns they generally see are from rising stock prices when the company is doing well. Sometimes the company pays dividends as well. Stocks can be advantageous in that there is no limit to what someone can make. If they choose a stock in a company that skyrockets, they can literally make a fortune on what started as a small investment. The downside is that there can be a lot of risk. Just as the stock price can rise dramatically, it can also fall dramatically and become practically worthless. Thus, an investor could lose everything. Some stocks are riskier than others, and diversifying stock lowers the risk.

Stocks change in price minute to minute, and you pay a commission to buy or sell. **Common stocks** offer a chance to hit it big if the price skyrockets. Since common stockholders are actually owners of the company, they will receive their prorated share of the earnings and dividend income only after the company's other obligations have been met. Common stockholders need to be aware that it is possible no return on investment is a possibility.

Bonds are a type of long-term debt; when you purchase bonds, you are a **creditor** of the company and that company pays you back over the life of the bond. Stocks provide higher rates of returns than bonds but they are far less stable. Additionally, bonds stabilize and diversify a portfolio. People who hold common stock have ownership or equity position whereas bondholders do not.

BONDS

Bonds are publicly traded IOUs in which the bondholders lend money to the issuer of the bond. Investing in bonds is popular because they can provide a high current yield and can generate substantial gains when market interest rates fall. Bonds can be used aggressively for individuals who actively seek capital gains, and conservatively for individuals who seek high current income. Due to the high quality of bond issues, they may also be used for the long-term preservation and accumulation of capital.

Investing in bonds means an investor is loaning money to an institution, which is the borrower. In exchange, the borrower is providing the investor (or lender) with a coupon or premium. Thus, the investor will get money for lending money. In addition, when the bond reaches maturity, its face value will be given back to the investor. The advantage of bonds is that they are a less risky form of investing than many other methods such as stocks. Most of the time, investors receive the money they are promised. The disadvantage is that the return does not generally have the potential to be as great as with stocks. While stocks can return an almost unlimited amount, bonds are limited greatly. They offer less risk, but less reward. Many people invest in a combination of bonds and stocks.

A single issuer of bonds can have many bonds outstanding at a time. While bonds can be differentiated from one another due to maturities and coupons the kind of collateral behind them also distinguishes them. Bond issues are either senior or junior standing, with senior bonds being backed by a legal claim on the issuer's specific property. This claim acts as the collateral for the bonds. Senior bond issues include mortgage bonds (secured by real estate) and equipment bonds (secured by certain types of equipment and favored by airlines and railroads). Junior bonds are only backed by the issuer's promise to pay interest and principal in a timely manner; there is no collateral.

Copyright © Mometrix Media. You have been licensed one copy of this document for personal use only. Any other reproduction or redistribution is strictly prohibited. All rights reserved.
This content is provided for test preparation purposes only and does not imply an endorsement by Mometrix of any particular political, scientific, or religious point of view.

Segments of the Bond Market

The four segments of the bond market are the treasury, agency, corporate, and municipal. **Treasury bonds** were created by the US Treasury to help meet the federal government's ongoing needs, have a maturity of more than ten years and pay interest twice a year. **Agency bonds** are issued by divisions of the US government and usually provide higher yields than Treasury bonds. **Corporate bonds** are issued by corporations, and can come in the form of industrials, public utilities, rail and transportation bonds, and financial issues. **Municipal bonds** are issued by states, counties, cities, and other government divisions, and unlike other bonds, their interest income is federally tax free.

Sinking Fund

A **sinking fund** is the pool of money set aside by a business or the government to repay a bond issue over time. How the bond will be paid off is important to investors. Some bonds specify the yearly repayment schedule as well as how much principal will be retired each year. Sinking funds usually start one to five years after the issue date and continue each year thereafter until the issue is all or mostly paid off.

Call Features

A **call feature** specifies whether a bond can be retired before its scheduled maturity date, and if it can, under what conditions. There are three main types of call features: free call, noncallable, and deferred call. A freely callable bond can be retired early. A noncallable bond means the issuer cannot retire the bond before it matures. A deferred call keeps the bond from being retired until after a certain period of time passes from the date of issue, meaning the issue cannot be retired during the deferment time but becomes available for retirement thereafter.

Convertible Bonds

Convertible bonds are only found in the corporate market and have features of both corporate bonds and common stocks. They are issued as unsecured, but are allowed to be converted into a particular number of shares of the issuing company's stock during a certain time period. A convertible issue has a conversion privilege that accompanies it, and this clearly states the conditions and specific nature of the conversion feature, such as exactly when the bond can be converted. The **conversion ratio** states the number of shares of common stock that the bond can be converted into.

Bond Rating System

Bonds receive letter grades for their investment quality and these **bond ratings** are widely understood and used in the corporate and municipal bond markets. Two of the best known rating agencies are Moody's and Standard & Poor's. When a new corporate or municipal issue appears on the market, professional bond analysts calculate both its default risk exposure and its investment quality. The issuing organization's financial records are looked at carefully and its future prospects assessed. This allows a bond rating to be assigned that is indicative of how quickly and efficiently the issuing organization will repay its debt. Once after a new issue is rated, it is not finished: outstanding, older bonds are reviewed regularly to make sure their assigned ratings are still valid.

Pricing of a Bond

Figuring the fair price of a bond is known as **bond valuation**. Theoretically, the value of a bond is calculated using the present value relationship, or the cash value it would be expected to generate. Pricing the bond is done by determining the appropriate discount rate. Once the pricing and its relative sensitivity has been estimated, the yields and coupons can then be determined. In

Copyright © Mometrix Media. You have been licensed one copy of this document for personal use only. Any other reproduction or redistribution is strictly prohibited. All rights reserved.
This content is provided for test preparation purposes only and does not imply an endorsement by Mometrix of any particular political, scientific, or religious point of view.

corporate and municipal markets, bonds are priced in decimals. Treasury and agent bond quotes are given in thirty-seconds of a point, with1 point equaling $10.

Mutual Funds

A **mutual fund** is an investment strategy in which money is collected from many investors and professionally managed. The fund manager trades the collected money, investing it in bonds, stocks, short-term money market accounts and other investment vehicles. Any net proceeds or losses are paid out to the investors on a yearly basis. Mutual funds are a popular investment choice for individuals because they offer a number of investment opportunities and services that are appealing to investors. Mutual funds are one of the three basic types of investment companies in the United States (the other two are unit investment trusts and closed-end funds).

Mutual funds are businesses that take money from a variety of investors and put it in a portfolio of bonds, stocks, securities, and assets. Each mutual fund has a different combination. A person who buys into a mutual fund will hold a portion of ownership of the portfolio and reap the rewards when the portfolio gains value. The idea is that an investor enjoys the benefits of diversification by not investing in one single asset. There is risk involved with mutual funds—they can lose value—and there are fees and other costs that can lower the value. The government does not guarantee them. Some are riskier than others, depending on the combination of the portfolio. Still, they are a good way to balance risk and reward and are a popular retirement and investment option.

Mutual funds can invest in several types of securities with the most common being cash instruments, bonds, and stock although there are a lot of other categories. **Sector funds** are any stock funds invested primarily in a particular industry's shares, like technology. Both stock and bond funds can invest in mainly US securities (**domestic funds**), US and foreign securities (gl**obal funds**), or foreign securities (**international funds**). Bond funds differ according to their risk, issuers type (e.g., government agencies, corporations, or municipalities), or maturity of the bonds (short- or long-term).

Mutual funds are subject to a special set of regulatory, accounting, and tax rules. Unlike most other types of US businesses, mutual funds are not taxed on their income as long as 90 percent of it is distributed to shareholders and the funds meet certain diversification requirements as set by the IRS. Also, the earnings from mutual funds usually do not change as it passes on to the shareholders. Mutual fund distributions are tax-free to the shareholder if they are tax-free municipal bond income. Depending on how the mutual fund earned the distributions, taxable distributions are either ordinary income or capital gains. (Net losses are not distributed or passed through to the investors of mutual funds.)

Fund Manager

Professional fund managers try to choose investments they think will align with the purpose of the fund's investment, predict the future performance of chosen investments, oversee cash flow for mutual funds, and constantly adjust the mutual funds' investment portfolios. The fund manager is hired by a management company to administer the fund, and this company can also fire the manager. Fund managers charge a fee for their services, and this fee is a percentage of the fund's average assets during its management. A fund can be managed by one person, by two people who act as co-managers, or by a team of three or more people. When looking for a fund manager, look for someone with a history of long-term, consistent fund performance.

Copyright © Mometrix Media. You have been licensed one copy of this document for personal use only. Any other reproduction or redistribution is strictly prohibited. All rights reserved.
This content is provided for test preparation purposes only and does not imply an endorsement by Mometrix of any particular political, scientific, or religious point of view.

The Economist

The Economist is an authoritative weekly newspaper that provides anonymous (collaboratively written) opinions and analysis of business and finance. It is a good, objective financial resource to consult when investing. It covers the latest world and American stock indices as well as commodity prices, live stock prices, intraday and historical stock charts, financials for numerous companies, weekly economic and financial indicators, currency information, and rankings and ratings. A weekly economic statistics feature addresses items such as employment statistics as well as special statistical features.

The Wall Street Journal

The Wall Street Journal is a newspaper that primarily covers national and international business and financial news and issues. Sections include marketplace (which covers health, technology, media, and marketing industries), money and investing (which covers and analyzes international financial markets), economic issues, and personal investments. Its personal investments section has such regular columns as Cheapskate, The Intelligent Investor, Deals and Dealmakers, Fundtrack, Investing, Marketwatch, Tip of the Day, Starting Out, Encore, Reinvent, Ask Dow Jones, Common Sense, and Family Money, which can be quite helpful to an individual doing personal financial planning.

Banking and Financial Services

M1, M2, and M3 Measures of Money

The composition of the money supply in a country can change quite a bit over time. For instance, in the past, hard currency accounted for a much larger portion of money than it does now, while the proportion of checkable deposits has gone up in recent years. Governments have two official measures of money, known as M1 and M2. **M1** is the sum of all the currency held by businesses and individuals, all the traveler's checks, and all the checkable deposits held by businesses and individuals. **M2** contains all of the funds included in M1, as well as savings deposits, small-time deposits, money market funds, and some other deposits. Obviously, M2 is much larger than M1. Finally, **M3** is a classification of money that includes M2 as well as the long-term repurchase agreements held by banks and large-denomination time deposits.

Financial System

Finance consists of savings and investment. Money not immediately spent is either saved or invested. **Savings** refer all income and monetary holdings that are not spent. **Investment**, on the other hand, is money put to certain use in the hope of obtaining a future benefit. Investments can be either economic or personal. Economic investments are loans to businesses, while personal investments are the purchase of financial assets like mutual funds, stocks, and bonds. The financial system consists of the set of institutions that enable saving and investing. As such, this system includes bond markets, insurance markets, stock markets, and banks.

Liabilities

A **liability** is a debt that has to be repaid. Installment loans, credit card charges, mortgages on housing or other real estate result in liabilities. There are two types of liabilities, short-term (current) and long-term. Short-term liability refers to a debt that requires repayment within a year of the date on the balance sheet. Short-term liabilities include taxes, medical bills, insurance premiums, utilities, and rent. Long-term liabilities refer to debt that needs to be paid one year or more from the date of the balance sheet. A good example of a long-term liability is a student loan or real estate mortgage.

Copyright © Mometrix Media. You have been licensed one copy of this document for personal use only. Any other reproduction or redistribution is strictly prohibited. All rights reserved.
This content is provided for test preparation purposes only and does not imply an endorsement by Mometrix of any particular political, scientific, or religious point of view.

Federal Open Market Committee (FOMC)

The **Federal Open Market Committee (FOMC)** is the primary maker of policy within the Fed. It has 12 members: the president of the Federal Reserve Bank of New York; four presidents of other regional Federal Reserve Banks; and the seven members of the Board of Governors. The regional Federal Reserve Bank presidents rotate out every year, so each region is represented equally and often. Every six weeks, the Federal Open Market Committee gathers and discusses the economy. On occasion, the committee decides upon some strategic actions undertaken by the Federal Reserve Bank of New York.

Board of Governors of the Federal Reserve System

The seven-member Board of Governors is the highest authority in the Federal Reserve System. These members, usually renowned economists, receive appointment by the President, confirmation by the Senate, and serve terms of fourteen years. The board's main responsibility is creating and implementing monetary policy, although the board also must supervise the financial activity of banks, Reserve Banks, bank holding companies, and Federal Reserve System banks. The board decides how much money to loan these institutions and the rate of interest on these loans. Additionally, the board oversees any bank mergers and acquisitions for American banks, as well as those international member banks. The Board of Governors must report its activities to Congress.

Chairman of the Board of Governors

The Chairperson of the Board of Governors is the most important member of the Federal Reserve System. The chairperson controls the agenda of the Board of Governors, as well as the agenda of the Federal Open Market Committee. In Federal Open Market Committee meetings, the person has the most influence over the proceedings. The chairperson constantly receives reports from economists and other experts, so he or she usually has the best information on a given problem. The chairperson also serves as a spokesperson for the Federal Reserve in meetings with Congress and the President, as well as in meetings with economic representatives from foreign countries.

Great Depression

In 1929, the United States experienced the financial catastrophe known as the Great Depression. In large part, panic among depositors caused a massive run on the banks; many banks had insufficient funds and failed, hence causing the Great Depression. In 1933, Franklin Roosevelt led the passage of the Banking Act. This act established mandatory interest rates and prohibited risky bank transactions. Around the same time, the federal government created the Federal Deposit Insurance Corporation (FDIC), which guarantees bank deposits under a certain amount. These measures helped restore consumer confidence in the banks, although the United States did not rise fully from the economic doldrums initiated by the Great Depression until the Second World War.

Bank Mergers

In the 1980s, the federal government took many steps to deregulate banks. Perhaps most importantly, the federal government reduced restrictions on interstate banking, which enabled a number of small banks to merge. In particular, some large banks acquired small banks and used the existing infrastructure to enter new markets. In 1998, approximately 500 commercial banks were in existence, and in 2003, less than 200 commercial banks were in existence. Because of all these mergers, competition between the remaining banks has increased, thus creating more consumer services and low interest rates. Although fewer different commercial banks exist, more branches of each bank exist. Also, the remaining banks have larger funds with which to develop new technologies to aid consumers. However, some economists fear that the rise of enormous banks will diminish customer service in the long run.

Copyright © Mometrix Media. You have been licensed one copy of this document for personal use only. Any other reproduction or redistribution is strictly prohibited. All rights reserved.
This content is provided for test preparation purposes only and does not imply an endorsement by Mometrix of any particular political, scientific, or religious point of view.

Financial Services Modernization Act of 1999

In 1999, President Bill Clinton signed the **Financial Services Modernization Act** (also known as the Gramm-Leach-Bliley Act), which made it possible for investment companies, banks, and insurance companies to sell similar products in competition with one another. In other words, banks could now sell insurance, stocks, and bonds. Conversely, insurance companies and investment companies were now allowed to offer banking services. This act constituted a partial repealing of the Glass-Steagall Act of 1933. This legislation enabled consumers to complete all their financial transactions with one organization. However, each institution has suffered some growing pains while learning to perform the services of the other institutions.

Federal Funds Market

Commercial banks and other thrift institutions keep reserves at regional Federal Reserve banks in order to fulfill transactions and reserve requirements. These reserves, or federal funds, do not accumulate interest. Money constantly flows from banks whose reserves exceed the requirement to banks whose funds are less than the requirement. These exchanges occur on the federal funds market. The federal funds market evens out disparities in reserves, but it does not change the overall level of reserves. Funds acquired in this manner are available immediately. Most of the transactions in the federal funds market take place overnight, although some transactions, known as Term Fed Funds, are made for longer periods.

Reserve Requirement Ratio

The **reserve requirement ratio** (also known as the fractional reserve requirement) is the percentage of total deposits a bank is required to keep in reserve. When raised, the reserve requirement mandates that banks retain more money, which means they can make fewer loans. Although the total amount of reserves stays the same, the overall money supply decreases because loaned money can be deposited elsewhere, thus multiplying its presence in the monetary system. The Fed usually raises the reserve requirement ratio in order to avoid inflation, which many economists believe is proportionate to expansion of the money supply. The Fed typically lowers the reserve requirement ratio in order to encourage lending and investment. Reducing the reserve requirement ratio has the effect of increasing the velocity of money and the money supply in general.

Defensive Open Market Operations

The Fed undertakes **defensive open market operations** in order to counteract the effects of uncontrollable influences on the level of reserves. Tax collection is a classic example of a force that defensive open market operations must offset. When individuals and businesses pay their taxes in April, they are more likely to withdraw funds from commercial banks. The Fed anticipates this trend and buys securities to bolster reserve levels. Temporary repurchase agreements and timed repurchase agreements are among the most common tools for dealing with cyclical reserve changes. In some cases, the Fed makes repurchase agreements with an option to renew. This option means that the original deal can extend indefinitely at the Fed's behest. Finally, these deals give the Fed the ability to micromanage the money supply.

Repurchase Agreements

In a **repurchase agreement**, the Fed temporarily purchases securities with the understanding that the dealer will buy them back in the near future. These repurchase agreements temporarily increase the money supply and bank reserves. Often, repurchase agreements take place overnight, and the securities are repurchased on the next business day. These transactions have become a popular way for the Fed to make small adjustments to the money supply. Before arranging a

Copyright © Mometrix Media. You have been licensed one copy of this document for personal use only. Any other reproduction or redistribution is strictly prohibited. All rights reserved.
This content is provided for test preparation purposes only and does not imply an endorsement by Mometrix of any particular political, scientific, or religious point of view.

repurchase agreement, the Fed typically declares the duration. The Fed makes these transactions at the discount rate and credits these transactions with federal funds.

Reverse Repurchase Agreements

In a **reverse repurchase agreement**, the Fed temporarily sells securities with the understanding that the dealer will sell them back to the Fed later. Reverse repurchase agreements diminish bank reserves and money supply and can generate a small amount of short-term investment income. These transactions are secured because the government backs these securities. Additionally, securities dealers use reverse repurchase agreements in order to build up inventory and purchase other securities. In this case, temporarily owned securities serve as collateral to obtain longer-term securities.

Dynamic Open Market Operations

Dynamic open market operations are performed to tighten credit, ease credit, or increase or decrease reserves. Dynamic operations are not performed in advance of a predicted change, or in response to recent events. The Fed's ability to use dynamic operations has increased along with the rise of the monetarist philosophy among economists. Many economists believe that the Fed should concentrate on monitoring and adjusting the supply of money as a way of controlling inflation. Economists have paid more attention to regular, predictable changes in the money supply such as those changes that take place at the beginning of the week or month.

The Fed's Supervisory Functions

The Fed has numerous supervisory functions. Specifically, the Fed distributes currency and manages transfers of funds between member banks. The Fed also issues and redeems federal debt. The Federal Reserve ensures that banks maintain reserve requirements so the banks will have sufficient liquidity to meet their customers' withdrawal demands. The Fed is responsible for processing payments and checks. In this capacity, the Fed acquires a great deal of information regarding economic activity and trends. The Fed is also responsible for researching the economy and staying abreast of changes that could influence the economy in general and the money supply in particular.

Announcement Effect

When federal regulatory agencies make an announcement or issue a report, the market reacts. This reaction is described as the announcement effect. For instance, the market rates typically move in the same direction that the Fed changes the discount rate. Also, the market responds to reports of a growth in the money supply, adjustment of other interest rates, and borrowing by the Treasury Department. The market perceives these announcements as heralding potential changes in credit and interest rates and seeks to adjust ahead of time. Sometimes, traders are aware that the Fed is about to make an announcement, but the traders have no advance knowledge of what the announcement's content. In such a situation, the market is especially volatile.

Credit Multiplier

The **credit multiplier** is a measure of the change in credit and in the money supply resulting from bank deposits. The credit multiplier is calculated as the change in credit divided by the monetary base. In the banking system, a deposit can more than triple itself in the form of deposits and credit. As an example, imagine a $50,000 deposit in a bank with a reserve requirement of 20%. The bank is required to keep $10,000 in reserve, but it loans out the other $40,000. The recipient of the loan deposits it in his bank, and that bank can then loan out $32,000 of the deposit to some other customer. The original deposit now is several times its original value. This is an example of the credit multiplier.

Copyright © Mometrix Media. You have been licensed one copy of this document for personal use only. Any other reproduction or redistribution is strictly prohibited. All rights reserved.
This content is provided for test preparation purposes only and does not imply an endorsement by Mometrix of any particular political, scientific, or religious point of view.

Discount Rate

The **discount rate** is the rate of interest charged to banks that borrow funds from the Federal Reserve. Changes in the interest rates of banks and money markets follow changes in the discount rate. When the discount rate rises, in turn banks must charge a higher interest rate to customers. As a result, customers are less likely to seek loans, and the money supply is reduced. The money supply is reduced because money does not multiply itself in numerous deposits. On the other hand, a reduction of the discount rate encourages banks to borrow more money from the Fed and increase their lending by lowering their own interest rates. The net result is an expansion of the money supply.

Rates Affected by Discount Rate

The discount rate is the interest rate charged when member banks borrow money from the Fed through the discount window. The **base rate** is the benchmark against which adjustable rates are made. Sometimes, banks will give a base rate but indicate the possibility of a future adjustment within certain parameters. The **repo rate**, otherwise known as the **official bank rate**, is the discount rate the Bank of England uses in its loans to commercial banks in the United Kingdom and United States. The repo rate typically resembles the discount rate in the United States. The **prime rate** is the best rate of interest offered by a commercial bank; it directly ties to fluctuations in the discount rate.

Manipulation of the Discount Rate

One of the ways the Federal Reserve regulates the amount of money in the American economy is by manipulating the discount rate. The Federal Reserve loans money to commercial banks that need funds to meet the required reserve ratio. The discount rate is the interest rate at which the Fed loans this money. In order to change the discount rate, one of the twelve regional Federal Reserve Banks to the Federal Open Market Committee initiates a proposal. If the Federal Open Market Committee approves the change, it passes the recommendation on to the Board of Governors. The Board of Governors makes the final decisions regarding changes in the discount rate.

Discount Window Programs

The Fed uses the discount window to extend seasonal credit, exceptional circumstances credit, and 14-day adjustment credit. When banks borrow at the discount window, they receive the discount rate. Banks typically borrow money at the discount window when they want to avoid problems with liquidity. In addition, the discount window is able to ensure financial market stability by offering a permanent venue for financial transactions. At one time, the discount window was only available when banks already had exhausted other sources of funds. Gradually, however, the Fed has relaxed the restrictions on transactions made at the discount window and has traded with banks at any time as long as the banks can prove financial stability.

Required Reserve Ratios

The Federal Reserve's primary responsibility is to control the amount of money in the American economy. One of the ways the Fed accomplishes this task is by establishing minimum amounts (expressed as a percentage of deposits) for bank reserves. In other words, every bank and thrift institution must keep a certain percentage of its deposits as reserves, in case there is a large withdrawal from the bank. Every type of deposit requires different required reserve ratios. The larger the deposit type, the larger the percentage each bank is required to keep in reserve.

Monetary Base

The Federal Reserve is responsible for maintaining a solid foundation of money for the American economy. The supply of money maintained by the Fed, called the monetary base, consists of all the

Copyright © Mometrix Media. You have been licensed one copy of this document for personal use only. Any other reproduction or redistribution is strictly prohibited. All rights reserved.
This content is provided for test preparation purposes only and does not imply an endorsement by Mometrix of any particular political, scientific, or religious point of view.

coins, bank reserves, and Federal Reserve notes held by the Fed. If the monetary base is large, it can support a large amount of money in the economy. All of the Federal Reserve notes and bank reserves held by the Fed are liabilities, since they are owed to other institutions. The Fed's assets include loans made to banks, government securities, and gold and other deposits made with other central banks. While the United States economy still is based partly upon gold, American currency is not directly tied to the amount of gold held by the federal government. The Federal Reserve also makes deposits in other strong central banks around the world.

Open Market Operations

One of the ways that the Federal Reserve System adjusts the amount of money in the American economy is by buying and selling government securities, a process known as **open market operations**. The Fed sells government securities, including United States Treasury bills and bonds, to banks and private interests. When the Federal Reserve sells government securities, it reduces the amount of money in the American economy. When the Federal Reserve buys back government securities, it increases the amount of money in the American economy. The Federal Reserve does not sell government securities to other federal government organizations.

Open market operations are the primary policy tool used by the Federal Reserve to adjust the amount of money in circulation. The Federal Reserve buys securities with money and with the creation of new bank reserves. The purchase of securities by the Federal Reserve decreases the federal funds rate, because the presence of more reserves in the banking system increases the number of interbank loans and decreases along with demand for interbank loans. The opposite occurs when the Federal Reserve sells securities. Banks and other institutions purchase securities with money and bank reserves. The sale of securities by the Fed diminishes the reserves in the banking system and decreases the supply of interbank loans. This in turn increases the demand for interbank loans and raises the federal funds rate. Typically, the Fed has a particular federal funds rate target in mind when it begins open market operations.

Effects of Open Market Operations on Lending

Open market operations (that is, the buying and selling of government securities by the Fed) directly influence the amount of lending by commercial banks and thrift institutions. When the Federal Reserve purchases securities from banks, it increases the reserves in those banks, thus enabling them to lend more. When banks lend money, they in effect create new money through the collection of interest. However, when the Federal Reserve sells government securities to commercial banks and thrift institutions, it diminishes the bank reserves and therefore diminishes the amount of lending done by banks. This means that less money will be created by interest payments from loans.

Multiplier Effect and Open Market Operations

When the Federal Reserve purchases securities from commercial banks and thrift institutions, it is in effect increasing the monetary base. This makes sense, since the money used to purchase the securities goes into the bank reserves, which then can be lent to individuals and businesses. Some of the loaned money will make purchases, buy new equipment, and continue business operations. However, some of the loaned money will be invested back in the bank. At this point, the money will exist in the banking system twice: both as an outstanding loan that the bank considers an asset, and as a bank deposit which the bank can use to make investments of its own. This phenomenon is known as the multiplier effect.

Copyright © Mometrix Media. You have been licensed one copy of this document for personal use only. Any other reproduction or redistribution is strictly prohibited. All rights reserved.
This content is provided for test preparation purposes only and does not imply an endorsement by Mometrix of any particular political, scientific, or religious point of view.

Check Clearing Service

The Federal Reserve offers check-clearing services to banks, in which it records all the receipts and expenditures of the bank clients. The high volume of checks in each Federal Reserve District makes this a substantial undertaking, but the Federal Reserve speeds financial transactions and guarantees payment for banks. Unlike commercial banks, the Fed never has to worry about being unable to cover transactions. Because the Fed is in charge of printing the money, it has no liquidity problems. This generates confidence in banking transactions. However, in recent years, private companies have begun to take over check clearing services, and the Federal Reserve's role in this task has diminished.

Regulation of Bank Holding Companies and Bank Exams

The Federal Reserve is responsible for supervising the activities of bank holding companies, institutions that own a controlling interest in more than one bank. As part of this supervision, the Federal Reserve administers bank exams that require the banks to supply detailed information on their accounts and practices. In particular, the Federal Reserve wants to assure banks are not involved in risky lending practices. Trained bank regulators review the institution's assets and liabilities and pay particular attention to the soundness of the bank's investments and the adherence to law. The Federal Reserve also wants to maintain competition among banks and protect borrowers from predatory loans.

Creation of Currency

One of the main tasks of the Federal Reserve is to create the paper and metal currency used in economic transactions. Only one official currency circulates in the United States, the fiat money produced by the Federal Reserve. The Bureau of Engraving and Printing, a part of the Department of the Treasury, prints the Federal Reserve notes and sends the notes to the district banks. Then the district banks lend to commercial institutions. From there, currency makes its way to individuals and businesses. The currency produced by the United States Federal Reserve lasts approximately three years, although larger denomination bills tend to be exchanged less and thus have a longer lifespan. The US Mint produces the coins used in the United States.

Monetary Transmission Process

The **monetary transmission process** is the response of the product, financial, and labor markets to actions of monetary policy. For example, when the Fed sells securities, bank reserves and thus the money supply decrease, interest rates rise, and investors buy securities. These actions deplete the money supply further and decrease aggregate demand. On the other hand, when the Fed buys securities the money supply and bank reserves increase, so interest rates decline. When interest rates decline, investors are less likely to purchase securities of their own, so the money supply will remain high. This abundance of cash in the system is likely to increase aggregate demand. An increase in aggregate demand is good news for retailers and other vendors.

Recognition Lags

The goals of the Fed are to limit inflation, minimize unemployment, maintain a strong real GDP, and maintain stable prices in the financial and international markets. However, the Fed's ability to make accurate and timely adjustments to the monetary supply is hampered by recognition, response, and implementation lags. A **recognition lag** is the delay between an economic shock and the government and economic experts' observation of the shock. The duration of a recognition lag depends on the severity of the event. Events that may have a recognition lag include recessions and depressions, because these problems require assembly of economic data prior to their diagnosis.

Copyright © Mometrix Media. You have been licensed one copy of this document for personal use only. Any other reproduction or redistribution is strictly prohibited. All rights reserved.
This content is provided for test preparation purposes only and does not imply an endorsement by Mometrix of any particular political, scientific, or religious point of view.

Response Lags

The actions taken by the Fed rely on imperfect information and uncertain predictions regarding future economic events. The **response lag**, the delay between a policy's implementation effect, is one of the problems associated with action by the Fed. Most of the Fed's actions do not yield immediate results. For instance, if the Fed sells securities, the diminution of the money supply does not instantaneously lower interest rates. Economists estimate that the economy can take six months to respond to changes in the federal funds rate. To an extent, the Fed can consider the response lag when implementing policies. However, the duration of the lag is unpredictable.

Implementation Lags

Unfortunately, the Federal Reserve does not have the luxury of perfect information and immediate implementation. When a large macroeconomic event occurs, a significant gap, known as the **implementation lag**, emerges between the event and the implementation of a response policy. The implementation lag is longer than the recognition lag but shorter than the response lag. The Fed attempts to minimize the implementation lag by meeting regularly and giving the Board of Governors authority to call meetings at a moment's notice. Nevertheless, important decisions take time, and the delay between recognition and implementation invariably affects the utility of the Fed's policies.

Operating Targets vs. Intermediate Targets

Operating targets are short-term goals. For instance, in 1994, the Fed began setting a daily target for the federal funds rate. On the other hand, the Fed intends intermediate targets, as steps toward a larger goal. For instance, the Fed set intermediate targets for monetary aggregates, nominal GDP, exchange rates, and interest rates. The Fed does not set intermediate targets for the federal funds rate; rather, it seeks to control this rate through managing the money supply. In setting intermediate targets, the Fed monitors debt level, net borrowed reserves, total reserves, total federal funds trading, and other economic indicators.

Advantages and Disadvantages of Saving in a Bank

One of the advantages of saving money in the bank is the low level of risk involved. The bank provides a stable interest rate, so there is very little market risk. Also, all deposits up to a certain amount are insured by the FDIC, so there is little risk of default. Conversely, investments in stocks and bonds are much riskier. On the other hand, savings placed in a bank do not have any protection from inflation. If the money's value decreases, the depositor has no way to recoup the loss. Also, the relatively low interest rate means that the investor will receive a lower long-term return on his or her investment.

Commercial Banks

Commercial banks are institutions with the authority to accept deposits and make loans. Commercial banks receive this authority either from the Comptroller of the Currency in the United States Treasury or from a state agency. At present, approximately 10,000 commercial banks exist in the United States. There are actually fewer commercial banks today than there were 10 years ago, because a trend of mergers has combined many formerly independent banks. Commercial banks accept checkable deposits, time deposits, and savings deposits. The highest interest rates are paid on time deposits, while the lowest interest rates are paid on checkable deposits. The interest rate on checkable deposits is often zero.

Copyright © Mometrix Media. You have been licensed one copy of this document for personal use only. Any other reproduction or redistribution is strictly prohibited. All rights reserved.
This content is provided for test preparation purposes only and does not imply an endorsement by Mometrix of any particular political, scientific, or religious point of view.

Operations

Ultimately, a commercial bank wants to increase its stockholders' long-term wealth as much as possible. A bank makes money by charging a higher interest rate for loans than it pays out for deposits. However, this policy presents some risk, because the chance that loans will not be repaid always exists. If unable to pay depositors who wish to withdraw their money, the bank will fail. While it is very uncommon for a bank to be unable to pay its depositors, in some situations depositors become very concerned and a large number of them seek to withdraw their money. This is called a **run on the bank**. In order to avoid runs, a bank must be especially prudent regarding the manner in which it makes loans.

Cash Assets

The assets of a commercial bank are divided into four parts: securities, loans, interbank loans, and cash assets. A commercial bank's **cash assets** consist of the combination of reserves and all the funds to be received from other banks as payments for checks. The **reserves** of a commercial bank include all of the currency in the vaults and the bank's balance on its reserve account at a Federal Reserve Bank. Commercial banks make deposits in a Federal Reserve Bank much the same way an individual or business makes a deposit at a commercial bank. In order to maintain operations, commercial banks are required to keep a minimum percentage of deposits as reserves. This safety precaution is intended to protect the bank from "coming up short" during large withdrawal periods. The percentage of deposits that must be held in reserve is called the **required reserve ratio**.

Using Interbank Loans, Securities, and Loans

Sometimes commercial banks have reserves in excess of the required reserve ratio. When this occurs, these banks are allowed to lend their excess reserves to other banks with a shortage of reserves. These **interbank loans** take place in the federal funds market. The Federal Reserve Bank sets the interest rate, also known as the **federal funds rate**, for these loans. Indeed, establishing the federal funds rate is considered the most important monetary policy enacted by the Fed. After cash assets and interbank loans, a bank's remaining assets are composed of securities and loans. **Securities** are bonds created either by the United States government or by another large, stable institution. Banks buy and sell these bonds depending on the interest rate. Finally, banks make money by loaning funds to businesses and individuals and assessing a high interest rate.

Comptroller of Currency

The **Comptroller of the Currency** (sometimes known as the **OCC**, or Office of the Comptroller of the Currency) is an agency of the United States Treasury responsible for chartering new banks as national banks. As national banks, these banks may be given surprise annual inspections, and they become subject to all federal regulations. Besides chartering national banks, the Comptroller of Currency also regulates services offered by banks, with the goal of promoting competition. The OCC also monitors the banking system in order to ensure that all citizens have access to services. The OCC investigates and enforces money laundering and financing of terrorist organizations involving commercial banks. Finally, the OCC oversees the conduct of national bank agents and affiliates, thus ensuring that these employees maintain the highest ethical standards.

National Banks

The United States government charters certain private banks as national banks. Specifically, these banks receive their charter from the Comptroller of Currency, a part of the United States Treasury Department. Law requires national banks to become members of the Federal Reserve System. Also, they are required to join the FDIC. Thus, national banks must maintain a certain amount of reserves with the central bank in their region in order to guarantee stability. National banks buy and sell government bonds, which helps to regulate the supply of money. Only about 30% of the commercial

Copyright © Mometrix Media. You have been licensed one copy of this document for personal use only. Any other reproduction or redistribution is strictly prohibited. All rights reserved.
This content is provided for test preparation purposes only and does not imply an endorsement by Mometrix of any particular political, scientific, or religious point of view.

banks in the United States are national banks, although national banks are the most powerful banks in the country.

The federal government places certain restrictions on national banks in exchange for those banks' rights to buy and sell government securities and the banks' respective memberships in the FDIC. National banks cannot lend more than 15% of their equity to one agent. Also, limitations exist regarding loans that national banks can make to their own directors and officers. As of 1999, national banks are allowed to engage in all financial activities with the explicit exceptions of real estate development, merchant banking, and insurance underwriting. It should be noted that designation as a national bank does not mean that the institution does business in all fifty states.

Savings and Loan Associations

Savings and loan associations are thrift institutions that make personal, commercial, and home loans and accept checkable and savings deposits. Savings and loan associations have reserves, and like commercial banks, they are required to meet the minimum reserve ratios established by the Federal Reserve Bank. Most of the assets of savings and loans are held as home mortgage loans; for this reason, they sometimes are called building and loan associations. Savings and loan associations must register with the Federal Deposit Insurance Company (FDIC), which means that individual deposits up to $250,000 are guaranteed. In the 1980s, lax regulation led to a number of defaults by savings and loan associations, costing many depositors their entire savings. Since this debacle, the federal government has taken a much more aggressive stance towards savings and loan regulation.

Savings Banks

Savings banks are thrift institutions that primarily make consumer and home loans and accept savings deposits. In essence, the savings bank redistributes money from those persons who wish to spend less money than they make to those persons who wish to spend more money than they make. This arrangement enables borrowers to pursue the business projects that help fuel the economy. Sometimes the depositors actually own the savings banks, in which case the banks pay dividends rather than interest. Such institutions are called **mutual savings banks**. A savings bank holds reserves and must meet the minimum reserve ratio established by the Federal Reserve Bank. Savings banks do not accept demand deposits, thus differentiating them from commercial banks. The general category of savings banks includes mutual savings banks, municipal savings banks, postal savings systems, credit unions, and savings and loan associations.

Credit Unions

A **credit union** is a thrift institution that mainly makes consumer loans and accepts savings deposits. Credit unions are owned either by an economic group, like the employees of a particular firm, or by some other social group, such as the employees of a particular state government. In essence, the members of a credit union loan money to one another. The interest rates are very low, in part because the loans usually are for small amounts. Most often, credit union loans are for medical emergencies, car payments, and household appliances. Credit unions hold reserves, and like commercial banks, credit unions are required to meet the minimum reserve ratios established by the Federal Reserve Bank.

Federal Deposit Insurance Corporation

The Federal Deposit Insurance Corporation (FDIC) insures deposits up to $250,000. The deposits insured by the FDIC include retirement and savings accounts, among others. National banks are required to join the FDIC, but state banks are not required to join. The purpose of the FDIC is to promote depositor confidence and to prevent runs on banks. The FDIC occasionally buys or sells assets in order to enable a proposed bank merger. The organization was developed in 1933 as a

Copyright © Mometrix Media. You have been licensed one copy of this document for personal use only. Any other reproduction or redistribution is strictly prohibited. All rights reserved.
This content is provided for test preparation purposes only and does not imply an endorsement by Mometrix of any particular political, scientific, or religious point of view.

response to the Great Depression. Member banks and thrift institutions pay for the operations of the FDIC. There are five members of the FDIC Board of Directors. The President of the United States selects the five members of the FDIC Board of Directors, and these appointments are confirmed by the Senate.

FEDERAL REGULATION OF DEPOSITARY INSTITUTIONS

The purpose of federal regulation of depositary institutions is to maintain efficiency, solvency, liquidity, and most of all to reduce risks for consumers. Unfortunately, federal regulation does not always meet this goal. Accordingly, the financial crisis of 2008 illustrated the failures of the regulatory system. In the wake of these problems, the federal government has instituted a series of stress tests for major depositary institutions. A **stress test** is a computer model that measures a bank's performance after some cataclysmic event. In order to remain in business (that is, to avoid being closed or forced into merger by the federal government), banks must prove their durability and stability. At the same time, the government is said to be developing a systemic risk regulator that would measure the stability of the economy as a whole.

HOLDING COMPANIES

Most commercial banks are run by holding companies, classified as corporations that own controlling shares of stock in a number of different businesses. A holding company can run many businesses without going to the trouble of merging or consolidating them. In addition, the holding company only has liability for the business to the extent of its ownership; since the holding company does not own the entire business, it is not solely liable. Holding companies enable banks to provide services not explicitly allowed by the Fed. These services include tax planning, investment advice, and data processing. Holding companies that administer a number of related businesses sometimes are referred to as parent companies.

BROKERAGE COMPANIES AND INSURANCE COMPANIES

Brokerage companies are the primary depositories of investment accounts for the purpose of trading stocks and bonds. Formerly, brokerage firms appeared more distinct from banks than they are now. The main difference at present is outlined by the Glass-Steagall Act of 1933, which forbids banks from underwriting corporate securities. The Securities Investor Protection Corporation (SIPC) insures brokerage firms. Insurance companies are the primary vendors of life, health, property, and disability insurance. According to the McCarran-Ferguson Act, the federal government can regulate insurance if the state governments are not doing a good job. The National Association of Insurance Commissioners is composed of the commissioners of insurance from each state; this group has no power over insurance regulation but is charged with administering the law and recommending new laws.

MUTUAL FUND COMPANIES

Mutual fund companies typically start open-end and closed-end mutual funds. The mutual fund companies then sell these funds to investors. The Federal Deposit Insurance Corporation insures these groups. The FDIC will reimburse a depositor for any losses up to the amount of $100,000, even if the depositor is not a US citizen or resident of the United States. The FDIC insures all types of deposits regularly received by a financial institution except for Treasury securities. Deposits made in different institutions are insured separately, as are deposits maintained in different categories of legal ownership. IRA and Keogh funds are insured separately from any nonretirement funds the individual may have at that same institution.

Copyright © Mometrix Media. You have been licensed one copy of this document for personal use only. Any other reproduction or redistribution is strictly prohibited. All rights reserved.
This content is provided for test preparation purposes only and does not imply an endorsement by Mometrix of any particular political, scientific, or religious point of view.

Regulation of Savings and Loans

In the 1970s and 1980s, the federal government limited the deposit interest rates that savings and loan associations could offer. This limitation created a problem when the interest rates rose dramatically, because customers rapidly withdrew their funds in order to invest in securities. This run caught many savings and loans by surprise, and in some cases institutional failure caused depositors to lose their investments. In the wake of this crisis, the federal government expanded the rights of commercial banks and insurance companies to include the services previously offered exclusively by savings and loans. At this point, the tarnished brand name made it better business for savings and loans to operate as components of other financial institutions. This arrangement remains to the present day; namely, to the extent that savings and loans still exist, they are called banks.

Computation and Quantitative Analysis

Calculating Annual Profits from Sales Data

Companies calculate **annual profit** to ascertain how much money they have brought in through the year. The first step in getting the annual profit is to add up all of the revenues. This may include sales from different products or other sources of income. Next, all of the costs for the year must be added together. This may include many different types of costs. Companies need to subtract to account for returns. They need to consider all expenses, including but not limited to operating expenses, depreciation expenses, interest, etc. Finally, they will take the total costs and subtract that from the total income. This will give the profit. For instance, if a company has revenues of $100,000 and costs of $50,000, then it made $50,000 in profit. One of the best ways to get all the data for this calculation is from the income statement, which lists revenues and expenses.

Profit Margins

The **profit margin** statistic makes it possible to compare companies of different sizes because it is expressed as a percentage. To calculate profit margin, first the raw profit is calculated. This is done by subtracting total costs from sales revenue. For instance, if sales of a product made $10,000 for the company and costs were $8,000, then raw profit will be $10,000–$8,000, or $2,000. Next, the gross profit is divided by the revenue. Thus $2,000 would be divided by $10,000 for an answer of 0.2. The profit margin is this number expressed as a percentage. To get this, a person would multiply the decimal by 100, thus 0.2 is equal to a 20 percent profit margin.

Sale Prices

The **sale price** of an item is the price minus the discount, which is calculated by the percentage off. To calculate the discount, one should multiply the percentage off and the full price. For instance, to calculate the sale price of an item that is $100 and 20 percent off, first the percentage should be transformed to decimal form, which is done by moving the decimal point to the left by two digits. Thus 20 percent is the same as 0.2, five percent is the same as 0.05, and one percent is the same as 0.01. To calculate the discount, one would multiple 0.2 by 100. This equals $20. The sale price is calculated by taking the full price and subtracting the discount. In this example, it is $100 – $20. Thus the sale price is $80.

Commissions

Many employees are paid on commission; thus, it is important to understand how to properly calculate them. First, the employee must understand the amount of money that is eligible for commission. For instance, a sales professional might receive commissions when selling certain products but not others. Some people get a commission on sales while others receive profit-based

Copyright © Mometrix Media. You have been licensed one copy of this document for personal use only. Any other reproduction or redistribution is strictly prohibited. All rights reserved.
This content is provided for test preparation purposes only and does not imply an endorsement by Mometrix of any particular political, scientific, or religious point of view.

commissions. Next, employees should ascertain the percentage commission they receive. This may vary. For instance, a sales professional might receive a different percentage of commission depending on what he sells. Once he knows the commissionable amount and rate of commission, he will then multiply them together. For instance, if an employee receives a 10 percent commission on $100, then he will receive $10 in commission (0.1 × $100). The employee will then need to calculate taxes on the commission to ascertain his final pay.

Calculating Hourly Wages from an Annual Full-Time Salary

It is simple to calculate hourly wages from an annual full-time salary. First, the amount of hours worked in the year must be calculated. If the person worked 40 hours a week, then the number of hours worked in the year would be 40 × 52, or 2,080 hours. If they worked 35 hours a week, then it would be 35 × 52, or 1,820. Generally, full-time indicates a 40-hour work week, so 2,080 should be assumed if there is no other information except that it is full-time. To calculate the hourly wage, simply divide the full-time salary by 2,080. Thus if the person earned $41,600, then the hourly salary would be $41,600/2080, or $20 an hour.

Percentages

To calculate a percentage from a decimal, one has to simply multiply it by 100. Thus, 0.15 is 15 percent. To increase a number by a certain percentage (like when a product is marked up by a percentage), a person would first calculate the increase by multiplying the percentage by the cost. For instance, if the cost of a good is $100 and the company wants to mark it up 50 percent, then the markup would be $100 multiplied by 50 percent (which is the same as 0.5), and that would equal $50. Thus, the cost plus the markup would be $150. A person can also use it to find wholesale prices. If the wholesale price is 75 percent of the price of $100, then to get the wholesale price, a person would just multiply $100 by 75% or 0.75 to get a wholesale price of $75. Percentages are used in many business applications.

Compound Interest

Compound interest is when interest gets added back to the principal and then interest is calculated on that additional amount when the next compounding period happens. The formula to calculate compound interest is $A = P\left(1 + \frac{r}{n}\right)^{nt}$. In this formula, A represents the investment's future value (with interest). P is the principal or initial investment, r is the annual interest rate expressed as a decimal, n represents how many times the interested is compounded annually, and T is how long the money has been invested (in years). For instance, if an amount of $10,000 was invested, the interest rate was 0.1 and it is compounded monthly, then after 20 years, the investment value would be $A = 10000\left(1 + \frac{0.1}{12}\right)^{(12(20))}$,which equals $73,280.74.

Review Video: Compound Interest Formula
Visit mometrix.com/academy and enter code: 100366

Frequency Distributions

Frequency distributions are tables that show how often specific results emerged. For instance, a teacher might do a frequency table showing how often the students got an A, B, C, D or F. The teacher would create the table listing the grades on the left and then put the number of students that achieved each one to the right. To find out how many earned a grade, the person could look at the table.

Copyright © Mometrix Media. You have been licensed one copy of this document for personal use only. Any other reproduction or redistribution is strictly prohibited. All rights reserved.
This content is provided for test preparation purposes only and does not imply an endorsement by Mometrix of any particular political, scientific, or religious point of view.

Frequency tables are used often in business. For instance, if one needed to find out how often sales reached a certain level, he (or she) could put the data into a frequency table and see how often that occurred. Some frequency tables will also list a cumulative total; this is good if the person wanted to see how often sales reached at least a certain level.

Mean, Mode, Median, and Standard Deviation

Mean is simply the average of a group of numbers. This is calculated by adding all the numbers and dividing by how many numbers there are. For instance, if the numbers are 3, 2, 3, and 4, one would add them to get 12 and then divide by 4 to get 3 as the mean. The **mode** is simply the number that appears the most. In the group 3, 2, 3, and 4, the number 3 is the mode because it appears twice. The **median** is the number that would appear in the middle if the numbers were put in order. If the numbers are 7, 3, 9, 1, 5, the numbers would be put in order to 1, 3, 5, 7, 9, and the median would be 5 because that is in the middle. To get the **standard deviation**, the mean should be calculated first. Take each number and subtract the mean, then get the squared difference by squaring the result. Finally, take all the squared differences in the group and find the square root of their average. That is the standard deviation.

Review Video: Standard Deviation
Visit mometrix.com/academy and enter code: 419469

Sampling Techniques and Selection

There are different methods of sampling used when doing research. The basic categories are **probability sampling**, in which every individual has a chance of getting selected in a known probability; and **nonprobability sampling**, in which some units may not have a chance of selection, or their probability isn't known. Simple **random sampling** is the best probability method, but is often very difficult to achieve. Every individual in the population has the same chance of being selected. **Systemic sampling** (also known as Nth name selection technique) takes every Nth individual from the population. With **stratified sampling**, the population is divided into stratums, or groups with a shared characteristic such as gender or age. These are matched against how many actually reside in the population. Then the researcher uses random sampling to take the number from each stratum that represents its presence in the population. With **convenience sampling**, the researcher finds a convenient sample. This is not as accurate as other methods. With **judgment sampling**, the researcher uses his judgment to find the sample. **Quote sampling** starts out like stratified sampling but, instead of random sampling, they use judgment or convenience sampling to pick the individuals from the stratums.

Line Graphs

A **line graph** shows the connection between information. It is often used to show changes over time. For instance, a company may want to show how sales changed from month to month. On the vertical axis, they would label the different sales levels, including both the lowest and highest possible amount. On the horizontal axis, the months would be listed. For every month, a dot would be placed on the sales level. Once all the dots are posted for the different months, a line would be drawn to connect the dots to more easily show the relationship. In this case, managers could see whether sales went up, went down, stayed stagnant, or had no general pattern as the months went by. Line graphs can be useful visual aids for businesses.

Bar Graphs

A **bar graph** can be used to show data in a way that is clear and easy to understand. The first step is the title. For instance, a baseball coach may create a bar graph of hits made by players and call it "Hits Made By Players." Next, a label for each axis must be given. There will be a grouped data axis

Copyright © Mometrix Media. You have been licensed one copy of this document for personal use only. Any other reproduction or redistribution is strictly prohibited. All rights reserved.
This content is provided for test preparation purposes only and does not imply an endorsement by Mometrix of any particular political, scientific, or religious point of view.

representing the groups such as "Baseball Players." This can be either the horizontal or vertical axis. In this case, it will be at the bottom of the graph. A label should be created for the frequency axis such as "Number of Hits." This should be on the left side of the graph. A range also needs to be produced. If the best hitter had 18 hits, then the scale might go from 0-20. The scale interval should be considered. There could be one mark for each hit or a marker to signify every five hits. Now the data is used to draw in bars to the correct height. For instance, the player that made 10 hits will have a bar that rises to the 10 marker. This will be repeated for all the players.

Circle Graphs

Circle graphs are useful visual aids that show a variety of data. First, a circle is formed. Then the circle is divided into different sectors to represent the different elements that the graph is representing. The sectors should be the size of their percentage. For instance, a company might make a circle graph representing sales of different colors of a product like a shirt. If half of consumers bought the blue shirt, then half the circle would be a segment representing the blue shirt. If a quarter bought the red shirt, then a quarter of the circle would be a sector representing the red. Once all the sectors are created, they should be labeled with what they represent and the corresponding percentage. The business can then view the graph to easily get an idea of which colors sold the best.

Scatter Plots

A **scatter plot** shows how two variables are related to each other. A company can plot the different values of the variables to see how they relate. For instance, a company may want to see how sales are at different price points. On the vertical axis they can put sales while on the horizontal one they can put price. They can then adjust the price of their product and figure out the sales level for one day of each price. They will then plot the numbers on the graph and look for a relationship. Depending on the variables, there may or may not be one. In this case, the expected relationship will be that the higher the price, the lower the sales. They can use the graph to work out what is the best price point to make the best profits. Scatter plots can give a good visual representation of the relationship between two variables and are often used in business.

Random Variable for a Quantity of Interest

In order to graph a random variable and analyze its distribution, it's helpful to quantify it, i.e., to assign a numerical value to each possible event. This is more useful when there is some number that naturally corresponds to the event, rather than just arbitrary assignments. If the random variable represents the colors of the cars passing by, there's little gained by defining 1 to correspond to blue, 2 to red, and so on. However, if you want to quantify a student's attendance in a class, for example, one can derive a suitable number by adding together the number of days the student has been absent plus one fourth the number of days he has been tardy. This then gives a numerical value that can be graphed and otherwise analyzed.

Probability Distribution

A probability distribution is a set of values of a random variable, with a probability assigned to each one. All possible values of the random variable should be represented in the distribution, and the sum of all their probabilities must equal 1, or 100%. For instance, suppose our random variable represents the number of tails that come up if we flip a coin five times. The probability that no tails will come up is $\frac{1}{2^5} = \frac{1}{32}$, the probability of one tails is $\frac{5}{32}$, the probability of two or three tails is each $\frac{5}{16}$, the probability of four tails is $\frac{5}{32}$, and the probability that the coin will come up heads all five

Copyright © Mometrix Media. You have been licensed one copy of this document for personal use only. Any other reproduction or redistribution is strictly prohibited. All rights reserved.
This content is provided for test preparation purposes only and does not imply an endorsement by Mometrix of any particular political, scientific, or religious point of view.

times is $\frac{1}{32}$. Note that as required, the sum of all these probabilities is equal to 1: $\frac{1}{32}+\frac{5}{32}+\frac{5}{16}+\frac{5}{16}+\frac{5}{32}+\frac{1}{32}=\frac{1+5+10+10+5+1}{32}=\frac{32}{32}=1$.

Probability in Terms of Relative Frequency for a Finite Distribution

Probability is expressed as a relative frequency. For a discrete distribution, the probability that a variable X has certain values is defined as the sum of relative frequencies for each of those certain values of X,

$$\sum_{i=1}^{i=N} \delta_i f(x_i)$$

where $f(x_i)$ has the property that

$$\sum_{i=1}^{i=N} f(x_i) = 1$$

and $f(x_i)$ is the relative frequency that x_i occurs in the population, and $\delta_i = 1$ if x_i is one of the values of X whose relative frequency you wish to determine, otherwise $\delta_i = 0$.

Example: If two dice are tossed, the variable X is the outcome (sum of the two dice),

DIE #1	DIE #2	POSSIBLE OUTCOMES FOR X
1	1 2 3 4 5 6	2 3 4 5 6 7
2	1 2 3 4 5 6	3 4 5 6 7 8
3	1 2 3 4 5 6	4 5 6 7 8 9
4	1 2 3 4 5 6	5 6 7 8 9 10
5	1 2 3 4 5 6	6 7 8 9 10 11
6	1 2 3 4 5 6	7 8 9 10 11 12

Calculate the relative frequency of each outcome,

X	2	3	4	5	6	7	8	9	10	11	12
RELATIVE FREQUENCY	1/36	2/36	3/36	4/36	5/36	6/36	5/36	4/36	3/36	2/36	1/36

Calculate the probability, or sum of the relative frequencies, that X<8,

$$\sum_{i=1}^{i=11} \delta_i f(x_i) = \frac{1}{36}+\frac{2}{36}+\frac{3}{36}+\frac{4}{36}+\frac{5}{36}+\frac{6}{36}=\frac{21}{36}=\frac{7}{12}$$

Probability in Terms of Relative Frequency for a Continuous Distribution

For a continuous distribution, the probability is the integral of the probability distribution function (pdf) over the range of values for the variable whose probability one wishes to determine.

$$\int_A^B p(x)\,dx + \int_C^D p(x)\,dx + \cdots$$

Due to the definition of the integral, the relative frequency of a specific value for x is zero because, $\lim_{\Delta x \to 0} p(x)\Delta x = 0$. However, the relative frequency or probability is generally non-zero when

Copyright © Mometrix Media. You have been licensed one copy of this document for personal use only. Any other reproduction or redistribution is strictly prohibited. All rights reserved.
This content is provided for test preparation purposes only and does not imply an endorsement by Mometrix of any particular political, scientific, or religious point of view.

integrated over a range of possible values for x. The pdf has the property that when integrated over all possible values of x,

$$\int p(x)\,dx = 1$$

Example: The probability that variable X is greater than A and less than B is 1/2. This is written,

$$\mathrm{P}(A < X < B) = \int_A^B p(x)dx = 1/2.$$

Example: The probability that variable X is less than A and greater than B is 1/2. The domain for $p(x)$ is $[0,\infty)$. This is written,

$$\mathrm{P}(X < A, X > B) = \int_0^A p(x)dx + \int_B^\infty p(x)dx = 1/2.$$

Graphing a Probability Distribution of a Random Variable

A probability distribution of a random variable may be graphed similarly to a data set. You can plot the value of the variable on the *x* axis and the probability corresponding to that outcome on the *y* axis. Since the probabilities add to 1, the individual probabilities are likely to be small, and the axis should be scaled accordingly.

For example, consider the random variable corresponding to the sum of the numbers on three fair dice. The probability that this sum will be 3 is $\frac{1}{216} \approx 0.0046$. The probability that the dice will sum to 4 is $\frac{3}{216} \approx 0.014$, and so on; the largest probabilities arise in the center, where we reach a probability of $\frac{27}{216} = 0.125$ that the sum of the dice will be 10, and the same probability for 11. If we plot the probabilities of each possible outcome on a graph, we get the following:

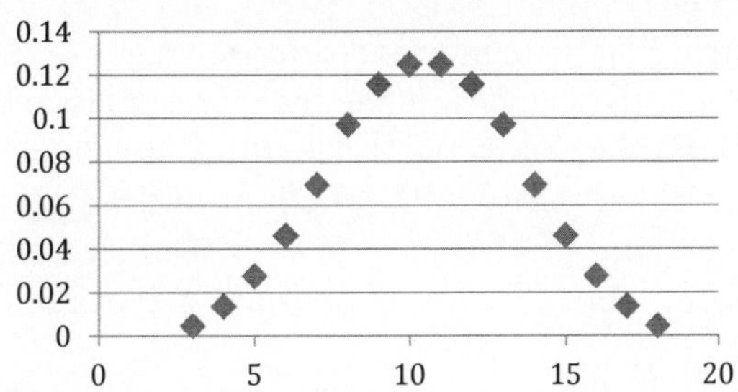

Value of a Random Variable Under the Probabilities of Various Outcomes

The expected value of a random variable is the sum of the possible values of the variable weighted by the probability of that value occurring. Mathematically, it can be expressed as $E(X) = \sum_{i=1}^{N} x_i P(x_i)$.

For instance, suppose you have a weighted die that has a probability $\frac{1}{3}$ of coming up 6, a probability $\frac{1}{6}$ of coming up 5, and a probability $\frac{1}{8}$ of coming up 1, 2, 3, or 4. The expected value of the die's result is therefore $6\left(\frac{1}{3}\right) + 5\left(\frac{1}{6}\right) + 4\left(\frac{1}{8}\right) + 3\left(\frac{1}{8}\right) + 2\left(\frac{1}{8}\right) + 1\left(\frac{1}{8}\right) = 2 + \frac{5}{6} + \frac{1}{2} + \frac{3}{8} + \frac{1}{4} + \frac{1}{8} = \frac{48+20+12+9+6+3}{24} = \frac{98}{24} = \frac{49}{12} \approx 4.08$.

Copyright © Mometrix Media. You have been licensed one copy of this document for personal use only. Any other reproduction or redistribution is strictly prohibited. All rights reserved.
This content is provided for test preparation purposes only and does not imply an endorsement by Mometrix of any particular political, scientific, or religious point of view.

Note that, as seen in this example, the expected value is not necessarily a value that you would actually expect to see; the weighted die will never show 4.08. Rather, it plays a role similar to the mean of a data set, providing a measure of central tendency of the variable's distribution.

Finding the Mean of a Probability Distribution

The mean of a probability distribution is synonymous with the expected value of a random variable. It can be calculated by summing all possible values of the variable weighted by their respective probabilities, $E(X) = \sum_{i=1}^{N} x_i P(x_i)$. For a uniform distribution, with all probabilities the same, $P(x_i) = \frac{1}{N}$ for all I, and this reduces to $(X) = \frac{1}{N}\sum_{i=1}^{N} x_i$, the more familiar formula for the mean of a data set. The more general formula for the mean of a probability distribution, however, holds for arbitrary distributions that may not be uniform.

The mean serves a similar role to the mean of a data set; it provides a measure of central tendency, and a rough idea of what a typical data point looks like. However, it also suffers from some of the same limitations as the mean of a data set, and does not by itself provide a complete picture of the distribution.

Confidence Interval

A confidence interval consists of three components: a statistic, a margin of error, and a confidence level.

The format is $sample\ statistic \pm margin\ of\ error\ with\ confidence\ level\ of\ XX\%$. The margin of error is proportional to the square root of the estimate of the variance is calculated from sample data.

When the distribution of the variable is known, the confidence level may be calculated by the area under the probability distribution function (pdf) and between the upper and lower limits of the confidence interval of the variable. This area is listed in the table for the distribution function, for example the standard normal table.

There is no single way of constructing the confidence interval of an unobservable population parameter, Θ. It depends on the statistical variable whose interval is to be estimated and the distribution of that statistical variable (if any exist). The first rule of constructing an interval is that the upper and lower end-points, U and L, are both functions of the statistical variable X. In other words, the confidence interval will be $(L(X), U(X))$. The probability Pr that the confidence interval $(L(X), U(X))$ includes the unobservable population parameter Θ at the $(1 - \alpha)(100\%)$ confidence level is:

$$Pr\big(L(X) < \Theta < U(X)\big) = (1 - \alpha).$$

Copyright © Mometrix Media. You have been licensed one copy of this document for personal use only. Any other reproduction or redistribution is strictly prohibited. All rights reserved.
This content is provided for test preparation purposes only and does not imply an endorsement by Mometrix of any particular political, scientific, or religious point of view.

How Large Must the Sample Size Be to Calculate the Confidence Interval with No More Than 10% Error?

When sample size is too small, the confidence interval at the $(1-\alpha)100\%$ confidence level

$$\hat{p} \pm z_{\alpha/2}\sqrt{\frac{\hat{p}(1-\hat{p})}{n}}$$

must be replaced with

$$\frac{\hat{p} + \frac{1}{2n}z_{\alpha/2}^2 \pm z_{\alpha/2}\sqrt{\frac{\hat{p}(1-\hat{p})}{n} + \frac{1}{4n^2}z_{\alpha/2}^2}}{1 + \frac{1}{n}z_{\alpha/2}^2}.$$

So, for the $z_{\alpha/2}^2$ terms to contribute less than 10% error in the interval for a $(1-\alpha)$ confidence level,

$$n \geq Max\left(\frac{z_{\alpha/2}}{0.21\hat{p}}, \frac{z_{\alpha/2}}{0.21(1-\hat{p})}\right).$$

Note: For a 95% confidence level, after rounding up to nearest integer,

$$n\hat{p}, n(1-\hat{p}) \geq \frac{1.96}{0.21} = 9.33 \to 10.$$

Example: What is the minimum sample size required to use the z-Table to calculate the 95% confidence interval so that there is no more than 10% error in the interval when $\hat{p} = 0.10$?

$$n \geq Max\left(\frac{z_{\alpha/2}}{0.21\hat{p}}, \frac{z_{\alpha/2}}{0.21(1-\hat{p})}\right) = Max\left(\frac{z_{0.025}}{0.21(0.10)}, \frac{z_{0.025}}{0.21(0.90)}\right)$$

$$= Max\left(\frac{1.96}{0.21(0.10)}, \frac{1.96}{0.21(0.90)}\right) = Max\left(\frac{1.96}{0.21(0.10)}, \frac{1.96}{0.21(0.90)}\right) = Max(93.3, 10.4) = 94.$$

Note: More samples are needed when $\hat{p}$ is very low or very high.

Meaning of a Confidence Level (i.e., 95% Confidence Level)

A confidence level of say 95% means that if the same sampling method were repeated a total of 100 times and the confidence interval was calculated each time, the true population parameter would fall inside 95 of the calculated confidence intervals.

Example: A normally distributed variable X is sampled 10 times. The standard deviation and 95% confidence interval is calculated. This process is repeated 10 times. For a normal distribution, 95%

Copyright © Mometrix Media. You have been licensed one copy of this document for personal use only. Any other reproduction or redistribution is strictly prohibited. All rights reserved.
This content is provided for test preparation purposes only and does not imply an endorsement by Mometrix of any particular political, scientific, or religious point of view.

of the values are between $\mu - 1.96\sigma$ and $\mu + 1.96\sigma$. The results for the 10 estimates of the 95% confidence interval are,

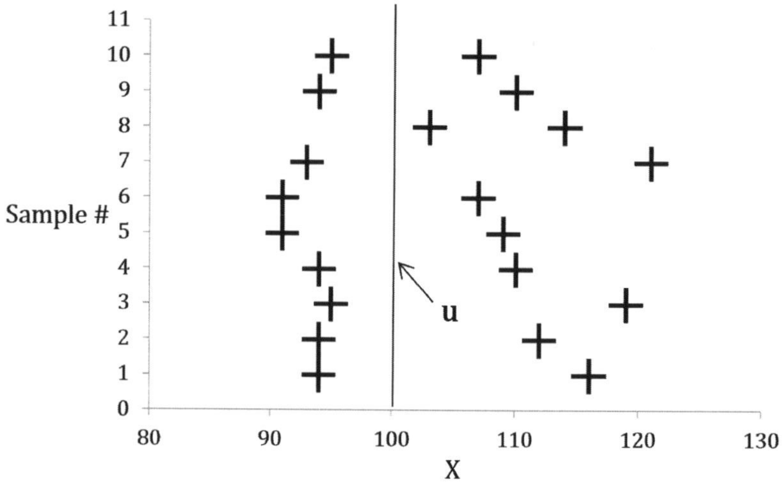

#	$\bar{x}_{10} - 1.96s_n$	$\bar{x}_{10} + 1.96s_n$
1	94	116
2	94	112
3	95	119
4	94	110
5	91	109
6	91	107
7	95	121
8	102	114
9	94	110
10	95	107

It turns out that $\mu = 100$, therefore, the true population mean does not fall in the confidence interval for sample #8, but it does fall within 9 of the 10 confidence intervals which is reasonably close to the 95% confidence level.

Processes Associated with the Binomial and Geometric Distributions

The process associated with a binomial distribution may be thought of as n independent trials each with probability p of a success, k is the number of successes, and

$$k \sim b(k, n, p) = \frac{n!}{k!\,(n-k)!} p^k (1-p)^{n-k}.$$

The binomial distribution function has two fixed parameters n and p, and one variable k.

$$E(k) = np, Var(k) = np(1-p).$$

The process associated with a geometric distribution may be thought of as independent trials each with probability p of a success, z is the number of trials until the first success, and

$$z \sim g(z, p) = (1-p)^{z-1} p.$$

Copyright © Mometrix Media. You have been licensed one copy of this document for personal use only. Any other reproduction or redistribution is strictly prohibited. All rights reserved.
This content is provided for test preparation purposes only and does not imply an endorsement by Mometrix of any particular political, scientific, or religious point of view.

The geometric distribution function has one fixed parameter p and one variable z.

$$E(z) = \frac{1}{p}, Var(z) = \frac{(1-p)}{p^2}.$$

Processes Associated with the Geometric and Negative Binomial Distributions

The process associated with a geometric distribution may be thought of as independent trials each with probability p of a success, z is the number of trials until the first success, and

$$z \sim g(z, p) = (1-p)^{z-1}p.$$

The geometric distribution function has one fixed parameter p and one variable z.

$$E(z) = \frac{1}{p}, Var(z) = \frac{(1-p)}{p^2}.$$

The process associated with a negative binomial distribution may be thought of as independent trials each with probability p of a success, w is the number of failures before r successes, and

$$w \sim b_{neg}(w, r, p) = \frac{(w+r-1)!}{(r-1)!\,w!} p^r (1-p)^w.$$

The negative binomial distribution function has two fixed parameters r and p, and one variable w.

$$E(z) = \frac{r(1-p)}{p}, Var(z) = \frac{r(1-p)}{p^2}.$$

Probability of a True Population Statistic Being Within a Confidence Interval Equal to $(1-\alpha)$ and Estimate of a Statistic $\pm$ Margin of Error at $(1-\alpha)100\%$) Confidence Level

$Pr\big((estimate\ of\ statistic - Std\ Error) < true\ population\ statistic < (estimate\ of\ statistic + Std\ Error)\big) = (1-\alpha) = 0.6826.$

$estimate\ of\ statistic \pm Std\ Error$ at 68.26% $confidence\ level.$

By contrast, the margin of error of the statistic can be defined for an arbitrary confidence level, $(1-\alpha)100\%$),

$$Pr\Big(\big(estimate\ of\ statistic - t_{\alpha/2}[n-1]\ x\ Std\ Error\big) < true\ population\ statistic < \big(estimate\ of\ statistic + t_{\alpha/2}[n-1]\ x\ Std\ Error\big)\Big) = (1-\alpha).$$

$estimate\ of\ statistic \pm t_{\alpha/2}[n-1]\ x\ Std\ Error$ at $(1-\alpha)100\%$ $confidence\ level.$

If the true population variance of the statistic is known, its square root is the standard deviation of the statistic, and the following equation applies,

$$Pr\Big(\big(estimate\ of\ statistic - Z_{\alpha/2}\ x\ Std\ Dev\big) < true\ population\ statistic < \big(estimate\ of\ statistic + Z_{\alpha/2}\ x\ Std\ Dev\big)\Big) = (1-\alpha).$$

$estimate\ of\ statistic \pm Z_{\alpha/2}\ x\ Std\ Error$ at $(1-\alpha)100\%$ $confidence\ level.$

Copyright © Mometrix Media. You have been licensed one copy of this document for personal use only. Any other reproduction or redistribution is strictly prohibited. All rights reserved.
This content is provided for test preparation purposes only and does not imply an endorsement by Mometrix of any particular political, scientific, or religious point of view.

Business Communication

Goals of Business Correspondence

There are a number of goals commonly seen on business correspondence, and at times they overlap. One of the major goals of business correspondence is to give information. One employee may be providing information to another employee, or the company may be sharing business happenings to customers. Another common goal is to sell the company's goods and services. Many companies create advertisements, blogs, social media posts, and other promotional materials to convince consumers to purchase their offerings. Business correspondence may also be used to convince an audience of something. A person may send a letter to a client to convince him that his product is better. An employee may try to convince another employee to try a new policy. Business professionals often correspond as a response to a question. If a consumer emails a question, customer service will respond with the answer. Businesses will often send out confirmation emails. This may be in response to a purchase or a question. Another form of correspondence may be sent out if an adjustment needs to be made. Correspondence may be through paper, email, the Internet, or other methods.

Communication Modalities

There are many different communication modalities used within a business, including emails, phone calls, and in-person meetings, each with its own uses. **Face-to-face communication** is very important in business, especially when delivering important or serious information. For instance, if there is a serious conflict with an employee, the supervisor is going to want to sit down and talk to him. If a business is going after a big client, a face-to-face meeting can show a lot of effort. Meetings can impart a lot of information to many people very quickly, engage people, and allow everyone to interact. **Email** is used very often for a wide variety of business matters because of its ease, speed, and convenience. This is often used in customer service because many customers prefer it. Also, it allows customers and customer service to interact even when the customer is not available during service business hours. The **telephone** is also commonly used, especially when it is a quick question that needs immediate attention. If there is a lot of back and forth required, a phone call can be quicker than an exchange of emails. Companies generally use many of these forms of communication.

Effective Communication Skills

Effective communication skills are important in business. First, it is important for people to practice active listening. This means perceiving everything about the communication by using all senses. Not only should a person listen, but they should also watch for body language and try to evaluate how the speaker feels. People want to feel like others are really listening to them and processing what they are saying. Eye contact is important. The person shouldn't interrupt or make it seem like he's making judgments. He should display interest. This can be done by nodding or making small comments. Nonverbal communication is also important. The person should appear engaged, relaxed, and open. He should not be fidgeting. He should use open body language. A person should be aware of what he says and how it comes across, choosing his words carefully. One can easily insult someone, even accidently. He should not argue, but try to work together to communicate effectively. In business, people should think logically and try to keep stress and emotion from influencing decisions. With practice, people can improve their communication skills.

Nonverbal Communication

Nonverbal communication can be just as important as verbal communication in business, thus it is important to know the best strategies to make it effective. First, eye contact is important because it shows that a person is interested, engaged, and actively listening. A person's facial expression can

Copyright © Mometrix Media. You have been licensed one copy of this document for personal use only. Any other reproduction or redistribution is strictly prohibited. All rights reserved.
This content is provided for test preparation purposes only and does not imply an endorsement by Mometrix of any particular political, scientific, or religious point of view.

express a lot. When one smiles, she is showing friendliness, encouragement and/or satisfaction with the work. When one frowns or displays an angry face, she is showing displeasure. It is important to show the expression that matches the feelings a person wants to convey when communicating in business, because otherwise the recipient may get the wrong idea. Gestures can show a lot. Someone clenching his fists may show anger. Hand movements can also help convey information. A person's posture tells a lot. Someone who crosses her arms may show resistance. A business professional who is standing or sitting tall may show off confidence. If someone is fidgeting, he may show discomfort or nervousness, which is not good for business. Business professionals should evaluate their nonverbal communication to make sure it enhances what they want to portray.

Proper Etiquette in Personal and Business Communication

Individuals should always practice proper courtesy. Business professionals should ordinarily address each other in a formal way and conduct appropriate cultural moves such as shaking hands. It is important to practice cultural sensitivity and know the rules and traditions of the person being greeted. For instance, in some cultures people may bow, while in another they may hug. People should make every effort not to show any bias or stereotypes as this can be very insulting to business contacts. Sometimes a person can come across as insulting or rude if she is ignorant of cultural customs. It is important to study the culture before interaction to make sure this does not happen. Otherwise, business communication should be formal and free of insults. It should be professional and without errors as well.

Communication Types Commonly Seen in Business

Business letters are sent for a wide variety of reasons and can be very formal. These may contain confidential and important information. Memoranda, also known as memos, are a less formal method of communication and may be used for announcements, information dissemination, and directions. They may be sent to a lot of people at once and are generally short and to the point. Emails are now commonly used in business communications because of their ease of use and speed. These may be less formal than written out business letters, or they can be just as formal. Publicity materials, such as press releases, are used to publicize an event or garner support. Recruitment communications are used in the process of hiring employees. For instance, a classified ad may be made when the company is hiring. Companies also make a lot of advertisements to draw consumers. These may be flashy advertisements or more subdued forms of communication and may appear in places such as newspapers and magazines.

Terminology Commonly Used in Business Communication

A memorandum is a short, informal form of business communication used to disseminate information. When a company writes "Enclosures," it means there is/are one or more enclosures. In email, an attached file is known as an attachment. The return address is the address of the person sending the letter. The inside address, or letter mailing address, is the recipient's address. The salutation is the greeting used, very commonly "Dear." The body is the main content of the letter. The complementary close is the closing at the bottom of the letter. There may also be reference initials at the end of the letter, which refer to the person who actually typed it, if different than the writer. Knowing these terms can help an individual write a professional business letter.

Writing Business Letters

A business letter should follow conventional professional practices. It starts with the sender's address (but not the name). Sometimes the address will be on the letterhead; otherwise it should be the first part. Next should be the date the letter was finished, written as month, day, and year. It should be two inches below the top and flush left (although some formats allow it to go in the

Copyright © Mometrix Media. You have been licensed one copy of this document for personal use only. Any other reproduction or redistribution is strictly prohibited. All rights reserved.
This content is provided for test preparation purposes only and does not imply an endorsement by Mometrix of any particular political, scientific, or religious point of view.

center). Underneath that will be the inside address, or the recipient's address, including the specific name and title of the addressee, always left justified. The salutation is under that and should include the personal title unless it is someone usually referred to by the first name. The body is next. Block format is common and is single spaced and flushed left. There is a line between each paragraph. The content should be succinct, to the point, and logical. It might start with an opening and the main idea of the letter, followed with information supporting or explaining the main point. The final paragraph may reiterate the point and ask for action. Below that is the closing. If there are enclosures, this should be stated under that.

Business Memorandum Format

A business **memorandum** is a relatively informal form of communication used in businesses to spread information, give announcements, explain company happenings, and provide similar functions. It is often sent out to a lot of people at once and does not generally contain confidential information. At the top it should state "Memorandum." Underneath that, flush left will be the word "TO:" along with the addressee(s). Underneath that and still flush left will be "FROM:" with the sender's name. If there are any CCs, this will be under that. Below that will be "DATE:" with the date. "SUBJECT:" is under that. Finally, the body of the memo will be underneath that, written in block format. A properly formatted memo is professional and succinct.

Presentations

Goals

Presentations can have one or more goals, and it is important for presenters to be aware of the specific objectives so they can tailor the presentation for maximum efficacy. One major goal of presentations is to give information to the audience. It might be to employees, the stockholders, the public, or another group, but the company may be presenting information about itself, its products, current news, or more. Reporting data is another common goal of presentations. For instance, a company may be reporting sales numbers to its stockholders. Sometimes presentations are made to convince an audience of something. For example, a company may give a presentation to a potential client in an effort to broker a deal. Inspiring is another common goal. This is often done in employee meetings. For instance, a company may have a meeting to motivate its employees to work harder to reach certain goals. It is vital for the presentation to match its goals and audience for the best chance of success.

Features of Successful Presentations

Presentations play a big part in business, so it is important to know the features of successful ones. First, the audience should be able to understand the presentation. It needs to be tailored to the audience so they can relate to it. It should be concise. The presenter should not carry on too long about the same thing because he or she could lose the audience. A good opening hook is important. It engages the audience from the start. Some people start with a story or quote. The presentation should also look good visually. Visual aids that can enhance a business presentation include graphs, charts, photographs, and videos. If the presentation contains a call to action, then it should be strong. The audience should be moved to do it. The presenter should be skilled. He should speak loud enough that everyone can hear, keep eye contact, and engage in good body language. He should appear confident. The presentation should flow well and keep the audience's attention. Many business presentations are participative because this can keep people's interest. All of these measures go a long way in making a business presentation successful.

Characteristics of Various Audiences

It is important for presenters to understand the characteristics of the audience for a business presentation because that can greatly influence the best presentation. The size of an audience

Copyright © Mometrix Media. You have been licensed one copy of this document for personal use only. Any other reproduction or redistribution is strictly prohibited. All rights reserved.
This content is provided for test preparation purposes only and does not imply an endorsement by Mometrix of any particular political, scientific, or religious point of view.

matters. The presentation will be different for a small room of 10 people compared to a large audience of 500. The cultural composition will matter. People of different cultures have different beliefs and may perceive a presentation differently. The other personal characteristics of the group, such as age, gender, and religion, can also affect how presentations are viewed. The level of knowledge matters. A health presentation on the same subject will be very different if given to a group of doctors as compared to a group of patients. Presenters should evaluate the audience to formulate the best presentation.

Preparation Steps

First, the presenter must understand his or her goals. What does he want to accomplish with the presentation? Once he knows this, he can select the exact topic, narrowing it down to fit the size and timing of the presentation. He will then need to evaluate the audience. The presentation of the same subject will be very different if given to customers as compared to employees or stockholders. The audience should be able to understand the topic, terminology, and references. The presenter should understand what is important to the audience and what they are thinking. Next, he should come up with the main points he wants to cover and make sure they are well illustrated in the presentation. He should find material to support these points such as graphs, charts, tables, photographs, data, and other visual items. This can give the presentation more substance and validity. Finally, the presenter should practice, ideally in front of someone who can evaluate the performance. By taking the time to carefully perfect the presentation, he will be more likely to reach his goals.

Adjusting Based on Needs and Concerns of Audience

To make the most impact, a presenter should adjust his presentation based on the needs and concerns of the audience. First, he or she needs to understand the audience and how they will likely feel about the presentation. He or she should do as much research as possible into the characteristics of the audience, including whether they will accept the presentation with acceptance or hostility and should plan to address their concerns. For instance, if he or she thinks the audience might be potentially hostile, the presenter should right away include things that will help to alleviate their concerns or ease the news to them. He or she should explain things so that they understand and will hopefully accept the content. It is important for the presenter to show empathy to the audience so they feel like the presenter is on their side. Oftentimes, the presenter allows the audience to ask questions and participate so that he or she can address their concerns directly. If they are worried about something that will not happen, then the presenter should be reassuring, personable, and friendly. The more the presenter comes off as a caring and competent individual, the better the presentation will proceed.

Delivery Strategies

Different strategies can make presentation delivery more effective. One decision is whether to use an extemporaneous (unscripted) speech or a scripted one. If the person is knowledgeable enough and wants to engage the audience without looking at a paper or prompter, he or she might choose the unscripted version. If he thinks he would be too nervous or forgetful without it, he might choose to use a script. Anyone might need it for a very technical speech with a lot of statistics. No matter what, it is important for the presenter to display only positive body language. He should make eye contact with members of the audience and not just look down. He should use positive gestures, facial expressions, and enthusiasm. He should watch his words to make sure nothing can be interpreted as biased or inappropriate. It is important for the presenter to be aware of the audience at all times and respond as necessary. If he senses that they do not understand something, for instance, he should go into more detail. If they are upset about something, he should try to address their concerns. With the right strategies, the presentation has a greater chance of success.

Copyright © Mometrix Media. You have been licensed one copy of this document for personal use only. Any other reproduction or redistribution is strictly prohibited. All rights reserved.
This content is provided for test preparation purposes only and does not imply an endorsement by Mometrix of any particular political, scientific, or religious point of view.

Visual Aids

Visual aids can enhance a business presentation. Graphs and charts can give a visual representation of the subject. For instance, if a person is talking about how sales numbers have changed, a line graph can make this very clear by showing how sales have changed over time or in response to certain variables. Diagrams can give a visual explanation of a concept. They can make a technical subject easier to understand. For instance, if someone is explaining a new product to investors, a diagram can help explain how it works. Slideshows are commonly used in business presentations. They can reinforce what the presenter is saying and draw interest. If a company is talking about its charity work, a picture of a smiling child the company helped would be more compelling than just talking about it. Videos can also show people a great deal. For instance, a company can make a video showing its factories or a new design. Computer projections are used as well. Most presentations use one or more visual aids.

Whiteboards, Presentation Software, and Multimedia Equipment

Whiteboards are often used in presentations. These are dry erase boards that the presenter can write on as he is speaking. This is also useful for a participative presentation in which the presenter asks the audience a question and writes down the answers as they are given. He can show step-by-step how something is done. Presentation software is also very commonly used. PowerPoint is one of the most commonly used presentation software programs and allows presenters to create detailed slides of photographs, charts, graphs, and more to enhance the presentation. They can make it easier to understand numbers and statistics. There are also various types of multimedia equipment a presenter might use. They might use a projector or a television. All of these can catch the audience's attention and bring the presentation to life.

Telecommunication Modalities Used in Business

The telephone is one form of telecommunication modalities. Individuals can get immediate access to someone to ask a question or have a discussion. A disadvantage is that there is no record of it (unless the call is recorded) and someone may not be available for a phone call. Another common form is a fax machine. This allows someone else to see a document. It is almost immediate. Both locations must have faxing ability, and it creates a physical document instead of a digital record, which many businesses prefer. Videoconferencing is commonly used. Individuals can discuss matters in real time. They can also share charts, graphs, and other visual aids. It has lowered the need for many business trips. Network email is also commonly used in business. It is delivered almost immediately and leaves a record. It can take longer to explain something than a simple phone conversation, however. An advantage is that it can be less intrusive and sometimes quicker.

Internet Modalities Used in Business

Email can be used to communicate with other businesses and with customers. Many customers prefer to email a company and it can be less time consuming for the company than a phone call. People like the convenience of being able to do it at any time. Message boards are also used. This is advantageous because customers can look up threads with topics similar to their issues and might get the answer to the problem without needing to contact customer service themselves. Mailing lists allow businesses to send out emails to many people at once. It is a great way for a company to disseminate information. Many companies also have instant messaging, both between its employees and for customers. This can be a great way to give customer service because customers like getting answers right away. One employee can be on several chats at once, which lowers the number of employees needed as compared to phone support. Chat rooms are also convenient because multiple people can see the answers. Many businesses use a combination of these.

Copyright © Mometrix Media. You have been licensed one copy of this document for personal use only. Any other reproduction or redistribution is strictly prohibited. All rights reserved.
This content is provided for test preparation purposes only and does not imply an endorsement by Mometrix of any particular political, scientific, or religious point of view.

Communication Technologies Used in Business

Many businesses have switched to solely wireless technology use, such as tablets and phones that use wireless internet. Cell phones are advantageous because people can take them while they're on the go and be reachable even when not sitting at a desk in the office. Of course, they do not always get service everywhere. Fax machines are used to communicate a document over long distances. They are almost instantaneous, inexpensive, and create a hard copy. Bluetooth is a wireless technology that provides convenience by letting data travel over short distances. It has lowered the need for wires. Streaming technology has allowed multimedia to be constantly delivered and received from one party to another. For instance, a person can watch a live newscast on a phone. Voice over Internet Protocol (VoIP) allows voice and multimedia to go over the Internet and other Internet Protocol Networks (IP). An example is Skype. It is advantageous for businesses because it is inexpensive and offers high bandwidth efficiency. Because voice and data communications can use one network, infrastructure costs are lower. In addition, it can be run on inexpensive standard interfaces like personal computers. It can be less reliable, however.

Etiquette in Electronic Communications

It is important to use professionalism in electronic communications, especially if it is a business letter. Just because a message is sent via email does not mean it should be sloppy. Of course, how professional it is will depend on the recipient, but if it is to a professional contact, it should be formed professionally. The sender should make a proper introduction and closing and avoid emoticons, writing in all capitals, and using excessive exclamation marks. It is very important to make sure it is free of typos and grammatical errors. Senders should proofread it just as they would proofread a regular letter. It is also important to not bombard people with unnecessary emails. Senders should be careful about including someone in a chain of unnecessary emails. They should make use of BCC and not share people's addresses with others. They should write an appropriate subject line so people know what it is. Senders should be careful about confidential information because users can easily forward them. By following these rules, the email will be more professional.

Chapter Quiz

Ready to see how well you retained what you just read? Scan the QR code to go directly to the chapter quiz interface for this study guide. If you're using a computer, simply visit the online resources page at **mometrix.com/resources719/mttcbusmmt** and click the Chapter Quizzes link.

Copyright © Mometrix Media. You have been licensed one copy of this document for personal use only. Any other reproduction or redistribution is strictly prohibited. All rights reserved.
This content is provided for test preparation purposes only and does not imply an endorsement by Mometrix of any particular political, scientific, or religious point of view.

Management

Organizational Management

Douglas McGregor's Theory X Assumptions

Douglas McGregor's Theory X focuses on three main assumptions regarding employee motivation and behavior. First, one must assume that employees, by their inborn nature, do not like to work and will try to do as little as possible. This leads to a management style in which a supervisor has no choice but to manage in a dictatorial manner, using coercion, strict control, direction, and threats in order to persuade the employee to actually work. It assumes money as the sole motivating factor for employees and that only great incentives or strict punishments will be effective in convincing an employee to work. It also assumes the person does not possess ambition and wishes for this direction, desiring security first and foremost. Furthermore, it assumes employees worry only about themselves and that the manager must assume control to get the most out of his or her employees.

Douglas McGregor's Theory Y Assumptions

Douglas McGregor's Theory Y provides a positive view of employees. It assumes that employees can be self-motivated and enjoy work just like they might enjoy play. It is natural to them. Although their talents are often under-utilized, most people do possess the talent, skills, imagination, ingenuity, creativity, and motivation to solve problems and direct themselves. They can control themselves, and accept and even search for responsibility and work to accomplish goals on their own. They desire success at work for the inherent satisfaction of performing well. Managers need not exercise strict control to force employees to work, but should instead organize, arrange, and allow for decision making in employees. These assumptions lead to a culture where supervisors work with employees and allow for positive communication and employee development.

Management Methods

Total Quality Management

Total quality management is a management method that strives for better internal processes and increased customer satisfaction. If done correctly, costs can be lowered, performance will be raised, and customers will be more pleased. There are various principles of total quality management. First, managers need to believe they can and should manage quality levels. If there is a problem, it is rooted in the process, not the employees. Instead of focusing on fixing just the symptoms, managers should look for the cure to what's really wrong. Quality is the job of every employee at the company. There must be a way to measure quality so a company can understand its position. The company should always work on improving quality. Quality investing is long term; it can take a while, but the resulting success can also be long term.

Management by Objectives

First coined in 1954 in Peter Drucker's "The Practice of Management," **management by objectives (MBO)** is a management model that focuses on the creation of objectives or goals. A key component of MBO is that both managers and employees create the objectives. The employees will then be more motivated to achieve them because they had a say in their formulation. In addition to making objectives, companies must formulate a way to measure performance to ascertain whether the objectives are being met. An advantage of MBO is that it can produce a better relationship between management and employees, as well as more employee commitment. A disadvantage is that its

Copyright © Mometrix Media. You have been licensed one copy of this document for personal use only. Any other reproduction or redistribution is strictly prohibited. All rights reserved.
This content is provided for test preparation purposes only and does not imply an endorsement by Mometrix of any particular political, scientific, or religious point of view.

focus on end results rather than on forming a comprehensive plan may make it more difficult to reach the results.

ACTIVITY-BASED MANAGEMENT

In **activity-based management**, managers examine activities to evaluate costs and value added. The goal is to eliminate or improve the activities that are not as valuable to the company. Managers look at overhead costs and try to allocate resources to where they will be the most valuable. One disadvantage to activity-based management is that some activities that do not show an obvious financial benefit may still have intrinsic value. For instance, if a company spends money on a luxurious work environment, this may not be obvious in a dollar amount gain. However, if it helps them attract higher quality workers who will be more effective, then it will produce financial results, even if they aren't easily measured. Companies use information about the value added by particular activities to make better decisions about their business operations.

FUNCTIONS OF MANAGEMENT

Managers perform many different roles, and Henri Fayol created a list of five basic management functions, four of which are generally recognized today. These include planning, organizing, leading, and controlling. **Planning** involves creating a plan of action to accomplish a goal for the organization. For instance, if the manager wishes to increase employee efficiency, then he or she may create a plan to give incentives to top performers. The leader will make a list of logical steps to accomplish the goal. **Organizing** includes resource distribution as well as organizing employees in the best way to carry out the plan. For instance, the manager will decide which employees can help with the plan. He or she might delegate work and direct employees to help implement it. When a manager is **leading**, he or she connects with the employees personally. He or she might inspire, motivate, and encourage. The employees should look up to the manager as a leader. **Controlling** occurs after the plan has been implemented. Managers evaluate whether the goals of the plan have been met. If not, he or she will take action to reach the goal.

PLANNING

One of the most important jobs of a manager is the planning function. Managers need to formulate detailed plans to reach their goals. They need to carefully design the steps that will reach these goals. These steps should be flexible, as they may need to change as the plan is brought to fruition. There are different types of plans within an organization. A **strategic p**lan deals with the company as a whole and is long term. It might be related to the objectives and vision for the business. A **tactical plan** outlines the tactics the company will utilize to fulfill the strategic plan. An **operational plan** deals with the daily running of the company. In this type of plan, short-term objectives are highlighted. Managers that plan well have a better chance of realizing their goals.

ORGANIZING

Once a manager has created a plan to reach a goal, the next step in management is organizing. This is an extremely critical step. In this step, managers must decide how to allocate the resources they have to best achieve their goals. For instance, a manager may decide how much money each department gets. Another important part of organizing is researching the talents and abilities of employees and delegating the work in a way to best take advantage of their skills. Managers will decide who will fill each role and how the work will be done. He (or she) must also make sure employees understand these roles and can accomplish them. The manager must also dictate how decisions are made and by whom, conduct problem solving, and create the chain of command and communication procedures. He should decide who has managerial power and how reporting will occur. Authority is often delegated to increase efficiency. Once organizing is complete, there should

Copyright © Mometrix Media. You have been licensed one copy of this document for personal use only. Any other reproduction or redistribution is strictly prohibited. All rights reserved.
This content is provided for test preparation purposes only and does not imply an endorsement by Mometrix of any particular political, scientific, or religious point of view.

be an organizational structure that dictates the roles, power, responsibility, and information distribution.

Review Video: Corporate Organizational Structure
Visit mometrix.com/academy and enter code: 752986

Controlling

Once a manager has created a plan, organized, and led it, he must perform the fourth and final management function—controlling. This is the process by which a manager evaluates the results of a plan to ascertain whether it has met his goals. When controlling, the manager must first decide how he or she will measure performance. For instance, if the goal is increased financial position, he might look at profits. Other common goals might involve efficiency, production, or customer satisfaction. Next, he will need to develop a way to measure this. He might look at sales data, customer satisfaction surveys, or production numbers. The data should be clear, objective, and measurable. Next, the manager will evaluate the new numbers compared to standards. For instance, he might look at customer satisfaction numbers this year as compared to the year before the plan. Did satisfaction increase as he'd predicted? Finally, he will decide whether corrective action is needed, then plan and take it if necessary. For instance, if customer satisfaction did not go up as he had hoped, he will investigate to see what happened and decide how to change the plan to reach his goals.

Levels of Management

Many companies have different levels of management, and each level is responsible for certain functions. Managers are typically broken into top-level management, middle-level management, and low-level management. The **top-level managers** are the managers in charge of running the organization as a whole and making the major decisions for the company. They oversee everything about the company and control it. They generally have the most experience, with skills in leadership, delegation, and making major decisions. The CEO and president are examples of top-level management. **Middle-level managers** bring organizational plans to fruition. They are delegated some authority and are a liaison between top-level management and low-level management. They will often have a decent amount of experience and are adept at solving problems, building teams, and developing talent. A department manager or general manager of a store is an example of middle management. **Low-level managers** spend their time leading, directing, and supervising employees. Employees can go to them with problems. They typically have more skills and experience than general employees, and they should be good at dealing with people. Examples include foremen and supervisors.

Leadership Styles

In an **authoritarian (autocratic) leadership style**, the rules and regulations are strict and the manager keeps firm control. The relationship is purely professional, and there is a lot of supervision. Problems can occur when employees become unhappy that their ideas and suggestions are not heard. A **democratic (participative) leadership style** is very popular. The manager does not make all the decisions, but instead shares them with the group. There is discussion and debate, and the employees are encouraged to provide ideas, which can contribute to the group. There is still guidance and the leader makes the ultimate decisions, but everyone helps throughout the process. Employees are often happy with this type of management. With a **paternalistic leadership style**, the manager acts almost as a parent and the employees as children who trust and are loyal to their leader. They follow his or her lead. The **laissez-faire (delegative) style** of leadership is one in which the workers make all the decisions without any managerial control. This can be problematic if the workers cease to be productive because no one is holding them responsible.

Copyright © Mometrix Media. You have been licensed one copy of this document for personal use only. Any other reproduction or redistribution is strictly prohibited. All rights reserved.
This content is provided for test preparation purposes only and does not imply an endorsement by Mometrix of any particular political, scientific, or religious point of view.

SWOT Analysis

SWOT refers to strengths, weaknesses, opportunities, and threats. A SWOT analysis is a powerful tool that allows managers to evaluate both internal factors and the outside environment with the goal of making the best business decisions. A company may produce a chart to illustrate the SWOT analysis. They will list **strengths** such as positive assets, a good work force, etc. Next to strengths, **weaknesses** such as financial limitations or government regulations that limit the company will be listed. Next, the company will look at **opportunities** such as increasing demand for a product. They will then look for **threats** such as a competitor's new patent. Once the company has identified as many of these as possible, managers will look to take advantage of the strengths and opportunities, minimize the weaknesses, and turn the threats into opportunities. For instance, if the threat to a cookie company is that people are more health conscious, the company may turn the threat into an opportunity by producing a healthier cookie. By understanding these factors, the company can take advantage of what it has and address the problem areas.

Types of Financing Businesses May Utilize

When large companies want money for short term debt obligations, they may give out commercial paper, a money-market security. This can be sold to a dealer and then to the market, or straight to a buy and hold investor. It does not cost as much as credit within a bank. It is not secured, and the maturity is between one and 364 days. Businesses can also get a long-term loan to finance their business. A number of banks and organizations offer loans. Rates and amounts vary. A business can also issue stock to raise money. This is essentially selling a small piece of ownership in a company. Many businesses use a combination of these strategies.

Time Value of Money

Because money has the ability to earn interest, the **present value** of money is worth more than the same amount of money in the future. For instance, the $100 an individual receives today is worth more than the same $100 he receives in one year. That is because he will be able to earn interest on the money he receives today and turn it into more money in the future. The sooner he receives the money, the more it is worth. The **future value** of money depends on the interest rate. For instance, if a person has $100 now and the interest rate is 10 percent, he will have $110 in one year. This can be calculated with the algebraic formula: $PV = \frac{FV}{(1+r)}$ in which PV is the present value, FV is future value and *r* is the interest rate. In this case, it would be $100 = \frac{110}{(1+0.1)}$. This formula can also be used to calculate missing values.

Budget Types

A **sales budget** is a budget that shows the expected sales for a period of time. This is shown in units and dollars and is often categorized by product categories or geographic location. A **production budget**, typically seen in a "push" manufacturing system, shows the number of products that should be made. The sales forecast and finished goods inventory are used to calculate this. A **cash budget** covers the inflows and outflows of cash that are expected. The four sections of a cash budget are receipts, financing, disbursements, and cash surplus or deficit. A **capital expenditure budget** covers investments in long-term projects and capital assets. Generally, it is for a time span of three to 10 years and may cover investments in buildings, land, plants, and equipment.

Master Budget

A **master budget** encompasses all of the budgets of a company to give an entire view of the business as a whole, allowing for comprehensive financial planning. It has two major components: the operating budget and the financial budget. The **operating budget** is created first because the

Copyright © Mometrix Media. You have been licensed one copy of this document for personal use only. Any other reproduction or redistribution is strictly prohibited. All rights reserved.
This content is provided for test preparation purposes only and does not imply an endorsement by Mometrix of any particular political, scientific, or religious point of view.

financial budget will depend on its numbers. The operating budget includes the sales budget, production budget, direct materials purchases budget, direct labor budget, overhead budget, selling and administrative expenses budget, and cost of goods manufactured budget. The **financial budget contains** a schedule of expected cash receipts from customers, a schedule of expected cash payments of suppliers, the cash budget, a budgeted income statement, and a budgeted balance sheet.

Budgeting Approaches

With a **zero-base budget**, the managers first decide on the outcome they want, then create the expenditures to make that happen. The budget needs to match the outcome. This is often used for governments and other service-level entities so that the desired outcomes are achieved. With **flexible budgeting**, varying sales levels are put into the model, and the planned expense levels change accordingly. This can be advantageous when the company has trouble predicting sales.

In a **static budget** the expenditures do not change in response to sales levels. This is often used for public entities with fixed grants. With **top-down budgeting**, the top management makes the budget for the firm as a whole and decides on all the allocations. The lower levels do not get a say in what they get. With **bottom-up budgeting**, the lower level managers have a chance to participate and help set their own budget needs. Those are then put together to formulate the budget of the company as a whole.

Review Video: Static and Flexible Budgets
Visit mometrix.com/academy and enter code: 352590

Cost-Benefit Analysis

A **cost-benefit analysis** is an important process to complete when making decisions in business. It is a way of looking objectively at all the costs and benefits of different options to make the best decision for the company. First, the company must decide on the different options available. Once it has the options, a cost-benefit analysis should be run on each. The company should compile all the costs of an option, being careful to not omit important factors such as overhead costs, costs of operation, and opportunity costs. It is important to measure in objective terms such as money. Next, all the benefits should be compiled. Benefits affecting the employees, company, customers, and all stakeholders should be considered. The time value of money should also be applied so values are accurate. The company will then compare the costs and benefits to see what the net benefit (or cost) of each option would be. The company can then move forward with the best strategy.

Production Methods

Continuous Processes

A **continuous process production system** is a method of production in which products are continually produced. This is advantageous when a great volume of products are needed. Businesses use this for products such as cars, paper products, and many food products. The production line may have a significant amount of machinery to make it semi-automated. People generally control the computers with a workforce that may be a combination of skilled and unskilled laborers. The production is steady and will continuously run at all times unless there is a maintenance break. There is less flexibility with this type of production and it can cost a lot of money to set up, but then the cost per item can be lower as there is less need for labor. There are typically numerous quality control measures, such as sampling, to ensure quality.

Copyright © Mometrix Media. You have been licensed one copy of this document for personal use only. Any other reproduction or redistribution is strictly prohibited. All rights reserved.
This content is provided for test preparation purposes only and does not imply an endorsement by Mometrix of any particular political, scientific, or religious point of view.

Batch Operations

With a **batch operations production method**, similar items are made together in batches. They proceed together through each stage of production and then all move to the next stage. An example is a bakery producing batches of cookies, desserts, or pastries. Advantages are that each batch can be customized—they can make one batch of chocolate chip cookies and another of oatmeal to suit customer needs. Also, it saves money and time to make them in batches as compared to doing them individually. Companies can save money by using the same production systems on more than one product. Also, many companies could not afford the expensive equipment needed for a continuous production method. It is a suitable method when companies don't know how many of a product they'll need, as well as for seasonal items. One disadvantage is that companies may have some downtime as they go from one batch to another. Another disadvantage is that companies need to have raw materials for different products in stock.

Inventory Systems

Traditional

A **traditional inventory system** involves ordering materials and storing them until they are needed. Companies may make agreements with suppliers to receive volume discounts. There will also be extra inventory on hand in case demand suddenly goes up, and a brief interruption in delivery will not halt the entire system. There are also disadvantages to this type of system. Generally it is not as efficient as a just-in-time system. Companies have to pay for the cost of storing the materials, which can be substantial. They could also potentially be stuck with extra materials if they ultimately do not need as many as they predicted. Companies should weigh the advantages and disadvantages when deciding which is best for them.

Just-in-Time

A **just-in-time (JIT) inventory system** is an inventory system in which materials come in just as they are needed for production. The idea is to keep inventory as low as possible, thereby lowering the costs of storage. Businesses spend less on carrying costs and can also save with the time value of money because they do not have to pay for materials until they need them. They will not end up with extra materials that go to waste. One consideration with this system is that companies need to be able to forecast the amount of materials they will need. They will not have extras on hand, so if there is a sudden increase in demand, they may not have the materials available to meet that demand. Also, if there is a problem with materials, they will not have any extras on hand to cushion them.

Organization Structures of Companies

Functional Structures, Team Structures, and Adaptive Structures

Companies can be structured in a variety of ways, and each type possesses its own advantages and disadvantages. A company with a **functional structure** organizes the employees, tasks, and supervision in the company by function. For instance, there will be a marketing department, a production department, etc. The advantage is that these functions can become highly specialized. A disadvantage is that it can hamper communication between the different departments. Companies that make a lot of standardized products may use this type of structure. A **team structure** is where people with different abilities are put together to build teams that can achieve more than the individuals alone. The teams can be flexible and draw on the strengths of the members. An **adaptive structure** has multifunctional teams instead of a rigid hierarchy. All levels are encouraged to contribute to give the most to the organization. This flexibility can be beneficial, but it may also be more difficult to manage.

Copyright © Mometrix Media. You have been licensed one copy of this document for personal use only. Any other reproduction or redistribution is strictly prohibited. All rights reserved.
This content is provided for test preparation purposes only and does not imply an endorsement by Mometrix of any particular political, scientific, or religious point of view.

Networks, Matrix Structures, and Product-Based Structures

There are various organizational structures a company can utilize, and the best one depends on the characteristics of the business. One type is a **network structure**. In this structure, business functions that can be accomplished with less cost and/or better quality by others are outsourced. Managers dedicate a lot of time to dealing with these external forces. For instance, a clothing company may find a company that can make the goods with fewer resources, allowing the main company to focus on other functions. In a **matrix structure**, employees are grouped by function and product for maximum efficiency. Teams are often employed. For instance, if a company sells both cars and boats, they might have a car sales department and a boat sales department. In a **product-based structure**, the company is organized by product. A grocery store will have a produce section, a meat section, a dairy section, etc. This is often used for larger companies.

Centralized and Decentralized Structures

In **centralized structures**, one individual makes decisions for the company, whereas in **decentralized structures**, there is a team and the decisions are made at different levels. Which structure is best for the business depends on the manager, the size, and other factors. Centralized structures allow for quick decisions and efficiency because only one person is making the decisions. Decentralized structures allow multiple individuals to contribute, which can be slower, but can also provide more information, insight, and ideas to the organization. Some centralized organizations have a lot of bureaucracy, which can slow things down, or they might inadvertently make decisions that are not the best for the lower levels. Decentralized structures sometimes struggle with too many differing opinions. Each method has its advantages and disadvantages.

Formal and Informal Structures

The **formal structure** is the exact chain of leadership and the formal hierarchy. It will start with the owner or CEO and then work its way down the chain of command with clear indications of who is in charge. The **informal structure** is often centered on project groups or even on friendship. Those who are more knowledgeable or just more natural leaders may take on an informal leadership role even without specific authority. Others might look to such people for guidance because they know more, are more willing to help or provide other leadership functions. The response from an informal leader may be quicker and more efficient. Both structures are utilized in many businesses.

Human Resource Management

Staffing Process

Planning Stage

It is important for human resource personnel to properly plan the staffing process. First, they need to perform **human resources audits**. This is the process in which all the functions, policies, and characteristics of a company's human resources department are examined to look for problems, find best practices, and increase efficacy and efficiency. It is also done to make sure practices properly protect the company legally and effectively. The company will then perform a job analysis to look at a job to understand all of its functions and attributes as well as those needed of the employee who will perform the job. Next, human resource employees can create a job description with specifications on what needs to be done and who could do it. They can then start to look for the employee. Sometimes they look inwards. **Succession planning** is the process of looking at existing employees and planning and preparing them to move up in the company to leadership positions. It can make things move more smoothly when the company grows or a key person leaves.

Copyright © Mometrix Media. You have been licensed one copy of this document for personal use only. Any other reproduction or redistribution is strictly prohibited. All rights reserved.
This content is provided for test preparation purposes only and does not imply an endorsement by Mometrix of any particular political, scientific, or religious point of view.

Staffing Procedures

There are a number of **staffing procedures** companies must perform. First, they must recruit potential employees. This can be done in a number of ways. They may send out job advertisements or contact a recruiting agency. They can go to job fairs. Once they have an employee, the company must train him (or her). They must have a good training program that prepares him to do his job satisfactorily. The company must also evaluate its employees. Many companies formally evaluate employees on an annual basis, but in reality, employees are constantly evaluated for performance. The company can help employees to improve themselves. Evaluations can be used as a basis for raises. At times, employees need to be terminated. This can be because of a company situation, or due to the fault of the employee. Procedures should be put in place so this is as smooth as possible for both the employee and the company. With the right procedures in place, the company will run more efficiently.

Addressing Diversity in the Workplace

It is important for businesses to embrace and promote **diversity**. People from different backgrounds have different ideas and can contribute in many positive ways. Companies should make sure that there is diversity at their office and no unfair hiring practices. Many companies make a concerted effort to hire people from all different backgrounds. In the office, it is vital to promote an atmosphere of acceptance and tolerance. There should be a zero-tolerance policy for discrimination of any type. This should be communicated to employees regularly. Avenues should be provided to report any problems. With diligence, every workplace can celebrate and enjoy the benefits of diversity.

Cross-Training

Cross-training is when employees are trained to perform functions outside of the typical functions of their job. For instance, someone who works in the copywriting department of a firm might spend a little time in the graphic design department. There are various advantages to cross-training. First, if an employee is absent, someone else may be able to take over without a problem, which ensures that the job functions are completed even when someone is absent. It can also help a person better do his or her job. For instance, the copywriter who learns about graphic design might get a better idea of how her copy is going to look as a whole. Employees might also be able to communicate better with other departments when they understand more of what they are doing. Additionally, it can promote teamwork and help motivate employees because it helps them to better understand the company. Employees who are cross-trained are easier to promote because they already understand multiple parts of the company and the organization as a whole, which is an advantage for both the company and employee.

Maslow's Hierarchy of Needs

In his work on human motivation, Abraham Maslow created **Maslow's hierarchy of needs**, a five-tiered approach to needs and motivation. The pyramid-shaped hierarchy places basic needs at the bottom, which must be attained before higher levels are reached. The desire for these needs will increase the longer they are denied. This level of the pyramid encompasses **physiological needs**. These are what a human needs to survive such as food, water, air, and sleep. The need for **security** comes next. These include important needs such as the desire for a safe home, medical care, and a secure job. Once these are achieved, a person moves on to **social needs**. People want love, affection, and belonging though friends, social involvement, and romance. The next tier is **esteem needs**. These make a person feel like they are worthwhile. People look for a sense of accomplishment and recognition from others. Once a person has achieved these four basic needs, they can progress to the **growth need**, the top tier of self-actualization. This is where people have enjoyed personal

Copyright © Mometrix Media. You have been licensed one copy of this document for personal use only. Any other reproduction or redistribution is strictly prohibited. All rights reserved.
This content is provided for test preparation purposes only and does not imply an endorsement by Mometrix of any particular political, scientific, or religious point of view.

growth and are reaching their potential. They do not worry as much about others' opinions and instead focus on their own growth.

Review Video: Maslow's Hierarchy of Needs
Visit mometrix.com/academy and enter code: 461825

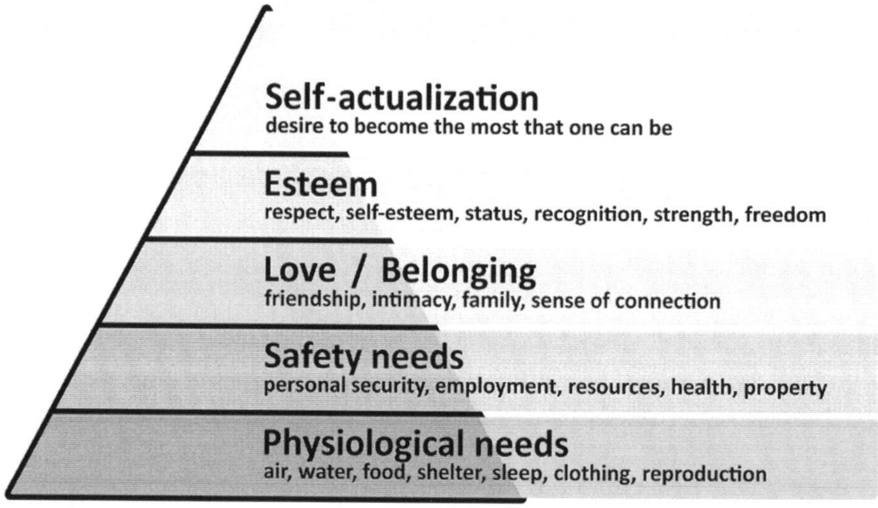

Collective Bargaining

Collective bargaining occurs when a company's management engages in talks with representatives of a workforce (often a trade union). They discuss numerous aspects of the business and its labor including working conditions, pay, hours, benefits, and more. It is advantageous to employees because they can have more bargaining power and more of a say when they band together. It is advantageous for the company because they just negotiate with one group and can get everything arranged and set without needing to go through the same process with every single employee. It avoids many future problems and arguments. Collective bargaining is commonly seen in many different industries and fields.

Conflict Resolution Strategies

When **conflict** occurs in the workplace, efficiency and efficacy can be impacted, thus it is important to employ conflict resolution strategies. There are numerous strategies a company can utilize. First, the company should address the situation right away. Small conflicts can grow into large ones with time. The manager should talk to the parties separately to get their side of the story. Sometimes the conflict is more of a misunderstanding than anything, and it can be simply solved by understanding the two points of view. The manager should understand what each person wants and see if there is a way to compromise and make everyone happy. They can try to mediate between the two people, allowing each party to speak. This meeting should be civil, calm, and constructive. Managers should try to come up with a solution that is beneficial for everyone. If necessary, a follow-up meeting should occur.

Effects of Group Dynamics on Individual Behavior

People can behave differently when in a group, and how groups act is an area of study called **group dynamics**. It is important for managers to understand these forces so they can promote positive behavior. **Groupthink** is a negative behavior that occurs when the people in a group want harmony so much that they minimize opposing viewpoints. They make a decision without considering all of the alternatives because the people do not want conflict. People will typically feel loyalty to certain

Copyright © Mometrix Media. You have been licensed one copy of this document for personal use only. Any other reproduction or redistribution is strictly prohibited. All rights reserved.
This content is provided for test preparation purposes only and does not imply an endorsement by Mometrix of any particular political, scientific, or religious point of view.

others that they identify with or respect. Also, they may have the mistaken impression that others agree it can't be wrong, even if many are harboring their own doubts. It is important to avoid this. Sometimes there can be conflict in a group and this can prevent the group from making decisions. Groups can also be good, especially if there is **group cohesion**, where people like and respect each other. If people are encouraged to speak their minds, then new opinions can emerge and the group can make the best decision possible.

Organizational Culture and Subculture Within the Workplace

Corporate culture encompasses many facets, including values, traditions, and customs. For instance, there may be a **formal culture** in which people dress formally and address each other in a formal manner. There might be a very **polite culture** in which people try to be very kind to each other. Management plays a big part in making the culture, which can have a large effect on the work that gets done. Within each culture, there are **subcultures** that may be very unique. For instance, the computer department in a firm may have a different subculture than the rest of the company, formed by their shared values, interests, etc. The various subcultures can affect the organization's culture as a whole. A positive culture can have a positive effect on the company.

Strategies to Promote Teamwork

Employees must work together even with differing and (at times) conflicting personalities. There are different measures employers can take to promote teamwork. One method is to incorporate **team-building exercising**. These might involve games or fun activities. There are companies that perform team-building sessions for companies. They can help employees get to know each other better and learn how to work together. There should be rules for teams to promote respect. For instance, employees should never insult others at the office. Employers should make sure employees adhere to the rules. If there is one person who is a problem, then management should talk to that person to address the situation. **Recognition** of teams is another way to promote teamwork. A company can recognize groups that work well together and accomplish their goals. The team members should have clear roles. This can help stop disagreements from a misunderstanding of roles and responsibilities. With strong teamwork comes better efficiency and productivity.

Influences on Employees' Morale and Motivation

First, employees should be fairly compensated. Employees who are underpaid may feel cheated and not motivated. Likewise, if a person is overworked, he or she will feel less motivated at the job. Jobs that allow the workers some flexibility can promote motivation. Also, workers who feel appreciated and valued have higher morale and motivation. Companies can accomplish this by praising employees or having recognition programs such as an **employee-of-the-month program**. Workers also like to have some say or responsibility in their work rather than just being told what to do. Workers will feel more motivated and have higher morale in a positive culture where people are respectful of each other. Working conditions affect employee motivation; employees will not feel very motivated if they are in a hot room crowded with 10 other people. The ability of the boss to lead well and create a good atmosphere also affects employee attitudes. Companies should work hard to control these factors to promote high morale and motivation.

Promoting Job Satisfaction Among Employees

If possible, employers can increase satisfaction by being flexible in employee schedules. When workers do not feel overworked, they are happier. Also, workers like to feel satisfied at their job—delegating some responsibility and letting them contribute instead of dictating every move can promote job satisfaction. Employers should be respectful of employees and provide a professional culture. Employees do not want to be talked down to or treated as if they are inferior. Employers

Copyright © Mometrix Media. You have been licensed one copy of this document for personal use only. Any other reproduction or redistribution is strictly prohibited. All rights reserved.
This content is provided for test preparation purposes only and does not imply an endorsement by Mometrix of any particular political, scientific, or religious point of view.

can show that they care about employees with something as simple as a manager recognizing when an employee is going through a difficult time, or offering a reward for a success. Employees like to be recognized for their hard work. Allowing employees to grow and feel like they are contributing is important. People will also be more satisfied if there is a place they can go with their complaints. It is worthwhile for a company to spend the time, effort, and money to promote job satisfaction. With higher satisfaction comes increased productivity.

Pertinent Factors When Determining Compensation

First, the company should consider the **experience** the employee possesses. An individual with 10 years of experience is generally more valuable than an employee directly out of college; he or she will expect and deserve higher compensation. The years the employee has been with the company also affects compensation. Many companies give a raise every year to reflect cost of living, merit, or both. **Skills** should also be considered. An employee with better or rarer skills should be compensated for them. The **education** of the employee matters as well. Generally, the higher the degree, the greater the compensation. Companies may have a salary range for the position based upon the wages paid for similar people in similar companies. This will depend on location and cost of living. Some companies pay a little more to attract higher quality employees or a little less to save money. Also, the company's **financial state** might affect pay. A company that is doing well will have more cash to spread around while one that is having difficulty might be more frugal. The other types of **benefits** offered will also affect pay.

Common Benefits Employees Receive

Employees receive many benefits in addition to financial compensation. Most full-time employees receive some type of paid time off. This may include sick, vacation, and personal days. Often, this number increases depending on the length of time the employee has been with the company. Companies also typically offer time off for holidays such as Thanksgiving and Christmas. The company may offer health insurance plans and even contribute to the premiums. Some employers also offer vision benefits, dental plans, and life insurance plans. Companies also often offer retirement benefits. It might be in the form of a pension, 401(k) plan, or an employee stock plan. The company may contribute to these as well. These benefits can be worth a great deal to an employee.

Retirement Plans

There are different types of retirement plans for which an employee may be eligible. A **pension** provides a fixed sum on a regular basis to an employee after retirement. This is often given to people who worked in public office or military service. Some employees are also eligible for an **employee stock ownership plan (ESOP)**. In this type of retirement plan, the company puts stock or money for stock into an account on behalf of the employee. This may have to vest over time. The employee does not control the stock directly until he or she leaves the firm, and then it is distributed. Many companies offer **401(k) plans**. These are tax-advantageous plans that allow people to defer their income taxes, both in earnings and contributions. A lot of employers will match a percentage of the contributions of the employee. A person can also get an individual retirement account that provides tax advantages.

Managing Employee Paid Time Off

Employers give employees paid time off in the form of vacation, sick time, and holidays. Companies may manage these by giving a certain amount of leave for each year of service, an amount that may increase when the person reaches a milestone such as five years. They will often do it as an accrual process, with each pay period showing how much the employee has accrued in time. Companies decide which holidays to give off to employees. Most offer New Years, Thanksgiving Day, Christmas,

Copyright © Mometrix Media. You have been licensed one copy of this document for personal use only. Any other reproduction or redistribution is strictly prohibited. All rights reserved.
This content is provided for test preparation purposes only and does not imply an endorsement by Mometrix of any particular political, scientific, or religious point of view.

Independence Day, Labor Day, and Memorial Day, but others also offer days like Veteran's Day and Martin Luther King, Jr. Day. Some companies have decided to combine sick, personal, and vacation time so people can use the time as they wish. People will typically ask for the time off from their managers or the human resources department. Some companies have a computerized system for this, which makes it easier to manage.

Workers' Compensation

Workers' compensation is insurance that companies pay for to protect themselves and their employees. It covers medical expenses and partial salary losses to employees who are hurt while on the job. It does not matter if the person is at fault (i.e., if the person tripped over his own feet), he would still be eligible (although not necessarily if it is intentional or due to drugs or alcohol). The injury must occur while the person is working. Employers pay all costs of the program. There may also be payment for economic loss. In the case of an employee killed while on the job, money may be paid to dependents.

Unemployment Insurance

Unemployment insurance provides benefits for workers who lose their jobs without fault of their own. These programs are usually run by the state and are typically funded by employers through taxes. It does not typically cover the entire salary, but instead a portion of it for a specific amount of time. This limit can be extended at times, especially when the economy is particularly bad. A number of factors determine eligibility into the program. The person must not have done something to lose his job. For example, a person will not get unemployment if he is fired for showing up late to work repeatedly. Also, many states require that the individual search for a job while receiving benefits. He might not be eligible if he is receiving other income. The employee must have been at the job for a certain amount of time before being laid off. It does not count for temporary employees or those who voluntarily quit. The amount is based on what the employee was earning.

Laws and Acts Preventing Discrimination

A number of laws have been created to prevent and punish discrimination. The **Americans with Disabilities Act (ADA)** protects those with physical and mental disabilities from discrimination, as well as provides many other protections. Those with disabilities must be reasonably accommodated in a number of areas. For instance, someone can't be fired for having a disability. **The Equal Employment Opportunity Commission (EEOC)** forbids discrimination against an employee or job applicant due to color, race, gender, religion, age, disability, national origin, or genetic information. Companies must adhere to this in all practices, including hiring, training, pay, termination, benefits, promotions, and harassment. The **Age Discrimination in Employment Act (ADEA)** is similar, but forbids discrimination based on a person's age. Strict penalties could be enforced for any parties violating the above laws and acts.

FMLA

The **Family and Medical Leave Act (FMLA)** allows employees who are eligible to take up to 12 weeks of unpaid leave while having their job and group health insurance protected for one of the following reasons:

1. To care for a newborn or child under one year of age.
2. To care for an adopted or foster child with the employee for one year or less.
3. To provide support to a spouse, parent, or child with a serious medical issue.

Copyright © Mometrix Media. You have been licensed one copy of this document for personal use only. Any other reproduction or redistribution is strictly prohibited. All rights reserved.
This content is provided for test preparation purposes only and does not imply an endorsement by Mometrix of any particular political, scientific, or religious point of view.

4. To deal with the employee's own health condition that does not allow him or her to work.
5. To deal with an eligible exigency due to a parent's, child's, or spouse's position as a covered military member on covered active duty.

If the employee is taking time off to care for an injured or ill covered military member (parent, child, spouse, next of kin) then the eligible leave is extended to 26 weeks.

FICA

The **Federal Insurance Contributions Act (FICA)** is a law in the United States that requires money be deducted from income to fund Medicare and social security. The social security portion has a maximum while the Medicare part does not. How much is deducted is dependent on the person's income. It is 12.4 percent for social security and 2.9 percent for Medicare. Those who work for someone else will only have to pay for half the FICA amount while their employer will pay the other half. Self-employed individuals pay it all, but can deduct half from their taxes as an expense of the business. There is an additional 0.9 percent Medicare tax for those making over $200,000 annually.

COBRA

The **Consolidated Omnibus Budget Reconciliation Act (COBRA)** is an act that allows employees and their spouses, ex-spouses, and dependent children to continue with group health coverage when it would have been otherwise terminated. Various events can trigger this continuing coverage, including the employee losing his job (without major misconduct), a reduction in hours that would result in losing the benefits, the employee's death, divorce or legal separation, a child becoming no longer dependent, and new eligibility for Medicare. The covered individuals may have to pay for the insurance in its entirety, including an additional two percent for administrative fees. State and local governments must adhere to COBRA, as do companies with 20 or more employees. Some states have laws that cover smaller companies. Coverage may be extended for a maximum of 18 to 36 months depending on the qualifying event.

HIPAA

The **Health Insurance Portability and Accountability Act (HIPAA)** provides broad protection for American workers concerning the privacy of health insurance. It gives patients and other individuals broad protections for their identifiable health information and limits who can see the information without permission. In addition, those who hold the information, such as doctor's offices, must put in safeguards so it is not accidently seen by unauthorized individuals. It includes medical records, patient/provider conversations, billing information, and other health information. Parties that must adhere to the rules include health plans, the majority of health care providers and health care clearinghouses, as well as their business associates.

Safety in the Workplace

The government plays a large role in promoting safety in the workplace. The Occupational Safety and Health Act of 1970 was implemented to prevent accidents at work by requiring safe working conditions. The **Occupational Safety and Health Administration (OSHA)** was formed by this act and gives and enforces rules and regulations about workplace safety. It conducts investigations, takes complaints, and issues fines. It requires employers to clearly label any hazards, create records of injuries and illnesses related to work, do OSHA-required tests such as air sampling and medical tests (depending on the industry), and tell OSHA if a fatality occurs or three workers go to the hospital. There are various requirements by OSHA, including providing employees with protective

Copyright © Mometrix Media. You have been licensed one copy of this document for personal use only. Any other reproduction or redistribution is strictly prohibited. All rights reserved.
This content is provided for test preparation purposes only and does not imply an endorsement by Mometrix of any particular political, scientific, or religious point of view.

equipment, preventing exposure to toxic chemicals, adhering to noise restrictions and more. Also, employees can't be discriminated against for making a complaint.

Review Video: Intro to OSHA
Visit mometrix.com/academy and enter code: 913559

Consumer Economics and Personal Finance

Personal Budget

A personal budget can be created through a series of straightforward steps. First, one should set a manageable time span for the budget, such as a month. Once the timing is set, the individual should formulate his ultimate financial goals. Creating a financial reserve is important in case there is an unexpected expense. He should decide how much money he wants to have left for his reserve or other savings. Next, the individual should calculate income. He must be careful to take out money for taxes, interest, and automatic fees. He should then make budget line items for recurring fees that are unavoidable such as rent, mortgage payments, car payments, etc. Next, he should add in needs such as food. He should consider how much he spends in each category and formulate ways to save. He should then add in other items such as leisure activities and unnecessary items. As time passes, he can make adjustments as necessary.

Banks, Savings Plans, and Checking Accounts

Banks vary greatly in the accounts, programs, and financial tools they offer, thus consumers should spend time comparing them to find the best bank for them. First, individuals should consider their banking needs. They might want a **checking account**, which typically pays little to no interest, but allows people to easily withdraw by writing checks. Alternatively, they may want a **savings account** that doesn't allow for checks but which offers interest. The characteristics of these accounts differ greatly. Factors that should be evaluated include fees, minimums, interest rates on accounts, services, special features, and more. They should also evaluate customer service. Some banks might be better for one product and worse for another, so people should evaluate exactly what they need. In addition, services, prices, fees, and other details change very often, so people should evaluate their options right before they are ready to commit to a banking product.

Strategies for Making the Best Purchase Decisions

First, it is important for people to research the products they are considering. The internet makes it easy to read ratings and reviews to compare the features, benefits, and prices of different products. There is often a quality versus price trade-off, but not always. In addition, this trade-off is not always significant, especially if someone is paying more for a brand name. It is important to know exactly what is in the product, so check the product labels carefully before purchasing. Second, comparison shopping is key to finding the best price. Oftentimes the same item can be found for far less from a particular source. You can look at advertisements to find the best deals, but be wary. Advertised deals are not always as good as they say, thus consumers should be sure to read the fine print. Consumers should also investigate any service plans and warranties offered to ascertain their value. The more research a customer does, the better the chance of getting the right product at the right price.

Factors Affecting a Purchase's Total Cost

Many factors affect a purchase's total cost beyond the retail price. For example, consider all the additional costs that come with purchasing a car. There are taxes as well as various fees. And one must consider what else he may need to purchase to be able to use the car, like a license tag. The

Copyright © Mometrix Media. You have been licensed one copy of this document for personal use only. Any other reproduction or redistribution is strictly prohibited. All rights reserved.
This content is provided for test preparation purposes only and does not imply an endorsement by Mometrix of any particular political, scientific, or religious point of view.

cost of credit, if applicable, needs to be considered. If someone is financing a car, then he will pay more than the retail price because he will pay interest on the money. The costs to operate should also be considered. A car needs gas, so this is an additional cost that will be incurred. A car also needs maintenance. A person should consider how long the life of the product will be. Most cars do not last 20 years. Knowing how many years of life the product will last can give a better idea of the true cost. By considering all of these different factors, a consumer can get a better idea of the true cost of a product.

Lowering a Product's Cost

Consumers can save a great deal of money with various strategies for lowering a product's cost. First, they can take advantage of sales. Sales allow consumers to save a great amount of money on products, and many stores have significant sales such as buy one, get one free. Certain days such as holidays are often accompanied by sales. Consumers can also look for coupons for both in-person and online purchases. They can purchase items on clearance for even greater savings. Another option is to purchase in bulk. Consumers will generally get a lower per item cost by doing this. Consumers can also comparison shop to look for the lowest price on an item. This is easy to do on the internet. Discount stores and low priced websites are great places to shop to save money. Combining all the above strategies leads to even greater savings.

Ascertaining Needs and Resources Before Large Purchases

Consumers should ascertain both their needs and resources before making large purchases. They may find that a less expensive option will fit their needs or that they have other items that can substitute for the purchase they were about to make. Consumers also need to consider their resources. Products may cost more than the retail price when one considers tax, other fees and interest on a credit card. Customers should honestly ask themselves if they can afford to purchase the product. By taking these measures, you can wisely limit your spending to get the most out of every dollar you spend.

Factors Influencing Employment Opportunities

Economic factors can have a significant impact on employment opportunities. When the economy is doing well, businesses will also be doing well and may be more likely to be expanding and hiring new people. When the economy is doing poorly, a person may have more difficulty finding a job. There may be a lot more supply (people looking for jobs) than demand (jobs hiring). This ranges by job—certain jobs, such as nurses, will always have openings. Geographic location also makes a large difference in employment opportunities. There are many more opportunities for business professionals in New York City than in a small town in rural America. The opportunities also vary by industry. Some industries, such as computer systems design, grow faster than others, such as publishing. There are many personal factors that influence an individual's employment opportunities such as education, skills, and experience.

Factors Influencing Cost of Living

One factor that influences the cost of living is housing prices. Housing prices can vary a great deal and change by many percentage points, even when salaries remain relatively stagnant. When housing prices go up, so does the cost of living. This can vary greatly depending on the area. A person's family size also greatly affects her cost of living. Kids are expensive, with costs such as medical bills, housing costs, food, education, and so forth. Someone with a larger family will have a greater cost of living. Inflation also influences the cost of living. When there is high inflation, the cost of living can go up. Things will cost more, even though individual income may be the same. This can make it more difficult to afford the basics.

Copyright © Mometrix Media. You have been licensed one copy of this document for personal use only. Any other reproduction or redistribution is strictly prohibited. All rights reserved.
This content is provided for test preparation purposes only and does not imply an endorsement by Mometrix of any particular political, scientific, or religious point of view.

Factors Influencing Personal Income

A person's education influences their personal income. Someone with a higher degree, such as a master's degree or doctorate, will generally make more than someone with a lower degree or someone without a degree at all. Many companies offering higher paying jobs want people with higher educations. Some fields need people with certain certifications. Experience also matters—those with more experience will generally earn more money. Someone who is skilled will earn more money, especially if the skills are particularly unique or valuable. Factors outside the individual, such as the job market or the average wage in a chosen field, also affect income. When the economy is doing well and a lot of people are hiring, a person might earn more. The geographic location also makes a difference. An employee will generally earn more in a place like New York City as compared to a small town. A higher cost of living will balance some of that.

Income Tax Preparation and Tax-Reduction Strategies

Personal income taxes are taxes on the money a person earns. The federal government applies these, as do some states. Individuals pay a percentage of their income (after deductions and credits). The percentage is based on how much they make and goes up as income rises. The **Federal Insurance Contributions Act** (FICA) and **Medicare taxes** fund the federal programs of social security and Medicare, which provide money and health benefits to senior citizens, people with disabilities, and other eligible individuals. **Property taxes** are levied on properties and are generally based on the amount the property is worth. **Gains taxes** are based on profit from a non-inventory asset such as bonds, stocks, property, and precious metals. **Sales taxes** are paid on items people buy.

Individuals must prepare income tax returns yearly, and many use an accountant to do so. They can look for deductions such as dependents, charitable contributions, or business expenses, which can reduce the amount of wages eligible to be taxed. They can also claim credits, which reduce the taxes owed. Contributing to retirement plans can also reduce taxes. After all credits and deductions are account for, some will owe tax money, while others will enjoy a refund.

Credit

People use **credit** in order to buy things that cost more than they can currently afford. One reason people use credit is because it is convenient. Credit cards are accepted almost everywhere and are quicker and easier than writing a check. The second reason people use credit is to make large purchases, such as homes and cars, without having to use cash. Sometimes people borrow part of the purchase amount and repay it on a loan schedule basis. This way, people can receive an expensive asset immediately and make small payments over time. Credit also provides a way to cover a financial emergency in unforeseen situations like illness or employment and can be used to partially fund finance investment options.

Types of Credit an Individual May Possess

Credit cards allow people to make purchases in advance and then pay it back monthly. People can keep a balance on the cards, but the interest can be very high. **Auto loans** are loans that are tied to cars. They allow people to pay off their cars slowly, but they could lose the car if they can't pay. **Mortgages** are loans made to let people purchase homes. Generally these come from the bank and allow homebuyers to slowly pay off the house with interest. Foreclosure could occur if the loan is not repaid. **Student loans** help students pay for education. **Home equity loans** are loans in which the person's home equity is put up as collateral in case the person defaults on the loan. People may use this for large expenses. A **variable loan** is a loan in which the interest rate changes along with the market interest rate, changing the payments. Alternatively, a **fixed interest rate loan** has the

Copyright © Mometrix Media. You have been licensed one copy of this document for personal use only. Any other reproduction or redistribution is strictly prohibited. All rights reserved.
This content is provided for test preparation purposes only and does not imply an endorsement by Mometrix of any particular political, scientific, or religious point of view.

interest rate stay the same during the life of the loan. How high the interest rates are and the length of the loan determine which is best.

Establishing Credit

Opening a checking and savings account will show lenders that you are financially responsible and will help you establish credit. Opening one or two credit card accounts and using them now and then (being careful not to overdo it) will also prove that you are a reliable credit customer. Even if you do not need a loan, getting a small one (and putting it in a CD or money market account) can help establish a good credit history. Any interest that accumulates can be used to cover the expense on the loan, especially if you pay it off ahead of schedule. Do not pay off the loan too quickly since lenders are looking for evidence of financial responsibility over a period of time. You may want a larger loan in the future, and your ability to get this will be based in part on your past history of paying off small loans.

Building a Strong Credit History and Maintaining Credit-Worthiness

You can build a strong credit history and maintain credit-worthiness in a number of ways. When first applying for credit, be honest; credit agencies will do a thorough background check and misinformation will only hurt your credibility. Avoid overextending yourself and only use credit when you can afford the repayment schedule. Make sure that you live up to all of the terms of the credit card and be on time with monthly payments. If you will not be able to make a payment, let the lender know; often they will work with you.

5 Cs of Credit

The 5 Cs of Credit are the five things a lender looks at when trying to determine how well a borrower will be able to repay a loan. **Character** is demonstrated by how well a borrower lives up to the loan's requirements. **Capital** refers to the borrower's assets. **Collateral** secures the loan and can be claimed by the lender in the event of default. **Capacity** is whether the borrower will pay back the loan in a timely manner. **Condition** looks outside the individual borrower's profile to any economic factors that could affect whether the borrower can pay back the loan.

Line of Credit, Cash Advance, and Base Rate

Line of credit is the most credit a customer can have at any given time as determined by the issuer of the credit card. An applicant can request a certain amount, and this is taken into consideration along with the applicant's financial status. A cash advance is a loan that banks or other financial institutions offer a credit card holder. The advance happens at a bank but the transactions are like merchandise purchases. Instead of receiving a good or service, the person receives a check or cash. When giving loans to individuals and small/medium size business, the rate of interest banks use is called the **base rate**.

Factors That Could Affect Personal Credit

Bankruptcy has a major impact on personal credit. Chapter 7, 11, and 13 bankruptcies remain on credit reports for as long as a decade, although Chapter 13 may come off in seven years. Negative reports about delinquent accounts that lower credit may stay for seven years, although positive closed accounts can stay for longer. Credit can go down with collections and these can stay for seven years as well. Credit score can even be slightly lowered for two years when an individual just applies for credit. Late payments also lower credit rating. Balances on credit cards can cause credit rating to drop, thus if an individual is only making minimum payments, he will have a lower credit rating and thus less ability to get and use credit. Inflation may make it harder for some people to pay their credit cards. Credit cards are governed by many laws and regulations.

Copyright © Mometrix Media. You have been licensed one copy of this document for personal use only. Any other reproduction or redistribution is strictly prohibited. All rights reserved.
This content is provided for test preparation purposes only and does not imply an endorsement by Mometrix of any particular political, scientific, or religious point of view.

MANAGING PERSONAL CREDIT AND DEBT

Consumers should work to manage personal credit and debt. They should try to get rid of unhealthy, high-cost debt such as credit card debt by paying off loans and balances. They can start by creating a budget. They should separate things into needs and wants and try to focus on only the needs until they have managed their debt. They should not buy things they cannot afford. People can also try to increase their income. People may also be able to talk to the creditors and come up with a payment plan or a reduction in their debt, which will make it easier to pay back. They should try to do this as soon as possible before a debt collector begins to make collection calls. There are debt relief services that offer credit counseling. These can be very useful, but consumers should be careful because many involve scams. Debt management plans and debt settlement programs can be done if researched properly (again, there are a lot of scams out there) and if there aren't other options. This may help get a person out of unmanageable debt.

TRUE COSTS OF CREDIT

Credit has a much higher cost than many consumers realize, especially if they are only paying the minimum amount and have high interest on credit cards. The cost of the interest is based on the annual percentage rate (APR) and the amount. For instance, if someone buys a television for $100 on a credit card with 20 percent APR and paid it in one year, then they would pay $120. The interest would be the APR multiplied by the principal amount. This calculates to $100 × 20% (0.2), or $20 interest. Sometimes the credit cards have such a low monthly minimum payment that it does not even cover the interest. If people are only paying the minimum, they might continue to owe more and more money. For instance, if in the last example the minimum payment was only $10 a year, then after the year, the consumer would still owe $110. Then the interest for that year would be $110 × 20%, or $22. The exact cost of the credit depends on APR and how long it takes a person to repay the loan.

CREDIT DANGER SIGNS

There are a number of credit card danger signs to watch out for. Taking sixty to ninety days to pay bills that used to be paid in thirty; struggling to make minimum payments; or ignoring bills altogether out of fear are signs of credit danger. Using a credit card for impulse purchases, exceeding borrowing limits, and using cards to pay off other debts are clear warning signs. You should also be concerned if you have no savings, are using more than 20 percent of your take-home pay to pay credit card bills and personal loans, are postdating checks to keep them from bouncing, or borrowing money for simple day-to-day standard living expenses. Finally, it should serve as a red flag if collection agencies repeatedly call.

CREDIT PROBLEMS FOR WOMEN

Lenders once vieweed women as credit risks because they could become pregnant and lose their jobs. **The Equal Credit Opportunity Act (ECOA)** removed creditors' ability to consider marital status or child-bearing plans, and mandated lenders must consider a woman's income on the same basis as the man's. Divorced and widowed women may not have an established credit history, making it difficult for them to get credit. This can be avoided by using one's own name when filling out credit card applications, reporting any information to the credit bureau using the maiden name, and keeping a separate credit file.

IMPORTANCE OF CREDIT TO BUSINESSES, GOVERNMENTS, AND CONSUMERS

Credit allows individuals and companies to purchase goods and services when sufficient cash is not available. It allows businesses, governments, and consumers to make transactions and supply the goods and services consumers demand. Credit allows businesses and governments to employ people and provide various projects and programs; these boost the economy and raise our

Copyright © Mometrix Media. You have been licensed one copy of this document for personal use only. Any other reproduction or redistribution is strictly prohibited. All rights reserved.
This content is provided for test preparation purposes only and does not imply an endorsement by Mometrix of any particular political, scientific, or religious point of view.

standards of living. Consumer credit permits the purchase of expensive items without jeopardizing the budge; however, the buy now, pay later mentality can lead to serious financial problems, including bankruptcy.

Credit Cards

Economists do not consider credit cards to be money since credit cards do not make payment at the point of sale. For example, if you use your credit card to buy a pair of shoes at the mall, you do not actually pay for the shoes when you swipe your card. Instead, you pay for the shoes when you pay your credit card bill a few weeks later. At the shoe store, basically you have obtained a loan from the bank that issued the credit card. The credit card, then, is really just a piece of identification ensuring that the proper account is charged for the value of the shoes. Payment is not made until later, however, so economists do not count credit card transactions as money transfers.

Electronic Checks

Electronic checks likely will become a more popular means of making purchases, especially online purchases. An **electronic check** is not considered money, because it merely instructs the bank to move currency to another account in order to complete a transaction. As such, an electronic check has no paper basis; although the early versions were designed to resemble paper checks. The Financial Services Technology Consortium developed these prototypes. Many banks and financial institutions are excited about the advent of electronic checks, which they feel will reduce paperwork and lag time in transactions.

Debit Cards

A **debit card** functions much like a credit card, except that it draws from the cardholder's funds rather than from the bank's funds. When a debit card is used to complete a transaction, the bank receives instructions to transfer a certain amount of money from the cardholder's account to the recipient's account. As a result, the debit card functions just like a paper check. It is not considered money; instead, the debit card serves as a means of instructing a bank to move deposits. For most consumers, the advantage of a debit card is that it can complete transactions much more quickly than a paper check.

Electronic Cash

Governments, banks, and other financial institutions hope that electronic cash will become a viable method of payment in the future. However, in order for this to happen, electronic cash needs to be secure, convenient, and recognizable. Most designers envision a system in which cards are assigned certain amounts of money and then can be used to make purchases in stores. The difference between this model of electronic cash and a debit card is that the value of the electronic cash is in the card itself, rather than in the card's ability to move bank deposits. At present, the online company PayPal offers the most popular electronic cash venue.

Automated Teller Machines

Automated teller machines (ATMs) are one of the most important advances in personal banking over the last two decades. In 2020, more than 3.5 million ATMs were in operation around the world. An automated teller machine is linked to a central computer, which in turn has connections to the computers of specific banks. When an identification card is inserted into the machine, the account holder can check his or her balance, withdraw money, transfer money, make loan payments, and make deposits. ATMs have increased the convenience of personal banking, although some critics say that they encourage frequent withdrawals and irresponsible spending.

Copyright © Mometrix Media. You have been licensed one copy of this document for personal use only. Any other reproduction or redistribution is strictly prohibited. All rights reserved.
This content is provided for test preparation purposes only and does not imply an endorsement by Mometrix of any particular political, scientific, or religious point of view.

Savings Account

While savings accounts typically yield only around 2 percent, they are safe because they are insured. After thousands of banks failed in the Great Depression, the federal government created the Federal Deposit Insurance Corporation (FDIC) to insure money in savings accounts up to $100,000. In this way, if a credit union or bank were to go out of business, your money would still be safe. Sometimes, a low minimum balance is required to keep a savings account active without being charged a fee, but sometimes there is no minimum balance required, depending on the type of bank and account.

A bank savings account pays interest because the bank is borrowing the money from you. The bank lends your money to other people, and by charging a higher interest rate on that loan than the interest rate they are paying you, they are able to make money. Since the interest in a savings account is compounded daily and paid monthly, you can also receive interest on the money that has been earned as interest.

The two types of savings accounts that banks offer are a basic savings account and a money market account. A basic savings account usually does not require a minimum balance, but it also has a very low interest rate. However, you can take money out of a basic savings account whenever you want. A money market account pays a higher interest than a basic savings account but it also may require a higher minimum balance. Also, you can only write a maximum number of checks (usually three) each month and you may only be able to make a certain number of withdrawals each month.

Starting a Savings Program

To help start a savings program, look at your spending habits to see where you can cut back. Have your employer regularly deduct money from your paycheck and automatically deposit it into your savings account. Deposit any unexpected extras like raises and bonuses in your savings account, and reinvest the interest and dividends made from your savings account. Work a little more to earn extra money, and if any loan payments end, write checks for those same amounts but deposit them into your savings account. Keep track of the returns you receive on your savings account, and if it's only 2 or 3 percent, consider opening a money market account. Establish a retirement plan and contribute to it on a regular basis. It is all right to splurge every now and then to have a bit of fun and make saving money easier.

CDs

CDs (certificates of deposit) differ from other savings types because the money deposited has to stay put for a certain amount of time. With a CD, you deposit your money for a specified amount of time, usually anywhere from three months to a number of years; the longer the period of time, the higher the interest rate. CDs earn more interest than savings accounts and money market accounts, but there is a penalty if you take your money out before the time is up.

Treasury Bills

Treasury bills (T-bills) are a simple way for the government to raise money to help pay off the national debt. T-bills are popular because they are affordable (they start in denominations of $1,000), are risk-free since they are backed by the US government, and are exempt from state and local taxes. T-bills are issued through a bidding process at auctions, and the bids can either be noncompetitive (you receive the full number of securities you want as determined at the auction) or competitive (you specify the return that you want, but if it is too high, you may only receive a portion of the securities or none at all). The one downside to T-bills is that they are so safe that they do not yield great returns.

Copyright © Mometrix Media. You have been licensed one copy of this document for personal use only. Any other reproduction or redistribution is strictly prohibited. All rights reserved.
This content is provided for test preparation purposes only and does not imply an endorsement by Mometrix of any particular political, scientific, or religious point of view.

Microeconomics

Microeconomics is the branch of economics that studies how individuals and small organizations act and make decisions. This includes how buyers, sellers, and their decisions affect supply and demand, price, and output. It not only covers the decisions buyers and sellers make but how they reach these decisions given limited resources, market failure, and perfect competition. It looks at preference relations, and the choices people can make. Microeconomics also covers supply and demand to see what affects them and how equilibrium can be reached. It also covers elasticity, consumer demand theory, theory and costs of production, and the types of markets such as perfect competition and monopolies. Additional topics include game theory, labor economics, economies of information, welfare economics, and opportunity costs.

One of the key assumptions of microeconomics is that individuals possess **preferences**. They may like brand A more than brand B. They also try to maximize their happiness while minimizing the cost. Essentially, people want to get as much happiness for as little as possible, due to limited resources. Another key assumption is that individuals must engage in competition for resources that are limited. Microeconomics also assumes that people typically make rational decisions. These assumptions make it easier to apply the theories of microeconomics and account for complex human behaviors.

Adam Smith's Theories of Microeconomics

Adam Smith (1723–1790) was a Scottish philosopher who is known as the founder of modern economics. He felt that, when people work in their own self-interest and get the products they need, the market will self-regulate and produce the best outcome for all. Supply and demand will come together if the market is just left to its own devices. This is known as the **invisible hand**. He promoted laissez-faire policies and was a free-market capitalist. In 1776, he published *The Wealth of Nations*, which describes self-regulation. Many economists used his theories as a springboard for their own work.

Elasticity

Elasticity refers to how one variable changes in response to another, such as how consumers respond to a change in a product. For instance, if the price of a product changes, will the demand change a lot or a little? The price elasticity of demand can be calculated with the equation:

$$\text{Price Elasticity of Demand} = \frac{(\%\text{ Change in the quantity demanded})}{(\%\text{ Change in the price})}$$

For instance, if the price of a good goes up by 50 percent and the quantity demanded goes down by 10 percent, then the price elasticity would be -10% / 50%, or 0.2 (technically there would be a negative sign, but this is usually discarded). If the price elasticity is greater than one, then the demand is considered elastic. This means that there will be a greater change in quantity demanded than the percentage change in price. Thus a higher price will cause lower revenues, and a lower price can increase revenues. If the price elasticity is less than one, then it is inelastic and a percentage change in price corresponds to a smaller percentage change in demanded quantity. Thus a higher price equals higher revenue. A price elasticity equal to one means price changes won't affect revenue.

Scarcity

Scarcity refers to how there are limited resources for unlimited wants in people. This means resources must be carefully allocated because using them for one thing means giving up another. Resources that are scarce include land, labor, and capital. Scarcity can affect price. If something is

Copyright © Mometrix Media. You have been licensed one copy of this document for personal use only. Any other reproduction or redistribution is strictly prohibited. All rights reserved.
This content is provided for test preparation purposes only and does not imply an endorsement by Mometrix of any particular political, scientific, or religious point of view.

scarce, then it can have higher prices. Scarcity can change, for instance, a crop may become less available due to weather conditions, and the price can vary with it. A good is considered scarce if there are fewer units available than the amount people want. Individuals and companies try to decide how best to allocate these limited resources for the maximum return.

EQUILIBRIUM

Equilibrium refers to when there are balanced economic forces. For a product, this is when demand is equal to supply. The spot where the demand curve and supply curve meet is the equilibrium price. The equilibrium price will not change on its own, but can change with the emergence of external factors. For instance, if consumer preferences change, then the demand might go down and thus the supply may rise. Due to this, a short time of disequilibrium might occur as the market adjusts. Subsequently, a new equilibrium price will emerge, and equilibrium will be reestablished. Equilibrium can also refer to other variables in economics. For instance, there may be an ideal interest rate for growth.

OPPORTUNITY COSTS

Opportunity costs are what a company gives up when making a decision. For instance, if a company can make five laptops or five desktop computers with the same resources, and it chooses to make the laptops, then the opportunity cost will be the five desktops. When managers make decisions, they need to consider the opportunity costs of various paths to determine the best path. Sometimes what they give up may be more worthwhile than what they are making, and then they need to consider a path where they won't incur the opportunity cost.

Opportunity costs help determine which party has a comparative advantage. For instance, if a company can make 10 shirts in one hour or 20 pants in one hour, then the opportunity cost of the 10 shirts is the 20 pants and the opportunity cost of the 20 pants is 10 shirts. It has a comparative advantage with the pants because it has a lower opportunity cost. The company that has the lowest opportunity cost for a product has a comparative advantage in that product. It makes sense to spend its resources making that product and purchase the other product elsewhere.

SUPPLY AND DEMAND

Supply is defined as how much of a good or service the market has to offer to buyers. The amount producers make changes based on many variables and is especially based on price. The law of supply states that the higher the price of a good, the more of it the producers are willing to make (with everything else being equal). If they will receive more money for a product, they will make more to increase their revenues. **Demand** is how much of a good or service buyers want. This also can vary due to price. The law of demand shows that the higher the price, the lower the demand (with everything else being equal). Buyers are willing to buy more of a product if it is cheaper. The supply and demand for a product or good can be shown in a graph by two intersecting lines.

CIRCULAR FLOW ECONOMIC MODEL

The circular flow economic model shows a simplified way of how money and products make their way through the economy. It divides the parties as households and firms and shows two distinct markets: goods and services markets and factor markets, which represent the market for the factors of production such as land, labor, and capital. The goods and services market shows the finished product moving from the firms to the market and then to the households while money moves from the households to the market to the firms. In the factors of production market, everything is reversed. The households are the "sellers"; for instance, they provide the labor. Thus, the factors of production move from the households to the market and to the firms. The firms pay

Copyright © Mometrix Media. You have been licensed one copy of this document for personal use only. Any other reproduction or redistribution is strictly prohibited. All rights reserved.
This content is provided for test preparation purposes only and does not imply an endorsement by Mometrix of any particular political, scientific, or religious point of view.

for this, so the money moves from the firms to the market to the households in this part of the model. The money then flows through the households and firms, leaving a sustainable economy.

Factors Influencing Economic Change

Individual wants can influence economic change, as do the choices people make. The production of goods influences it. When production rises or falls for different reasons, the economy will be affected. Of course, competition plays a large part in the economy. Scarcity, or when items are in short supply, also plays a part. Prices can go up when this happens. The amount of consumption, the purchase of goods and services, influences the economy as well. All of these factors combine to contribute to economic change.

Effects of Supply and Demand on the Price of Goods

Demand and supply affect the price of goods. The price is where supply equals demand on the demand curve. If demand goes up and supply stays the same, then the price will rise. More people will be competing for the same number of products. Alternatively, if demand goes down and supply stays the same, then the price will go down because fewer people will want it. If supply goes up and demand stays the same, then the price will go down. There will be more products for the same demand. If supply goes down and demand stays the same, then the price will go up because there will be fewer products for the same demand.

Complements and Substitutes

A high supply on a related product can affect both products. First, the higher supply on the related product will drive prices down for that related product. If the related product is a substitute (i.e., pens versus pencils) and the price has gone down, then buyers will move to that product and have less demand for the original product. When the demand goes down for the original product, the price will go down too. Thus, both prices may go down.

Margins

Marginal benefits describe the utility or satisfaction an individual gets from one more unit of a service or good. It is how much they will pay for that extra unit. Oftentimes this amount will go down with more units. For instance, someone may be willing to pay five dollars for a hair bow, but once she has bought five bows, she would only pay four dollars for another. **Marginal costs** describe how much it costs to make one more unit of something. Companies may use it to find the best level of production. **Marginal utility** refers to the satisfaction a consumer will get from one more unit. This can be positive or negative. **The law of diminishing returns** refers to the fact that, as there is an increase in a factor of production (holding all other factors steady), eventually the per unit output of that factor will go down. For instance, if there is one cook in a busy kitchen, adding one more will make a big difference. Once you add 10 more cooks, however, then each additional one will not make as big a difference.

Perfect Competition

In the market structure of perfect competition, all companies make products that are exactly the same. They are identical, and because of this, no one firm has a large market share. The companies all have a small share. These firms do not have control over pricing. The buyers know the pricing for each firm as well as complete information regarding the product itself. There is complete freedom to enter or exit the market. Although there may be no one market that is exactly like this, some are close, such as agriculture. There are a lot of buyers and sellers in perfect competition, and supply and demand drive prices. The profit earned is modest and allows them to just stay in business because more firms enter when it rises.

Copyright © Mometrix Media. You have been licensed one copy of this document for personal use only. Any other reproduction or redistribution is strictly prohibited. All rights reserved.
This content is provided for test preparation purposes only and does not imply an endorsement by Mometrix of any particular political, scientific, or religious point of view.

Monopolistic Competition

Monopolistic competition is characterized by a market with many different producers that sell similar, although not identical, products. It is a form of imperfect competition. They are not perfect substitutes because of their differences, but they are very similar. The differences may be in quality, branding, or another area. One example would be restaurants. There may be a hundred Italian restaurants in an area that all serve Italian food, but none of them serve the exact same products in the exact same place. The consumers understand this and will often make decisions based on factors other than price. There are often a lot of consumers, and no one business controls the pricing of the market. There are not a lot of barriers to entry, so many competitors can go into the market. These competitors have some market power and make their own decisions without regard to the market, but they also have imperfect information.

Oligopoly

An oligopoly occurs when there are only a small number of businesses supplying a certain product, meaning there is very limited competition. At times, this occurs when companies collude together to reduce competition and gain the ability to charge higher prices for their products. Because there are so few competitors, companies are very aware of each other and will often make decisions based on the actions of the other companies. Sometimes the companies try to collude, although this is illegal in some places. A cartel occurs when this collusion is formalized. Some oligopolies do feature fierce competition, however, and prices can be lower for it. An example is the cellular phone market, which has several large firms controlling most of the market.

Monopoly

A monopoly occurs when one company is the only provider of a product. Everyone who wants to receive that product or service must get it through the one entity. There is no competition and no reasonable substitute that consumers can purchase. Because the company is the only seller and does not have to compete, it can charge high prices for the product. If a consumer wants the product, he will have no choice but to pay whatever the company is asking. A government may make them or they may form on their own. Many countries such as the United States have laws that restrict monopolies to promote healthy competition.

Effects of Competition

Competition affects the behavior of individual firms. Individual firms that have to compete against others may be forced to lower their prices in order to stay competitive. They may also make decisions on location based on where competitors are located. For instance, they may strive to stay away from a very heavy competitor. With a lot of competition, consumers may get more of a choice of products and services. Each company may work hard to differentiate its product and make it unique to attract more of the market. Consumers can benefit greatly from healthy competition.

Competitive Strategies

There are different competitive strategies that businesses employ to gain a competitive advantage. With **cost leadership**, a company charges less for the product to attract more customers. With **penetration pricing**, a business offers a low cost initially to get customers and then slowly raises it. With **economy pricing**, it strives to offer the lowest cost through the most basic items. With **skimming**, the initial price is high, but then it goes down to compete. In **bundle pricing**, a variety of products are offered together.

There are a wide variety of promotional pricing strategies such as **percent off sales**. There are many non-price competition strategies as well. One is **differentiation**, in which a company tries to produce a unique product. The differences may be real, or they may just appear to be real. They

Copyright © Mometrix Media. You have been licensed one copy of this document for personal use only. Any other reproduction or redistribution is strictly prohibited. All rights reserved.
This content is provided for test preparation purposes only and does not imply an endorsement by Mometrix of any particular political, scientific, or religious point of view.

may offer features that are better or different than the competitors' products, or they may try to increase the quality of the product. For instance, a phone manufacturer will try to produce innovative or higher quality features. Some strategies involve analyzing the market and customizing their strategy to different groups. These strategies may be used independently or in conjunction with each other.

PRODUCTION

There are four main factors of production: land, labor, capital, and entrepreneurship. **Land** encompasses the natural resources used in the production of goods and services. Besides literal land, it also includes wood, farms, fisheries, metal, and other natural substances. **Labor** encompasses all human resources such as the workers in businesses with the exception of the entrepreneur. The **entrepreneur** is his or her own factor of production because it is his idea that will make the business happen. He uses the other resources to create a good or service that will be profitable. He accepts the risks, reaps the rewards, and creates the business. The final factor of production is **capital**, which can be defined as either the money used to purchase the resources necessary for the business, or the large physical assets utilized in production such as vehicles, buildings, and equipment. These four factors of production can be combined to create a business.

DIMINISHING RETURNS

The **law of diminishing returns** refers to the concept that, as one factor of input is increased (while all others stay constant), eventually the marginal or incremental output will start to decrease. It is not that there will not be increased output (although at times this can occur) but that the incremental amount will not be as much. Take studying for example. The first hour you spend studying for a test will likely be very productive. You will be very motivated and will really remember what you've learned. By hour eight of continous studying, you'll likely be very tired and will not remember what you just went over. Each hour of studying produces less benefits, or *returns*, than the previous hour, until eventaully it is best to just go to bed. This law is true of many items as well as labor, and should be considered so that companies are not spending the resources to add an input that is not making a worthwhile difference in output.

ECONOMIES OF SCALE

With **economies of scale**, as the volume of output increases, it costs less per unit to produce it. This is true of a number of products, especially when overhead is high. For instance, a video game manufacturer might spend a lot of money to design, create, and program a video game. If they only make ten units of the game, the cost per unit would be very high. If instead they make 100,000 copies of the game, the cost of production per unit would be significantly less. This is true for products such as medications, which cost a lot to develop, but then may not cost a lot to produce.

ECONOMIES OF SCOPE

Economies of scope is when it is cheaper to produce a range of products rather than just one. The company may be able to benefit from one function for both, such as the same marketing department. A company that makes toys may use the same advertisements to advertise similar but not identical products. Other major departments such as IT may be the same as well. Also, the output of one might be used for another such as a company that produces chocolate chips and then also uses those to make chocolate chip cookies. Also, the company may be able to sell them near to each other such as a toy manufacturer that can sell the toys together.

SIZE OF A COMPANY AND THE DIFFERENT FACTORS OF PRODUCTION

The size of a company can affect the cost of the different factors of production. For instance, a larger company may have more land or use more natural resources. Because they use so much, they may

Copyright © Mometrix Media. You have been licensed one copy of this document for personal use only. Any other reproduction or redistribution is strictly prohibited. All rights reserved.
This content is provided for test preparation purposes only and does not imply an endorsement by Mometrix of any particular political, scientific, or religious point of view.

pay less for each unit; there is often a cheaper per-unit cost when things are bought in high numbers. Overall, they may pay more if they use more land. A larger company may have less difficulty attracting employees. Employees may be willing to take a lower salary knowing they will be working for such a large company. Of course, a bigger company will need more employees and some of these employees will be more skilled, higher-paid employees, which can increase the overall cost. A larger company is likely to need more in the way of capital and will therefore spend more money on that as well. Again, they may get pricing discounts, so it may be a lower per unit cost.

Macroeconomics

Macroeconomics is a branch of economics that examines the structure, performance, and behavior of an entire economy, focusing on large scale factors such as employment, distribution of wealth, sustainability, national income, growth rate, gross domestic product, prices, and inflation. There are many models that look for the reasons behind national income fluctuations and economic growth to find ways to maximize income and economic growth. Popular theories include those of Milton Friedman, John Maynard Keynes, supply-side economics, and monetarism. It looks at regional, national, and even global economies. Economic policies often come from macroeconomic model forecasts.

Terminology Utilized in Macroeconomics

Economic indicators are statistics that provide information about economic activity. These statistics let people evaluate economic performance and forecast the future based on it. It includes gross domestic product, the consumer price index, and bankruptcies. **Aggregate supply and demand** refers to the price level for the country as a whole and the total goods and services made by suppliers in the country. **Deflation** is when the general price of goods and services go down, while **inflation** is when it goes up. Fiscal policy is the government's use of spending and taxing to influence the economy. It must balance these two practices. **Fiscal policy** can have an effect on individual spending, interest rates, deficit levels, exchange rates, and more. **Monetary policy** can also lead to the growth or slowing of the economy, but it is done through the Federal Reserve. They can influence with open market operations such as transactions with US government bonds. By changing reserve requirements, the supply of money can be changed. In addition, they can make changes by altering the discount rate.

Taxes

Tax cuts greatly affect people, companies, and the economy. If they are done in the right way, they can be stimulating to the economy. With reduced taxes, people may spend more. If done incorrectly, it can cut the ability of the government to spend by too much, which can be a significant problem for governments and citizens. Taxes can be progressive, which means people earning lower incomes pay a lower percentage. This is how the income tax system is in America. This allows the lower income people to keep more of their money, and the higher income people who have more to spare give a greater proportion. A regressive tax is the opposite—those who make less pay a higher percentage. With a proportional or flat tax, everyone pays the same percentage no matter what they make. Taxes are a common source of discussion and dissention in the government.

Economic Theories and Systems

There are many different theories of economics. **John Maynard Keynes** (1883-1946) was an economist who helped create modern macroeconomics. He promoted government financial intervention to calm the results of the expansion and contraction phases of the business cycle. **Keynesian economics**, developed by Keynes, purports that increasing demand by lowering taxes

Copyright © Mometrix Media. You have been licensed one copy of this document for personal use only. Any other reproduction or redistribution is strictly prohibited. All rights reserved.
This content is provided for test preparation purposes only and does not imply an endorsement by Mometrix of any particular political, scientific, or religious point of view.

and increasing government spending can grow the economy. This is also known as **demand-side economics**. **Milton Friedman** thought people consumed an amount based on permanent income. He advocated free markets and thought government intervention should be reduced. **Monetarism** is a theory surrounding the government controlling the quantity of money in a market. It asserts that inflation is dependent upon the amount of money printed. Milton Friedman thought this amount should be relatively level. **Supply-side economics**, also known as "Reaganomics," is the **trickle-down policy**. It states that giving tax cuts for entrepreneurs and investors will allow them to invest more and give economic benefits to everyone as these benefits "trickle-down" to consumers through cheaper and more varied products. The three pillars it stands on are regulatory policy, tax policy, and monetary policy, and it asserts that supply is the most vital element to economic growth. All of these theories have both proponents and opponents.

There are various economic systems, including traditional, market, command, and mixed. A **traditional market system** is, as the name suggests, based on tradition. They make products because of customers, traditional beliefs, and cultural history. Many of these are in developing countries. A **command economic system** is one in which the government controls a great deal of the economic system. They may regulate resources or own everything. A **market economic system** is like a free market. Organizations are run by the people, and they shape the market, not the government. In a **mixed economic system**, the command and market system are combined. This is very common and can vary in the combination. The free market does a lot, but the government will control some things such as preventing monopolies. This is seen in the United States, as well as many other developed nations.

Open and Closed Economies

A **closed economy** is one that is wholly self-sufficient. There is no international trading of any kind, no exporting, and no importing. There is no investment in other countries, either by the country or by others into the country with the closed economy. Everything produced within the country is sold and used within that country. An **open economy** is the opposite of a closed economy. The people and businesses may export and import goods and services as well as exchange technology. Citizens can invest in projects in foreign countries and the country accepts investments from foreigners. This is advantageous in that the people can enjoy products and services from many countries, giving them a larger selection. It also gives them the opportunity to invest in other countries as well as an outlet to export items.

Capitalist, Communist, and Socialist Economies

A **capitalist economy** allows for private ownership and a free market. Supply and demand drive the market, and individuals can own businesses and personally enjoy the profits. Supply and demand keep prices in check. There is free competition without government interference. In **communism**, everything is owned communally. The point is to eliminate the gap between the wealthy and the poor with everyone owning everything and everyone seeing the benefits. In **socialism**, most of the production is run through the government for the benefit of all, although there can be some ownership of private property. There should be less of a gap between the wealthy and poor, although not a completely nonexistent one. The government should work to redistribute wealth to promote fairness. Most economies are not purely one of these but a combination of two or more.

Business Cycle

The **business cycle** describes the changes in the economy. These include production, trade, and the economy in general. **Expansion** is a time when production and pricing are being increased. Interest rates and unemployment are low while the GDP is higher. Some theorists feel that government

Copyright © Mometrix Media. You have been licensed one copy of this document for personal use only. Any other reproduction or redistribution is strictly prohibited. All rights reserved.
This content is provided for test preparation purposes only and does not imply an endorsement by Mometrix of any particular political, scientific, or religious point of view.

spending should be less at this time. The **peak** is when production and pricing are at their highest. **Contraction** is a time when the opposite is happening. Production and the GDP are going down while unemployment is going up. Some feel that the government should be spending more at this time to stimulate the economy. When it gets to its lowest, it reaches the **trough**.

Inflation

Inflation is the increase in prices that leads to a lowering of dollar value as time passes. Many economies experience about two to three percent inflation a year. If the inflation rate is three percent, for instance, then a candy bar that costs $1.00 at the beginning of the year will cost $1.03 at the end. **Hyperinflation** occurs when inflation is extremely high. This is very rare and can be disastrous for an economy. **Stagflation** is when high inflation occurs at the same time as stagnation in the economy. The opposite of inflation is **deflation**, in which prices decrease.

Inflation is caused by various factors. **Demand-pull inflation** occurs when demand is increasing at a higher rate than supply, so prices go up. Growing economies might see this. In **cost-push inflation**, companies have higher costs and increase prices so their profit margins do not go down. Inflation can show growth in the economy and the lack of it can show a weakening economy. Anticipated inflation is not usually a big deal, but unanticipated inflation can hurt the economy. For instance, uncertainty might mean people don't spend as much and the country might not be as competitive as other countries.

Gross National Product

The gross national product is comprised of the market value of everything produced by a nation's citizens in a one-year period. It is whatever goods and services are produced by one people. It does not matter where it is produced, but instead who produces it. Thus for the United States, it would include all products and services produced by Americans, both in the United States and abroad. It does not include items produced in the United States by foreign entities. It is calculated by taking the market value of the production in a country, adding the market value of goods and services produced by the people of that country in foreign areas, and subtracting the value of items produced by foreigners. The number can aid in government policy making as well as business decision making. It can also be used in the evaluation of economic theories. It can give an idea of the health of an economy.

Gross Domestic Product

The **gross domestic product** describes the value of goods and services produced within a country, typically annually. It is calculated by adding consumer spending (private consumption) within a country, spending by the government, capital spending, and net exports (exports minus imports). This is called the expenditure approach. It can also be calculated with a production approach and income approach. It does not matter who owns the products or services, only that it occurs within the country. It is used to evaluate the health of an economy, especially growth. It can give an idea of whether a recession is occurring and what the results of an economic policy are. It can affect the stock market and will often signal other things such as unemployment and wages.

Consumer Price Index and Producer Price Index

The **consumer price index (CPI)** looks at the weighted mean of prices of a basket of goods or services to see how the price changes. To calculate it, the prices of a variety of representative items are gathered for a period of time. The price changes for each item are averaged, and the items are weighted based on how important they are. This calculation can show changes in the cost of living as well as deflation and inflation. The equation for one item is current CPI = item price ×

Copyright © Mometrix Media. You have been licensed one copy of this document for personal use only. Any other reproduction or redistribution is strictly prohibited. All rights reserved.
This content is provided for test preparation purposes only and does not imply an endorsement by Mometrix of any particular political, scientific, or religious point of view.

price in base year × (current CPI/base − year CPI). It is not perfectly accurate in estimating the cost of living.

The **producer price index (PPI)** calculates the mean difference in selling prices domestic producers get over a period of time. The areas of production it considers are commodity-based, industry-based, and stage-of-processing-based companies. The PPI is often used because it can help predict the CPI.

Index of Leading Economic Indicators

The index of leading economic indicators is used to forecast the economy in future months. There are a variety of components used in its calculation. These include the following: manufacturing employees' weekly hours, unemployment insurance applications, orders going in to manufacturers for goods and materials for consumers, how quickly merchandise travels from vendors to suppliers, capital goods' new orders, residential buildings' new building permits, S&P 500 stock index, monetary supply adjusted for inflation, the difference between short interest rates and long interest rates, and the sentiment of consumers. These indicators can give an idea of where the economy is headed. Firms and investors look at it when making business decisions.

Unemployment

Unemployment occurs when people are actively looking for work but are unable to find it. There is always some unemployment, but the number varies. When there is a lot of economic growth and the economy is in a state of expansion, unemployment is lower; alternatively, when it is in a decline, unemployment is higher.

There are different types of unemployment. Structural unemployment occurs when the labor market has inefficiencies. There will be structural economic issues. For instance, the skills needed for the jobs and the skills of the workers might not match. This might occur when the technological needs of jobs increase and the workers do not have this knowledge. Frictional unemployment happens when a worker is moving between jobs. The worker might not have the information or the skills for the new job or may not get a good offer. Cyclical unemployment is due to contractions in the economy. For instance, if there is a recession, the job openings will go down. Seasonal unemployment is expected because of the time of year. For instance, there may be fewer employees at a ski resort in the summer.

Calculating of the Rate of Unemployment

The United States regularly calculates the rate of unemployment. To calculate unemployment, the government administers a survey every month called the Current Population Survey (CPS). These may be in person or on the phone. Census Bureau interviewers look at 60,000 households in a sample to replicate the United States. They ask about employment and find the percentage that is unemployed. Unemployed is classified as people who are not working, have been searching for work in the past four weeks, and are able and available to get a job. Interviewers also look at other statistics such as the characteristics of the unemployed workers.

The rate of unemployment can give an overall view of the economy and help shape policies. Unemployment is important because, when people are unemployed, the nation does not have the products or goods the worker would have made. Also, there is lowered purchasing power, and other workers may become unemployed because of it. The government will look at the statistics surrounding unemployment to make policy decisions that affect the economy and unemployment.

Copyright © Mometrix Media. You have been licensed one copy of this document for personal use only. Any other reproduction or redistribution is strictly prohibited. All rights reserved.
This content is provided for test preparation purposes only and does not imply an endorsement by Mometrix of any particular political, scientific, or religious point of view.

Rate of Inflation

Inflation is how much goods and services increase in price as time changes. To calculate inflation, a price index such as the consumer price index may be used. This shows the prices of goods and services for an average person. The government uses this to measure how prices change over a year. The following equation is used:

$$\text{Inflation} = \frac{\big((\text{current year price index} - \text{base year price index}) \times 100\big)}{\text{base year price index}}$$

For instance, if the price index went from \$100 to \$110 the next year, then the equation would be $\frac{((110-100)\times 100)}{100}$, or 10 percent inflation.

This can be negative if prices went down, which would show deflation. There are other price indices that can be used such as the commodity price index, cost of living index, and producer price index. Policymakers use the rates of inflation to make decisions. For instance, a government may change its monetary policy to influence inflation. This may involve changing interest rates or creating wage controls.

Federal Reserve System

Formed in 1913, **the Federal Reserve System** is the United States' central banking system. It works to keep employment up, keep prices stable, and moderate interest rates in the long term. It also works with monetary policy, oversees banks, keeps the United States financial system stable, performs research, and provides financial services. One of its primary roles is to help keep the balance between banking and government and provide aid in a time of financial crisis or panic. Essentially, the Federal Reserve is the bank of the government and of other banks. It acts as a lender of last resort, provides many payment services, and works to provide an elastic currency. Its policies and work provide many functions to the banking system.

The Federal Reserve System is the central bank in the United States, responsible for maintaining stable growth in the economy and creating monetary policy. The "Fed," as it is called, does not deal with individual accounts; rather, the "Fed" is the bank of private banks and other depository institutions. The Fed also regulates and supervises banks, distributes currency to the public through the banks, facilitates the collection and transfer of checks, and implements some of the regulations of consumer credit legislation. The Federal Reserve System consists of the Board of Governors, the Federal Open Market Committee, twelve Federal Reserve Banks around the country, various branches of these banks, advisory committees, and some member financial institutions.

The Federal Reserve System divides the United States into twelve regional Federal Reserve districts. A regional Federal Reserve Bank with nine directors administers each of these districts. The Board of Governors of the Federal Reserve Bank appoints three of these directors, and the commercial banks in each district elect the other six directors. Each regional Federal Reserve Bank has a president appointed by the directors in that district. The Board of Governors must approve the president. Regional Federal Reserve Banks are located in the following cities: San Francisco, Minneapolis, Chicago, Kansas City, Dallas, St. Louis, Cleveland, Atlanta, Richmond, Philadelphia, New York, and Boston. The Federal Reserve Bank in New York City is considered the most important of the regional banks, in part because of its proximity to the New York Stock Exchange.

Government Fiscal Policies That Can Affect the Economy

Tax policy has a big impact on the economy. There is a lot of debate on exactly how taxes affect the economy, but in some cases, a reduction in taxes may cause people to spend more, stimulating the

Copyright © Mometrix Media. You have been licensed one copy of this document for personal use only. Any other reproduction or redistribution is strictly prohibited. All rights reserved.
This content is provided for test preparation purposes only and does not imply an endorsement by Mometrix of any particular political, scientific, or religious point of view.

economy. Of course, there will be less money for the government to spend, which can also affect the economy. Another factor that can affect the economy is government bond sales. Bonds make a difference because they help to determine interest rates and therefore liquidity. Interest rates affect how easily people can buy things. Sometimes governments limit the price of a good or service in an attempt to keep the items affordable. **Price ceilings** and **price floors** are two examples of these **government price controls**. There is debate on just how effective these are, but it is accepted that all of these factors combine to affect the economy.

INTEREST RATES

In general, an **interest rate** is the percentage of interest charged by a lender to a borrower. Essentially it is what it costs to borrow money. A fixed interest rate stays the same for the length of the loan, while a variable interest rate can vary as the market rates change. The **annual percentage rate (APR)** is the percentage of interest for a loan based annually. This is often used for credit cards and makes it easier to compare various credit cards to each other. The **prime rate** is the benchmark rate of interest, which banks often use when calculating rates for loans. This is used in the United States. A **teaser rate** may be a special, limited time rate that is offered to attract people.

Chapter Quiz

Ready to see how well you retained what you just read? Scan the QR code to go directly to the chapter quiz interface for this study guide. If you're using a computer, simply visit the online resources page at **mometrix.com/resources719/mttcbusmmt** and click the Chapter Quizzes link.

Copyright © Mometrix Media. You have been licensed one copy of this document for personal use only. Any other reproduction or redistribution is strictly prohibited. All rights reserved.
This content is provided for test preparation purposes only and does not imply an endorsement by Mometrix of any particular political, scientific, or religious point of view.

Marketing

International Business, Marketing, and Trade

Benefits of International Trade

There are many benefits to international trade. One advantage is that a company has an entirely new market to which to sell. It can increase its sales and thus its profits tremendously by reaching these customers. A company may have surplus supply that would otherwise not be utilized. Customers can enjoy products that are not available domestically. If international trade was not available, they may not be able to get that product. Also, opening up international trade can make those products available for less money. They may get the foreign product for less, and even domestic companies may lower their prices to become more competitive. Consumers who wouldn't have been able to afford the products may now do so. Also, there is less dependence on a single market, so if something goes wrong, the item will still be available. A foreign market may be more profitable for a domestic company.

Drawbacks of International Trade

There are a lot of arguments against free trade. It can lead to job losses and company failures domestically. New domestic companies may not have a chance to catch up with foreign companies. Some feel that getting products from rival countries is risky, and there are concerns about working conditions. In some countries, there is little regulation and people work in unsafe and unsanitary conditions. Workers, including children, may work many hours for little pay. Also, the manufacturing processes may damage the environment. There might not be the same quality control for the products, and some of the products may be of lower quality or even hazardous. Also, when jobs are outsourced, there will be less opportunity in the United States. Domestic companies that have good practices and fairly compensated employees may have difficulty competing with international companies that do not. A company may also face barriers to trade such as quotas, tariffs, and cultural resistance.

Historical Patterns of International Trade

The United States has engaged in international trade for many centuries. The **triangular trade system** was a system that ran from the late 1500s to the early 1800s. It connected Africa, the American colonies, and the Caribbean and consisted of slaves, crops, and manufactured goods. Many countries export raw goods and import manufactured materials. The United States trades with a wide variety of countries, and many companies have gone international through trade. The United States used to practice protectionism, but has gravitated towards free trade in modern days. Still, protectionism is not eradicated and can be seen in policies today.

Review Video: The Triangular Trade
Visit mometrix.com/academy and enter code: 415470

Modern Trends in International Business

There have been many trends in international business. Much of the manufacturing has moved internationally to areas where the cost of labor is lower. China has emerged as a significant exporter, with many of the goods in the United States and other countries coming from there. Multinational businesses have a great impact on the growth and health of the economy, especially given their size. They add a lot to the growth of the GDP. Trade also plays a large part in economic growth, both in the United States and other countries. There have also been some trends specific to

Copyright © Mometrix Media. You have been licensed one copy of this document for personal use only. Any other reproduction or redistribution is strictly prohibited. All rights reserved.
This content is provided for test preparation purposes only and does not imply an endorsement by Mometrix of any particular political, scientific, or religious point of view.

the United States. The US has increased the importation of oil. Approximately half of the oil import originates from the Western Hemisphere. Also, the United States currently has a negative balance of trade, also known as a trade deficit. This means the United States is importing more than it is exporting.

Economic Factors That Influence International Trade

There are various economic factors that influence international trade. One is opportunity costs. **Opportunity costs** are what a producer gives up by choosing a different option. For instance, if a producer can make a dozen cookies in an hour or a dozen brownies in an hour for the same cost and he chooses to make the cookies, then the dozen brownies are the opportunity cost. Someone who has a higher opportunity cost for making a product may want to import that product so they do not have to incur the opportunity cost. **Comparative advantage** is given to the party with the lowest opportunity cost. It makes sense for them to produce and export the product. **Absolute advantage** is when a producer can make more of something with smaller inputs. For instance, if one country can make 10 shirts for the cost and effort that another country uses to make five shirts, then the country that can make more has the absolute advantage. It makes sense for the producer who can make it with the least inputs to make it.

Government Policies That Create Obstacles to International Trade

There are many government policies that create obstacles to international trade. These are done for different reasons, including protecting domestic businesses and raising revenues. **Quotas** put a restriction on the number of imports. Beyond that number, the products must be made by domestic means. This can make products more expensive because it may be more expensive to make domestically, although domestic companies gain because they can charge more. The government also wins with more tax revenues. **Tariffs** are taxes that apply to goods that are imported. Because the cost of imports is increased, domestic production is cheaper. This is advantageous for domestic manufacturers. **Voluntary export restraints** are self-applied rules that restrict what a country can export to another country. Oftentimes the importing country has requested the limit. **Embargoes** occur when a country restricts trade with a specific foreign country, often for political or economic reasons. These measures are often done concurrently.

Effects of Currency Exchange Rates on Trade

When a country purchases items from another country, they first change their money over to that currency. When the foreign currency is weaker, they can purchase more of it for their own money. They will then have more money and the items will be relatively cheaper. They will import more from the country with the weaker currency because these items are less expensive. Alternatively, if a country is trading with a country that has a stronger form of currency, then they will be able to get less of that foreign money and thus the goods will be more expensive. They might import less in this case. Exchange rates change constantly, thus so does trade.

Benefits and Drawbacks of a Weak/Strong Dollar

Whether the dollar is weak or strong can make a big difference for the economy and everyday people. If the dollar is weak, it has less purchasing power and it becomes more expensive to import from foreign countries. As prices increase, consumers spend less. Fuel costs tend to go up, too. Inflation can occur because of this. Central banks might raise interest rates to attract investors, but this can be problematic for the economy. A benefit of a weak dollar is that a trade deficit could decrease and domestic job growth can occur, especially in industries like manufacturing. Demand will also increase for exports because they are cheaper, which will also increase jobs. There could be some lost jobs, however, from businesses that are paying more for supplies. A strong dollar makes the opposite occur. Foreign goods cost less, so importing may increase while exporting or

Copyright © Mometrix Media. You have been licensed one copy of this document for personal use only. Any other reproduction or redistribution is strictly prohibited. All rights reserved.
This content is provided for test preparation purposes only and does not imply an endorsement by Mometrix of any particular political, scientific, or religious point of view.

domestically-produced items go down. Prices can go down as well. One is not necessarily bad or good. Overall, a strong economy will have a strong dollar, but sometimes a weak dollar is best.

Elements That Influence International Trade

The **balance of trade**, the differential between a nation's imports and exports, can influence international trade. So can the **balance of payments**, which is a compilation of economic transactions of a nation and the global companies with which it trades. It includes loan repayment, capital movements, money spent by tourists, and more. International trade is also affected by changes in the supply of labor as well as demand for labor. If a lower supply of labor exists, a country may need to import more and vice versa. Some countries also have practices such as **dumping**. This is where a country exports products at an extremely low price compared to what they would be available for domestically. This can be catastrophic for manufacturers in that country. Sometimes countries will also take retaliatory actions that can affect international trade. The exchange rates and values of the different currencies also matter. If a country's currency is strong, it has more power and might import more; if it is weak, it might import less. All of these factors combine to affect international trade.

GATT

The **General Agreement on Tariffs and Trade (GATT)** is a treaty that was formed after World War II to help the economy. It strives to lower obstacles to global trade such as quotas, tariffs, and subsidies. It played a huge part in increasing free trade throughout the 20th century. The main part was for trade to occur without discrimination. A country had its markets opened equally to other countries. If a country made an agreement to lower tariffs with the countries it had a significant trade with, then those went to other GATT members, too. The nations would specify the tariff rates they would provide to the other member countries. GATT also strove to promote tariffs rather than a limit on the number of items traded. There was an escape clause in case a country lost a lot because of concessions in trade. It was in effect until the World Trade Organization took over in 1995, at which point it had 125 nations signed to it and governed 90 percent of international trade.

NAFTA

The **North American Free Trade Agreement (NAFTA)** became active in 1994 and has had a profound effect on trade ever since. The agreement was signed by the United States, Mexico, and Canada and, as part of it, number restrictions and duties were terminated on January 1, 2008. The largest international free trade area was formed, and trade between the three countries increased tremendously, going to 1.2 trillion for US goods and services in 2012. Canada benefited economically from the agreement. Mexico has a lot of factories known as maquiladoras that take raw goods and make them into finished products. The United States has seen trade increase tremendously, but there has been loss of manufacturing jobs to Mexico. There were some issues about environmental concerns, thus the North American Agreement on Environmental Cooperation (NAAEC) was formed to address this. Despite some increases in pollution, there have been many benefits overall.

WTO

Started in 1995 by the Marrakesh Agreement, the **World Trade Organization (WTO)** is an international organization related to trade rules between different countries. WTO agreements are negotiated and created to form agreements that benefit producers, importers and exporters. It provides a place for companies to negotiate trade and work through problems, such as trade restrictions. It has formed trade rules. It works to promote safe and effective trade without conflicts between nations. If there is conflict, WTO works to resolve disputes and ensure nations comply

Copyright © Mometrix Media. You have been licensed one copy of this document for personal use only. Any other reproduction or redistribution is strictly prohibited. All rights reserved.
This content is provided for test preparation purposes only and does not imply an endorsement by Mometrix of any particular political, scientific, or religious point of view.

with the agreements they have made. It also helps nations come up with their own trade agreements. The WTO has a staff of more than 600 people in Geneva, Switzerland.

IMF

Part of the United Nations, the **International Monetary Fund (IMF)** promotes economic stability in 188 member countries. It strives for international growth by giving policy advice and helping developing nations reduce their level of poverty. Some of its primary roles are to keep exchange rates stable, balance international trade, provide financing to struggling countries, and give training and technical assistance. It also works with research and tries to keep the international financial system stable and looks at worldwide economic trends. The IMF performs surveillance to keep track of economic or financial problems. It will appraise financial situations and help countries create policies that are best. There is some criticism of the organization based on several issues, like reports that the loan conditions are too intrusive and intervene too much by forcing privatization, for instance. Critics also argue the policies of the Washington consensus are put forth without considering the special needs of that country, that policies are expected to be implemented together right away, and that the organization doesn't take criticism well.

World Bank

The **World Bank** works to reduce poverty by loaning money to developing countries for capital programs. This international financial organization is part of the United Nations and is based in Washington, D.C. It promotes foreign investment, international trade, and capital investment. It also works to improve health and fight diseases such as AIDS, tuberculosis, and malaria by sending vaccines internationally, along with other measures. It has also fought for environmental causes such as preventing climate change. It is now focused on 14 centralized global practices, including health and water. There has been some criticism, with some based on upcoming layoffs and lowered budgets.

Conducting International Business Through Licensing

International business is often conducted through licensing. **International licensing** occurs when one business makes an agreement with another, giving special permission to make the product in a foreign country. It might involve the resources to do it or the right. This might include a copyright, skills of managers, patents, technology, and more. It is advantageous in that companies can get into new markets they may not have been able to enter otherwise, because of restrictions in trade. It is also a way to enter another market without spending too much money or incurring too much risk because the company is just giving the rights and resources to make the product and not actually going in and doing it itself. The disadvantage is that there is a risk that the foreign firm will not adhere to the agreement. Also, with lower financial involvement and risk comes a lower expected financial return.

Conducting International Business Through Franchising

One way to conduct international business is through franchising. This is where an individual leases the ability to replicate a business model and brand. Generally, the individual will create a business that is a replica of a successful one. For instance, a franchise restaurant will have the same look, food, etc. McDonald's is a common franchise. There are both advantages and disadvantages to conducting international business through franchising. The model has already been successful and people are accustomed to it, so it may already have a built-in audience, which can stimulate business from the beginning. Domestic success may not translate to international success, however. Tastes and preferences are different in other countries. One advantage is that much of the work is done—the person will already have the branding, products, and so forth created. The franchisee may be subject to laws and regulations in other countries, however. Also, the franchisee may have

Copyright © Mometrix Media. You have been licensed one copy of this document for personal use only. Any other reproduction or redistribution is strictly prohibited. All rights reserved.
This content is provided for test preparation purposes only and does not imply an endorsement by Mometrix of any particular political, scientific, or religious point of view.

little control and be unable to change things. Entrepreneurs should consider all these factors when deciding whether to franchise.

Conducting International Business Through Contract Manufacturing

Contract manufacturing is a popular method of entering a foreign market. With contract manufacturing, the company designs the product but then hires another company to manufacture and ship it. This can be a very cost effective way of doing business, especially in foreign markets where it might be more expensive to do business. Also, companies can find a manufacturer that is able to make a product that they do not have the ability to make. It will also free the company to focus on designing the products and other things. There are risks as well. The company will not have as much control over the product and it may not come out with the desired quality. Also, some foreign companies have poor practices with regard to working conditions or the environment. The company will also be sharing their intellectual property, which they risk losing. If there is a problem with the manufacturer, it will reflect on the company. Also, sometimes there are contract disputes or other issues with the relationship. Overall, contract manufacturing can be a great way to enter a foreign business as long as the risks are considered.

Conducting International Business Through Joint Ventures

One common method for conducting international business is through **joint ventures**. In this strategy, a company will form a partnership with a company in the international market it wants to enter. Both inputs and outputs, such as profits or losses, are shared. It can be short or long term, but is often temporary. It is advantageous in that the risk is shared, making it less risky to a business entering the foreign market. In addition, the business can take advantage of the fact that the foreign business is already familiar with the market in the other country. Also, consumers may be less resistant to them because they will seem to be part of the local business and not a foreign entity. Sometimes there are laws and regulations that would make it difficult for a foreign business to enter the market otherwise. The downside is the company will share the profits from the venture. Also, the company may have to give up some decision-making power. Sometimes disagreements arise from partnerships. With proper research it can be an excellent way to enter an international market.

Conducting International Business Through Strategic Alliances

A common method of conducting international business is through **strategic alliances**. It is similar to a joint venture in that two companies—one domestic and one foreign—come to an agreement to work on a project to benefit both of them, perhaps sharing resources or knowledge. Whereas in a joint venture the company may form an actual business entity together, with a strategic alliance they work together on a project, but the firms remain independent. Also, it is typically not as long or involved as a joint venture. It is advantageous because a company can get into a foreign market it may otherwise have difficulty entering. It can use the benefits of the foreign company's knowledge and reputation in that country and help avoid resistance to a foreign business. The businesses can also share the risk. Of course, the company will not have full control over the project and may be responsible if the other company does something wrong. They will also have to share the rewards, such as profit.

Conducting International Business Through Foreign Subsidiaries

When a company opens a new subsidiary in a foreign country, either by starting one or buying an existing company, it is called a **foreign subsidiary**. The advantage is that the parent company stays in charge of the subsidiary and makes the decisions. They can get the rewards of it, and also enjoy cost savings when the parent and subsidiary share the same resources, such as the same financial processes. A disadvantage is that they can be liable for the subsidiary's problems. If the parent

Copyright © Mometrix Media. You have been licensed one copy of this document for personal use only. Any other reproduction or redistribution is strictly prohibited. All rights reserved.
This content is provided for test preparation purposes only and does not imply an endorsement by Mometrix of any particular political, scientific, or religious point of view.

company starts a business from the beginning, it will have to deal with the difficulties of establishing a business in a foreign country such as finding customers and suppliers. Buying an established business can ease some of these difficulties. It can be very expensive to get into international business this way, and it is a large commitment. Still, it can expand a business' customers, sales, and profit.

Factors to Consider When Entering International Business

There are many factors that businesses should consider when entering international business. First, they should think about how their product is likely to do overseas. Consumers have different tastes and preferences in different areas. The company should make sure there is a demand for their product by conducting market research. Sometimes a product can be successful but only with changes to the product, branding, pricing, or marketing. They should also consider the competition. Businesses should look at the laws, regulations, and licensing requirements, which may be very different from those in the United States. The company should consider the logistics and costs of expanding internationally. It may cost a lot more to ship products overseas. The company needs to consider exactly how it will penetrate the international market. There are many methods for international penetration; the company should research these to find out what is best for them. They may want to research alliances with others in the foreign area. They should make a clear business plan for penetrating the market.

Influences of Cultural, Economic, Sociopolitical, and Language Differences

Laws and regulations, including those pertaining to business, can be different in different countries. Business professionals need to be sure to understand the laws in the country in which they are doing business. The culture can have a significant effect. Some cultures are much more formal than others. Certain practices, such as touching someone, are taboo in certain cultures. Business professionals need to know what is acceptable. Also, there can be language barriers, and someone may accidently convey the wrong meaning. It is important to have someone who knows the language well and can translate successfully. There can also be political issues as well. Some countries are more restrictive on what can be advertised and how. Businesses should understand how distribution channels work. When a business plans to enter a foreign market, they should do research to make sure they understand the cultural, economic, sociopolitical, and language factors at play.

Ethnocentrism and Stereotyping

Cultures across the globe are very different, and it can be difficult to communicate across these lines. This has led to some mistaken beliefs and practices. **Ethnocentrism** occurs when a people believe that they and their culture are superior to those of others. It is extremely common and can affect international business greatly. People of one culture may be very resistant to businesses from other countries because they feel they are not as good. Stereotyping can occur in which people believe certain things about a people just because of who they are. They may believe everyone from a certain country is bad, for instance. When consumers are ethnocentric and have stereotypes, they may reject products from international companies and prefer those from their country. Certain countries display these characteristics more than others. This can affect international business greatly.

Review Video: Stereotypes
Visit mometrix.com/academy and enter code: 569262

Copyright © Mometrix Media. You have been licensed one copy of this document for personal use only. Any other reproduction or redistribution is strictly prohibited. All rights reserved.
This content is provided for test preparation purposes only and does not imply an endorsement by Mometrix of any particular political, scientific, or religious point of view.

Marketing

FOUR PS OF MARKETING

In 1960, Jerome McCarthy defined a framework for understanding and making decisions in marketing called the Four Ps, which make up what is called the **marketing mix.** The marketing mix includes the **product** itself, the **price** at which it will be sold, the **places** the product will be sold, and how the product will be **promoted.** Determining these four aspects of a prospective product is useful in that doing so provides objective considerations for developing a plan to sell what you plan to create. Since its proposal in the 1960s, McCarthy's Four Ps have been almost universally accepted in marketing models.

PRODUCT

The product itself is a very important part of marketing. A **product** can be a physical good or an intangible service. The company needs to pay attention to the quality of the product to ensure it meets customer needs. They should consider its design; physical features (if it is a good) such as color, shape, and texture; and the packaging it is in. For both goods and services, customer service needs to be considered before, during, and after the sale. If it is a service, the exact service and how it will be carried out should be considered. All of these factors should be pleasing to the consumer.

PRICE

Pricing is a very important decision for a product because it can impact sales and opinions on the product. There are many factors that go into pricing decisions. This includes the costs, including fixed, variable, and direct and indirect costs. It also includes the competition. If the market is saturated, the company may have to lower the product's price to compete. It also depends on the group they are targeting and how much they would be willing to pay. Some companies also price as part of a positioning strategy. **Penetration pricing** is when companies offer the product at a low price initially to increase sales and market share. **Skimming** is when a company instead has a high price and then lowers it to make it available to more and more of the market. With competit**ion pricing**, a company looks at competitors when pricing. In **bundle pricing**, they tie the product to other products. **Cost-based pricing** is done based on costs and the desired profit. With **premium pricing**, companies price their product high to show that it is exclusive. Companies use a variety of pricing practices depending on the product.

PLACEMENT

The **placement** element of the four Ps of marketing refers to the distribution or how the product gets from the company to the consumer. It focuses on the distribution channels utilized as well as the elements involved such as order processing, inventory management, warehousing, and transportation. The goal is to make an efficient and effective distribution system that is as cost-effective as possible. It also includes where the storefront or business is located. Of course, many companies utilize the internet to sell their goods and services and then ship the items to their customers. Placement must be convenient to the customer and cost efficient for the company.

PROMOTION

No matter how great a product is, it will not do well if no one knows about it. This is why promotion is so important. **Promotion** is the act of marketing a product so that people become aware of it and hopefully want to purchase it. This can include many facets. One is **public relations**, including press releases, sponsorships, trade fairs and other unpaid promotions, and advertising and sales promotions. There are also different promotional strategies. In **push marketing**, businesses bring their products to customers. New products can benefit from this. In **pull marketing**, businesses try

Copyright © Mometrix Media. You have been licensed one copy of this document for personal use only. Any other reproduction or redistribution is strictly prohibited. All rights reserved.
This content is provided for test preparation purposes only and does not imply an endorsement by Mometrix of any particular political, scientific, or religious point of view.

to convince consumers to come to them through sales promotions, brand loyalty, and advertising dollars. Both are commonly used.

Expanded Marketing Mix

In the 1980s, Booms and Bitner proposed an additional three Ps to add to McCarthy's Four Ps of Marketing, which together are often called the **7 Ps of Marketing** or the **Expanded Marketing Mix.** The three added elements include consideration of the **people**, the **process,** and the **physical evidence.**

- **People** refers to all human factors in sales, including customer interaction, employees, and general relationship mechanics. Often this is expressed through decisions regarding policy, uniforms, and customer service.
- **Process** refers to the flow of service delivery. This varies greatly between business types, but often has to do with operations and efficiency. This is usually expressed as particular training policies, checklists and standardization, and best practices in business.
- **Physical evidence** refers to the actual physical environment that customers will interact with, which goes on to influence the customer experience. For instance, souvenirs are tangible, physical products that remind the customer of the experience. Another example might be the noise-level at a basketball game, which can be either appealing or irritating to a particular customer base.

Advertising

There are many forms of **advertising**, including print, television, online, and radio. Within each of these are subsets. For instance, **online advertising** includes social media ads, banner ads, and pop-up ads. Many companies use an assortment of different advertising techniques, some of which can support each other. The goals of advertising include reaching consumers, teaching consumers about a business' products, convincing people to purchase the product, building brand loyalty, increasing sales, and more. Typically, marketers build advertising campaigns with a step-by-step process. First, they perform research to find out how best to advertise the product to their target market. Then, they create a budget. Next, they create the advertisements, often using a specific theme or idea. They decide on the type of media to be used and schedule it in the best way. Finally, they set the campaign in motion.

Marketing Research

Companies perform **market research** to learn about their customers and the factors that affect their company. It can go a long way to producing quality marketing campaigns. There are different types of marketing research. **Sales research** involves looking at the sales numbers and the strategies the company was taking when sales were high as well as when they were low. They could look at the times they did not do anything, and see how sales were then. The goal is to recreate the wins and avoid the losses. Companies also do **product research**. In this research, companies try to identify the characteristics of a product or service that will fulfill the customers' needs. It is done to help produce the best product that will satisfy the customer. Companies will also look at what products can be developed with existing and upcoming technology. **Advertising research** aims to make advertising more effective. For instance, a company may show an ad to a sample audience before releasing it widely to test its efficacy.

MIS

A **marketing information system (MIS)** helps marketers make good decisions. It collects and analyzes internal and external data and then sends out that information so marketers can better make decisions. It includes user interfaces, which allow the marketers to evaluate and understand

Copyright © Mometrix Media. You have been licensed one copy of this document for personal use only. Any other reproduction or redistribution is strictly prohibited. All rights reserved.
This content is provided for test preparation purposes only and does not imply an endorsement by Mometrix of any particular political, scientific, or religious point of view.

the data; application software; marketing databases; and system support. There are many software programs that create an MIS. It helps the company make decisions based on actual information and data. Business managers use it to better understand their customers and the right decisions to make. It can help them understand the marketing environment and its changes. A business manager might use it to come up with the right marketing plan.

Collecting Market Data

Marketers collect as much **market data** as possible to help make marketing and business decisions. Marketing research can take many forms. Companies may give out surveys to ask consumers about their behavior. These can be done in person, by mail, by phone, online, or through email. They form focus groups to find out information. A group will come together to talk about and evaluate a product. They will also look at public records. The data may be primary data or secondary data. **Primary research** is when marketers do original research. For instance, they give out a new survey. With **secondary data**, marketers look for data that already exists. They may do an evaluation of several studies, for instance. Primary data can be specifically tailored to the company, but can be expensive. The company may not have the means or resources to collect it. It can be used to find the most up-to-date information, however. Secondary data can be much cheaper. Sometimes it is hard to find because companies don't always share their information. The data may be outdated or not exactly what the company needs.

Marketing Plans

A **marketing plan** is vital for any business. It gives a direction for marketing efforts, incorporates important research, and serves as a guide for the marketing team. It contains various information, including details on the target market, the company's competitive position, the various methods that will be used to reach the market, and strategies for differentiation. First, the marketing team should research the target market and the best ways in which to reach them. A marketing plan typically encompasses many tactics because different consumers can be reached different ways. **Marketing activities** may include print, television, and radio advertisements; sponsorships; press releases; a website; a social media presence; and more. There also needs to be a realistic **marketing budget** to support these activities. After the plan is created, they should constantly revisit it and make changes as necessary. It should contain both short-term and long-term goals, both of which should be realistic. It is also important for marketers to constantly evaluate the success of marketing activities by finding out the return on investment. They should try to measure as many of the activities as possible to evaluate where the money is best spent.

Marketing Strategies

There are a variety of **marketing strategies** a business can employ. With an **undifferentiated marketing strategy**, the company has the same marketing strategy and marketing mix (product, placement, promotion, and price) for the whole target market. It doesn't differentiate between anyone. This can be easier and less expensive because the company just needs one campaign, but it can also be less effective because the segments in markets differ in tastes and responses to marketing. They might benefit from different strategies. In a **differentiated marketing strategy**, the company divides the target market into segments based on similar characteristics and creates a marketing mix and strategy for each segment. Although more expensive, it can be more efficient. A third option is a **concentrated marketing strategy** in which a business focuses only on one segment of the target market and markets towards them. Again, they only need one plan, but they are risking everything on one market and possibly ignoring other potential customers.

Copyright © Mometrix Media. You have been licensed one copy of this document for personal use only. Any other reproduction or redistribution is strictly prohibited. All rights reserved.
This content is provided for test preparation purposes only and does not imply an endorsement by Mometrix of any particular political, scientific, or religious point of view.

Competitive Marketing Strategies

A company can choose from one of many **penetration strategies** to get sales from competitors. They may try price adjustments by lowering prices or increase the amount of promotion with an effort like an advertising campaign. They can try different distribution channels to make it easier for consumers to get their products. It is also a good idea to directly improve the product so that more people are interested in it and start to prefer it to competitors' products. Another type of marketing strategy is **horizontal diversification**. The company produces products that are different than its current offerings, but which might be desired by their current market. They might be able to increase sales this way and still target the same market.

Market Segmentation

Market segmentation involves breaking up a large target market into segments to try to find an ideal group to target. There are various ways a company can segment the market, including by the population's demographics; the physical location of the population; and psychographic characteristics such as lifestyles, values, attitudes, personalities, social class, and interests. Segments need to be measurable, large enough to generate a profit, stable, convenient to reach, and made of people who prefer the same products. Once a company has segmented the market, they may choose a concentration or multi-segment strategy. In a **concentration strategy**, the company chooses one segment to pursue. This will be good for a company that has a specific product that would appeal to one group. For instance, a very expensive car company such as Ferrari only focuses on people who choose to drive very expensive cars. The brand does not offer cheaper cars because they want their brand to be known as an ultra-luxury brand. With a **multi-segment strategy**, companies market to more than one segment and may change the marketing mix accordingly. More sales can be achieved because there are more possible customers.

Factors That Influence Decisions in Marketing

Business ethics should be considered during the decision-making process. Marketers have to be sure not to do something unethical when marketing or they can get in trouble with consumers or even the law. **Sociocultural factors** also affect marketing. Different cultures respond to different types of marketing. Marketers should take advantage of **available technology**. For instance, many organizations utilize social media because it is inexpensive and wide-reaching. Of course, marketers have to follow **laws and regulations** or they could be subject to fines or other penalizations. Marketers evaluate the market and use different methods to forecast sales to help them make marketing decisions. For instance, they may perform trend analysis to find patterns in sales data to get an idea of future sales. They can use that to evaluate past marketing strategies and help create the best ones for the future.

Product Life Cycle

A new product has a life cycle, characterized by introduction, growth, maturity, and decline. In the **introduction stage**, the goal is to make people aware of the product and create a market. There are different pricing strategies such as penetration pricing or high skim pricing. The company brands it and promotes to early adopters. In the **growth stage**, the company tries to get more market share. Promotions work to get consumers to prefer the product over other offerings. They may add new features to the product or add new types of distribution. It will be promoted to more people. Once a product reaches **maturity**, the sales growth decreases as competition may arise, causing a possible lower price. The company works to keep the market share it has as well as maintain its profit. They may improve the product to make it more differentiated and work to promote these differences to consumers. In the **decline stage**, sales begin to decrease. Companies may choose to keep the product with or without changes, harvest it with lowered costs, or discontinue it.

Copyright © Mometrix Media. You have been licensed one copy of this document for personal use only. Any other reproduction or redistribution is strictly prohibited. All rights reserved.
This content is provided for test preparation purposes only and does not imply an endorsement by Mometrix of any particular political, scientific, or religious point of view.

Product Lines and Product Mixes

A **product line** is a group of related products a company offers. They may be related by price, function, target market, or other characteristics. A **product mix** comprises all the products a company offers. Its **width** refers to the number of product lines with it, its length covers the number of products in a line, its **depth** covers the number of versions of the same product there are, and its **consistency** refers to the uniformity of those versions. There are various factors that influence decisions on product lines and product mix. Companies should consider how much products cost to make and their sales potential. They need to consider what products their target buyers will purchase. If there is a reason their main products won't sell, they might need to develop new products. Additionally, if a product is older, they may want to add new features to entice people to stay with it. Companies are constantly changing their product mix and lines.

Branding

Branding is very important for a company to make its product known in the market. It is how the company distinguishes its product or products as differentiated and may include logos, names, graphics, shapes, and more. It can help its product stand out and build loyalty to it, especially as it matures. There are different types of branding strategies. Sometimes they use **company branding**, where the brand is connected with the general company but not individual products, such as Rolex Watches. In **product branding**, the name of a product is important, such as Hershey's Kisses. **Attitude branding** involves connecting the product with a feeling. They may successfully connect the product to happiness, such as in Coca Cola's Open Happiness campaign. In **iconic branding**, the brand helps with the person's identity. For example, Apple is an iconic brand that has become synonymous with modernity, innovation, and aesthetic design. With a **no-brand strategy**, the packaging is simple as if there is no brand, such as the packaging for the Japanese brand Muji. In the previously mentioned brand strategies, the labels and packaging are crucial to promoting the brand. For instance, an expensive watch will generally be packaged nicely and elegantly. Brands are a very valuable intangible asset.

Distribution Channels and Channel Integration

Many companies use intermediaries to make the flow of products more effective and efficient. A **direct channel** takes the product straight from the producer to the consumer. This might be a face-to-face sale or an online sale. An **indirect channel** takes it through nonaffiliated retailers, wholesalers, or other parties. It may be a one-level channel with one intermediary such as a retailer, a two-level channel with a wholesaler and retailer, or have even more levels. Some companies take advantage of horizontal or vertical integration. **Horizontal integration** happens when a company acquires a similar company. A company that owns a popular website might take over another, for instance. In **vertical integration**, a company will also own another part of the production and/or distribution process. For instance, a company that makes chocolate chip cookies takes over a firm that makes chocolate chips or opens a bakery to sell their cookies. **Exclusive distribution** channels have just one distributor; **selective distribution** channels have a few; and in **intensive distribution**, the products are located in many outlets.

Distribution System Parts

A **distribution system** involves getting a product from the production line to the customer. It contains various parts. First is **order processing**, in which the consumer places an order that translates to the purchased products. It is important that this be both efficient and accurate. Next is **materials handling**, which is all of the processes involved with caring for, storing, and moving the materials of production and products. With **inventory management**, companies strive to keep the cost of inventory as low as possible while increasing the quality of the products. A good system can

Copyright © Mometrix Media. You have been licensed one copy of this document for personal use only. Any other reproduction or redistribution is strictly prohibited. All rights reserved.
This content is provided for test preparation purposes only and does not imply an endorsement by Mometrix of any particular political, scientific, or religious point of view.

reduce costs significantly. Many companies warehouse products and need to find ways to make that as efficient as possible to reduce costs. Finally, **transportation** to get the finished goods to consumers must be done as quickly and inexpensively as possible. Technology has helped distribution systems a great deal. One example is using bar codes so a company can always know where a product is. Many computerized systems run parts of the distribution system.

Retailers

Mass merchandisers are large retail stores that sell many different types of products. They may sell anything from furniture to clothing to appliances, all in the same store. Sears is an example of a mass merchandiser. **Discount stores** such as Wal-Mart generally sell items at lower price points than other sources, often at a lower quality. Many people like to buy at **chain stores**, which are stores owned by one company that sell similar products in many locations. People like shopping at familiar places because they are accustomed to them and feel comfortable in them. They know what to expect. **Specialty stores** specialize in a specific type of product and related goods. For instance, a small store that sells only bath and body items may be a specialty store. These sometimes offer higher prices, but employees will often have more knowledge of the items the store sells. **Supermarkets** specialize in all types of foods and drinks.

Factors That Affect Retailing Choices

One factor that affects what retailers a business chooses for its products is store location. A company should make sure the store is located conveniently for its market. The product mix also plays a factor. A company may want to look for a store that offers products that will aid in sales of its own products. For instance, a toy manufacturer will want to target toy stores where people are specifically going to shop for toys. The atmosphere also plays a part. The company will want the atmosphere to match the product. For instance, a company that manufactures high-end clothing may look for an exclusive boutique to sell their products. How the product will be displayed matters. Products that are displayed to stand out, such as the books that are on a special table at a bookstore, will garner more attention and sell better. Companies may look for these opportunities. All of these factors play a part in retailing choices.

Stages and Factors Involved in Consumers Decision Making

Many consumers go through a process when deciding to make a purchase. First, they may recognize a need such as a need for a new car. Next, they will search for information such as information on the new models. After that, they will evaluate the different alternatives such as looking at the prices and features of the models. They will make a decision on whether to purchase and what to purchase. Afterwards, they will evaluate their purchase and whether it met their expectations. Various factors affect decision making, including cultures, society, personal factors (how easily the person spends), and demographics. Various adverting strategies try to entice buyers at a specific decision-making spot, such as a call to action or information when someone is comparison shopping. There are many motives behind making a purchase. Some people buy emotionally—i.e., a buying a sports car to impress neighbors or feel younger. Some buy based on physical need, such as buying a basic car to fulfill basic needs. Different marketing strategies are made to fulfill different needs.

Selling Process

The selling process is made of a number of steps. First is **prospecting**, or the process of looking for new customers. Sellers should consider existing customers and their traits as well as where new customers might be. The **pre-approach** is researching and understanding potential customers. If a seller knows what the customer is looking for, he will be able to give the best sales pitch. The **approach** is the start of the relationship and is crucial because it will identify the seller as someone

Copyright © Mometrix Media. You have been licensed one copy of this document for personal use only. Any other reproduction or redistribution is strictly prohibited. All rights reserved.
This content is provided for test preparation purposes only and does not imply an endorsement by Mometrix of any particular political, scientific, or religious point of view.

a buyer isn't interested in or as someone offering help. The seller must engage the person and come off as knowledgeable, able, and willing to help. The **presentation** should be based on how the product will benefit the buyer. It's not just that a dress is beautiful, but that the dress will make the buyer beautiful. In the **closing**, the salesperson strives to effectively move it to a sale. They figure out what needs to happen to have the customer agree to the sale. Finally, the **follow-up** can help sustain a relationship and keep repeat customers. The car salesperson might call the customer to ask how he likes his new car.

Sales Support, Order Taking, and Creative Selling

There are many processes that are related to the sales process that can make a large difference in the success of selling. **Sales support** provides support services to salespeople. They may monitor the accounts of customers, gather data that is useful to the salespeople, answer the phone, work on scheduling, process sales leads, manage sales targets, and help with correspondence between the sales team and customers. Some people perform **order taking**. They do not attempt to convince anyone to buy but instead are responsible for takeing the orders. In **creative selling**, the salesperson follows a step-by-step process to engage the customer and hopefully secure the sale.

Factors That Influence Customer Satisfaction

Customer service is one factor that influences customer satisfaction. Customers want to feel like there is someone easily accessible to contact if something goes wrong and that the company hears their concerns and responds appropriately to the situation. Companies with good customer service will often be able to retain a customer even after a problem as compared to a company with poor customer service. Many companies focus on **relationship marketing**. They strive to form a relationship with the customer. They may provide more personalized service or reach out to customers. The customers will feel more valued. They may strive to increase customer satisfaction. Of course, customer satisfaction is influenced by the quality of the product as well as efficient service. They do not want to feel cheated by the company; instead, they want to feel like they're purchasing from a responsible company that cares about its customers. Companies that get satisfied customers will see more repeat customers.

Entrepreneurship and Business Plan Development

Effects of Entrepreneurs on Business and the Economy

Entrepreneurs drive innovation. In a large company, it can be difficult to get a new idea across with so many layers, but an entrepreneur has no such limits. Entrepreneurs also create jobs, both for themselves and the employees they hire. People who have difficulty finding a job may start a company on their own. They also fill niches. Entrepreneurs might see places where there is an unfulfilled need through their own or others' experiences. They can make a product or service to fill this need. At times, more established companies have to make changes to respond to entrepreneurs. Entrepreneurs play a large part in the economy and can make a significant difference.

Entrepreneurial Opportunities Due to Changes and Development

Changes in social, technological and economic factors can provide entrepreneurial opportunities. Technology has made it easy for people to start a home-based business without a lot of capital. For instance, someone who makes products at home can sell them on the internet and not have to open an actual store. It is also much less expensive to advertise if entrepreneurs take advantage of resources such as social media websites like Facebook and Twitter, where they can reach a lot of people without spending a lot of money. Home-based entrepreneurs can even sell internationally

Copyright © Mometrix Media. You have been licensed one copy of this document for personal use only. Any other reproduction or redistribution is strictly prohibited. All rights reserved.
This content is provided for test preparation purposes only and does not imply an endorsement by Mometrix of any particular political, scientific, or religious point of view.

thanks to the internet. With this lowered cost of entry, many entrepreneurs are forming startups. There is also more funding available to startups. In many societies, innovation and hard work are prized, and this can spur entrepreneurs. Many people are looking to fulfill their dreams of owning a business. Some may be having difficulty at regular jobs and want to be their own boss. Now that it's easier than ever, this is becoming a reality for many.

Established and Entrepreneurial Ventures

There are many differences between established and entrepreneurial ventures. An **established firm** might have a lot of money and a lot of customers. An **entrepreneurial venture** that is just starting out might be lacking in both. Oftentimes it can be difficult to bring new innovations in an established business. There might be many levels to go through, and the business may be set in its ways. An entrepreneurial venture can try new things more easily and be more flexible. They may be more willing to take a risk or to use new channels. With less money, they may need to be more creative in their business such as by using social media to position themselves. Of course, there is more risk in entrepreneurial ventures, but many do stick around to become established businesses.

Methods to Compete with Established Businesseses

It can be difficult for entrepreneurs to compete with established businesses, but a number of strategies can make a difference. First, they can try to differentiate their products so consumers will choose them. They may offer excellent and personalized quality and service that people will appreciate. They also can use innovative and yet low-cost methods to promote their products. For instance, many small companies became very successful using social media websites like Facebook and Twitter. They can promote their products with very little cost output. They can also use innovative ideas to promote brand loyalty such as a loyalty discount or club. Some companies will offer something for free such as a free premium service or bonus product. An entrepreneur might offer a range of products for a wider market. He should get to know his audience well to entice them. It is also important for entrepreneurs to make sure their companies are healthy internally.

Qualities of Successful Entrepreneurs

Successful entrepreneurs are typically good leaders. They are not afraid to lead others and can do so effectively. They have good interpersonal skills and are very motivated and enthusiastic. They are usually hard workers willing to put in the time and effort to make their business a success. Many new businesses fail, and this is often due to lack of a solid business plan. Successful entrepreneurs are generally organized and create good plans that account for contingencies, and can be flexible when things don't go according to plan. Successful entrepreneurs are thorough, meticulous, persistent, and do research into their market and competitors. They are also good at managing money and promoting themselves and their businesses. They are passionate and willing to take risks. They have a vision and believe in themselves and their business.

Benefits and Drawbacks of Entrepreneurship

There are both advantages and disadvantages to entrepreneurship. One advantage is that an entrepreneur can be his own boss. He will be able to control his working conditions such as location, time, and hours. Entrepreneurs often work from home, especially when starting a new business. He makes all of the business decisions and enjoys all the success of the business. If the business makes millions, he might become a millionaire as compared to someone who works for a company and just makes a salary no matter how well the firm does. The disadvantages to entrepreneurship are also significant. The entrepreneur assumes all the risk. If the company fails, the entrepreneur can lose a great deal of money. Many types of businesses cost a lot of capital up front and all the money invested by the entrepreneur is at risk if he fails. Also, entrepreneurship typically involves hard work and long hours. The entrepreneur will have to make risky decisions

Copyright © Mometrix Media. You have been licensed one copy of this document for personal use only. Any other reproduction or redistribution is strictly prohibited. All rights reserved.
This content is provided for test preparation purposes only and does not imply an endorsement by Mometrix of any particular political, scientific, or religious point of view.

without help. On top of all this, a significant number of start-ups fail in the first year, which can be very stressful, especially for someone who needs a secure form of income for a home, family, or other responsibilities.

Benefits and Drawbacks of Starting a Business from Home

Starting a business from home is easier than ever before, yet it is still wrought with challenges. There are both benefits and drawbacks to home-based businesses. One obvious benefit of a home-based business is the ability to work from the comfort of home. Entrepreneurs can enjoy their own personal environment. Also, some people have other responsibilities that preclude them from a job outside the home such as children or an ailing loved one. Entrepreneurs can save a significant amount of time and money with a home-based business. There is no commute, no gas money, and no need to rent an office. Entrepreneurs can also save money on taxes with business deductions. Entrepreneurs must also consider the drawbacks of a home-based business. Many people find it difficult to work at home; distractions such as the computer or phone may keep them from realizing the efficiency they'd see in an office. Also, a home-based business can be difficult if the entrepreneur needs a professional place to meet with clients. They might not have room for an office or a place to store products. Also, some have restrictions on where a commercial venture can be located.

Sole Proprietorships

A **sole proprietorship** is a simple and common form of business ownership in which an individual starts an unincorporated business. Everything with the business is connected to the individual, therefore she is responsible for all debts and liabilities. If there is a problem, she could be personally liable. She also enjoys all the profits from the business. It is not nearly as difficult or complex to start a sole proprietorship as many other types of businesses; although one must get the necessary licenses and follow regulations, it is not as complex as incorporating a business. Also, taxes are simpler because the taxes for the business are combined on the individual's personal income taxes, as opposed to having taxes just for the business. With a sole proprietorship, the individual has total control of the business and makes all of the decisions.

Benefits and Drawbacks

One advantage of a sole proprietorship is that the person has complete control over the company. He can make changes as he wishes and sell the company if he desires. There aren't any corporate taxes, and the legal costs and requirements are fewer and less complicated than when forming a corporation. Also, the sole proprietor will enjoy all of the profits and benefits of the company. A disadvantage is that a single person may find it more difficult to find investors. He can also be legally liable for all the debts and any issues that occur because of the company or its employees. It can be challenging and a lot of work to be the sole proprietor and have to make all the decisions. If the company loses, so will the entrepreneur. Entrepreneurs should look at the pros and cons to decide whether a sole proprietorship is right for them.

Partnerships

A **partnership** is formed when two or more individuals band together to form a business in which they share in the work, profits, liabilities, and other features of the business. It may be a general partnership, in which all partners share everything equally; a joint venture, which is similar to a general partnership but temporary and encompassing a single project; or a limited partnership, in which a partner can have both limited liability and limited input into the business. Partnerships are registered with the state and must obtain required licenses and follow regulations. They are a generally easy type of business to form. Taxes must be filed specifically for the business, including annual return of income, excise taxes, and employment taxes. The partners are personally liable for the actions of the business as well as responsible for the debts. They share the profits, and partners

Copyright © Mometrix Media. You have been licensed one copy of this document for personal use only. Any other reproduction or redistribution is strictly prohibited. All rights reserved.
This content is provided for test preparation purposes only and does not imply an endorsement by Mometrix of any particular political, scientific, or religious point of view.

can benefit from the expertise of each other. They all contribute to the business as well as the decision making. Partnerships are a common form of business.

Benefits and Drawbacks

There are both benefits and drawbacks to being in a partnership. One advantage is that the partners can bring different skills and qualities to the business. For instance, one partner might be great at creating a product but terrible at selling it, while the other might be a great salesperson. They can each complement one another. It takes the burden off of one person as far as the workload and decision making. In addition, it might be easier for the partners to share the cost and liabilities of the business. One person might not be able to afford to do it on her own. It is generally an easy type of business to form and relatively inexpensive. A business that lets employees become partners might find the employees are much more motivated. A disadvantage is that the partners might not agree on something and this can lead to adversity within the business. Also, the partners still have the liability of the business tied to them personally, including the decisions made by others in the business. Additionally, unlike sole proprietors, partners have to share their profits.

Corporation

A **corporation** is a type of business that is its own legal entity, although it is owned by shareholders. The liabilities and debts are incurred by the corporation, not by the shareholders. They can raise money by selling stock so that investors can own a small part of the company. It is a complex form of business structure and requires administrative fees and complicated taxes. Usually, corporations are bigger companies with numerous employees. They are formed when a party chooses a name and files forms to incorporate the business through the Secretary of State's office. There are various taxes that must be paid, including income taxes. This is a common form of business for larger businesses in the United States.

Benefits and Drawbacks

One benefit of operating a corporation is that the shareholders are shielded from the debts and liabilities of the corporation. In other types of business, such as a sole proprietorship, an owner could be legally liable based on the actions of the company. A corporation provides protection against this. Corporations also have the ability to gain funds by selling shares, or small portions of ownership in the company. Some of the profits may be taxed at a corporate rate, which is typically lower than the tax rate for individuals. Corporations also can often get better employees because of their size, benefits, and stock options. One disadvantage of a corporation is that it generally costs a lot more to start than other types of business. It can also take a lot more time and effort as it is more complicated and there is more paperwork. In some cases, profits can be double taxed when they are taxed both as income for the business and as personal income when shareholders receive dividends.

Franchise

When someone owns a **franchise**, they pay a company for the right to recreate their business. They typically use the same name, products, style, and look. They also enjoy benefits from the advertising. They usually have very limited control; the company will dictate what the franchise owner can and cannot change. Customers expect a certain experience when they go to the store or restaurant, so it should be as uniform as possible. The person who owns the franchise can get the benefits of using an already proven brand with proven products that have a built-in customer base. McDonald's is an example of a popular franchise.

Copyright © Mometrix Media. You have been licensed one copy of this document for personal use only. Any other reproduction or redistribution is strictly prohibited. All rights reserved.
This content is provided for test preparation purposes only and does not imply an endorsement by Mometrix of any particular political, scientific, or religious point of view.

BENEFITS AND DRAWBACKS

There are both benefits and drawbacks to owning a franchise. One advantage is that much of the hard work is already done. The company that owns the brand has already created a successful brand, product, look, etc. It can be very difficult to come up with all of these details. Another advantage is that there is a built-in audience of customers. For instance, people will seek out McDonald's because they know what to expect. This is different from starting a new business in which an owner has to convince consumers to give him a chance. One disadvantage of a franchise is that it costs money. Some of the profits will go to the brand owner. Another disadvantage is the lack of control. Even if someone owns a franchise, he can't just make whatever changes he wants. He might not be able to change much of anything, which might be frustrating to some owners. Entrepreneurs should balance the pros and cons to decide whether a franchise is right for them.

VARIATION OF TAXATION BETWEEN BUSINESS OWNERSHIP TYPES

The taxation of a business will vary greatly depending on the type of business ownership. In a sole proprietorship, there is no separate tax filing for the business. Instead, the taxes related to the business are absorbed into the owner's individual tax filing. Business earnings would just be reported as income. A partnership is taxed in much the same way as a sole proprietorship, except it is divided between the individual partners who will then include it in their returns. A corporation is considered a separate taxable entity, however, and will be taxed as such. A tax filing must be done for the company, and it will be subject to a corporate income tax rate. Any owners that receive dividends will also pay personal taxes on those.

LAUNCHING SMALL BUSINESSES

The first step in launching a small business is to come up with a solid business plan. This should include every part of the business such as a description of the offerings, who is going to be involved, the target market, pricing, promotions, the financial plan, and more. If possible, the person should consider getting business counseling or training from a source such as the **Small Business Administration**. Next, the entrepreneur should consider if his business needs a physical location. If the answer yes, it should be somewhere where it will get noticed and attract customers. Next, the person has to get financing for the business. This can be in different forms such as a loan or capital investment. The entrepreneur then needs to follow all the procedures for a business of his type such as registering the name, setting up taxes, and attaining required licenses and permits. The more attention he pays to each step, the more likely he will be successful.

FINANCING

One type of financing is through a **loan**. Some very beneficial loans are available through the Small Business Administration (SBA). They offer a loan called the 7(a) small business loan and another that is the 504 fixed-asset small business finance program. Various banks also offer similar loans. A small business may also try to attract a venture capitalist who invests in promising businesses. They typically want their money back relatively swiftly but can give management experience. A **capital investment** may be done by banks, angel investors, equity investors, or financial institutions. Usually, common or preferred **equity** is issued, but there could also be straight or convertible debt. Small businesses can also finance their company through other means such as through loans from family and friends.

OBSTACLES

It can be very difficult to get capital to start the business, especially if it is being started as a sole proprietorship. Lenders may not be willing to risk the money and thus the entrepreneur will have to work hard to finance the project. They must also be able to manage the money so it lasts until the business becomes profitable, which can take time even for a well-thought-out business that will

Copyright © Mometrix Media. You have been licensed one copy of this document for personal use only. Any other reproduction or redistribution is strictly prohibited. All rights reserved.
This content is provided for test preparation purposes only and does not imply an endorsement by Mometrix of any particular political, scientific, or religious point of view.

eventually succeed. Entrepreneurs must come up with a solid business plan and all the different aspects of their business, which means a lot of hard work, long hours, and perseverance. They must accept the risk; even good products and businesses may fail through no fault of the entrepreneur. They must find a way to make themselves stand out so people will choose them. There is a lot of competition in today's market, especially with how the Internet and technology has eased the ability to start a business, and entrepreneurs must contend with that.

SBA

The **Small Business Administration (SBA)** was started by Congress in 1953 with the goal of aiding small businesses and the entrepreneurs starting them. They provide a wide variety of functions, including giving loans, grants, and loan guarantees. They also offer counseling and information to small businesses. The counseling is both across the Internet and in person at one of their many offices. On their website, entrepreneurs can learn about how to start a business, including important information such as securing financing. They also help people with government contracting and advocate for small businesses with the legislature, as well as conducting research.

Factors That Influence Success of Small Businesses

There are various factors that influence whether a small business succeeds. First, the company has to be competitive and attract consumers. This might be through differentiation or providing better quality, value, or services. The company has to be able to secure stable financing. Depending on the business, it can cost a lot of money to start, and the company needs to make sure it has enough to see it through the beginning stages. Some companies that will eventually turn a profit fail to do so at the beginning. The location makes a big difference in whether a business succeeds. A restaurant in a busy shopping plaza will have a lot more exposure than one in a small and quiet strip mall. It's important for entrepreneurs to carefully choose the location of the business. Marketing decisions also make a large difference in whether the business succeeds. Companies that are very successful at marketing their business will attract more customers. They need to do a good job of retaining their customers, as well.

Business Plan

A **business plan** should be thorough and contain the necessary components to give the business the best chance of success. First, the business plan should provide a vision. This might be in the executive summary and show what the entrepreneur envisions his business will become. The plan should have a detailed description of the business, including the product, pricing, distribution, what makes it unique, and how it will gain a competitive advantage. It should discuss the background of the company, as well as the complete management team and key players. It needs to discuss the financial details of the company and should include a cash flow statement and projections of revenue. It should discuss the capital the company needs to start up, as well as give a detailed financial plan for the company that shows how profit will be made. A marketing plan also needs to be included. The target market should be clearly identified, as should a plan for marketing and advertising to them. A SWOT (strengths, weaknesses, opportunities, and threats) analysis should be conducted. A summary should wrap everything up at the end.

Strategies

A solid business plan can make a large difference in whether a business succeeds. Different strategies can help an entrepreneur create such a plan. First, the person might want to seek help. For instance, the Small Business Administration gives counseling and provides information on making a business plan. The plan should be as thorough as possible, planning for as many contingencies and details as possible, but also flexible. It should give detailed numbers. The entrepreneur should perform as much research as possible. For instance, to attract investors, she

Copyright © Mometrix Media. You have been licensed one copy of this document for personal use only. Any other reproduction or redistribution is strictly prohibited. All rights reserved.
This content is provided for test preparation purposes only and does not imply an endorsement by Mometrix of any particular political, scientific, or religious point of view.

may need to show exactly how she found her target market and how she is going to earn profits. She can show the investors that she "did her homework" and expects a certain return based not on wishful thinking, but on solid research and numbers. Entrepreneurs can also look at other successful business plans to help create their own.

Career Development and Professionalism

Business Career Paths

There are many different career paths one can take in business. One might try a traditional business position in which he or she applies for a business job at a company. The person then works her way up through the corporate ladder, either at that job or switching to other companies. Some people prefer an entrepreneurial path. With the internet and social media, there are numerous ways to start a low-cost business right from the comfort of home. The person might sell something online from a website or an auction site. Some people work in the business world on a freelance basis. Someone might work as a marketing consultant, for instance. This can be a good option for someone who has experience in the field, but wishes to work from home. Some people choose a combination of these options.

Sources of Information About Business Careers

Business schools can provide a great resource. Students can find out information about the different career choices as well as current trends. Many of the schools have career centers where students can talk to career advisors. Business and trade associations also offer information. These will often have websites that provide information as well as meetings where individuals can network and learn about careers. The internet provides a wealth of information about business careers. From business websites to free resources, many websites share business career information. Individuals can easily search for their particular interest on a search engine. Government publications also provide information.

Important Characteristics of Individuals Pursuing a Business Career

Personal Qualities

Individuals pursuing a career in business will find that certain characteristics can help them. For instance, someone in business should have initiative. He or she should be able to take steps without direction. A business professional should be dependable. Clients and customers depend on businesses to fulfill their promises, and companies need to be able to rely on their employees. A business professional should be enthusiastic. He can promote his products or offerings better if he is enthusiastic about them. He can motivate others with this enthusiasm. It is also very important for a business professional to be responsible. Colleagues, clients, and customers need to be able to trust that he will do the right thing. He should be competent. He needs to understand his job and be able to perform it well.

Education, Experience, and Skills

It is important for someone pursuing a business career to have the right education, experience, and skills. The exact experience necessary will depend on the job. Many employers prefer workers to have a college degree in business or a related field. A Masters of Business Administration (MBA) is very useful for those looking to get ahead in business. Individuals can go beyond that to a doctoral degree, but that is not nearly as common for those not in the education or research field. The more business experience, the better. Even those who haven't had a full-time job may have experience from an internship, part-time job, or apprenticeship. A professional business organization can provide some of this experience as well as information. Someone pursuing a business job should

Copyright © Mometrix Media. You have been licensed one copy of this document for personal use only. Any other reproduction or redistribution is strictly prohibited. All rights reserved.
This content is provided for test preparation purposes only and does not imply an endorsement by Mometrix of any particular political, scientific, or religious point of view.

have the ability to do the job effectively as well as reliability, responsibility, enthusiasm, and good communication skills. He should also have soft skills, i.e., the skills related to a person's emotional intelligence quotient, such as an ability to be friendly and work well with others.

Employee Rights in Business

There are a number of health and safety rights covered under the Occupational Safety and Health Act (OSHA). Employees should work in a safe environment with the proper safety precautions. Employees also have the right to equal employment opportunities. For instance, a person cannot be discriminated against because of gender, race, or religion. A person has the right to earn a fair minimum wage. He or she cannot be forced to work for less than that. Workers with disabilities and those in the military have special rights. Workers also receive rights from the Family and Medical Leave Act. For instance, eligible employees can get unpaid but protected leave for the birth of a child or to care for a sick family member. The exact rights range based upon the eligibility requirements, state, and position.

Strategies to Work Effectively with Business Colleagues

Certain strategies help business professionals work well with colleagues. First, it is important for a person to be responsible and reliable. Co-workers become resentful when they can't rely on someone, especially when it reflects on them. Business professionals should practice active listening. People appreciate those who really listen to them, and everyone can get their ideas heard. When a person communicates, he or she should do so in a constructive fashion. He should stay positive to the extent possible and explain himself instead of just dictating. He should not be insulting and should keep professional at all times. He should work to compromise with co-workers and show that he is willing to be flexible. People appreciate when co-workers help them and will often pay kind co-workers back with the same courtesy. He should try to solve problems, not make them. He should make sure to "pull his own weight" as workers can be resentful if someone is not doing his share. All of these can make a huge difference in professional relations.

Career Planning Strategies to Reach Career Goals

The first step in career planning is to create goals. These should include both short-term and long-term goals. Students should be realistic in considering the type of career that would suit them. They should evaluate themselves as far as their abilities, skills, and characteristics. There are many career assessment tools available at career centers, in books, and online. Of course, most people want to enjoy work, so they should consider the types of things they enjoy and look for a job that encompasses that. They should also consider both what they want from and what they want to give to a job. For instance, they should consider the salary they desire as well as the hours they are willing to put in to get it. Students should consider what needs to be done to get their desired job such as further education, work experience, and so forth. They should formulate a plan for how they will climb the ladder toward the ultimate goal and the steps along the way.

Steps in Career Planning

Career planning involves a variety of steps to increase an individual's chances of attaining a desired career. First, a person must do a personal assessment. He or she should consider his strengths, weaknesses, and abilities as well as his likes and dislikes. He should think about what he wants in a career such as salary, working hours, conditions, and other specifics. Next, he should research the available opportunities. He should first look at industries in general and narrow that down to specific jobs and companies, considering what is available in the areas he would consider working. He can look at trends in the labor market. He then needs to develop a plan for his career path. This might involve deciding on ways to get experience such as through an internship or volunteer position, and ways to learn such as through a student business organization. He should create a

Copyright © Mometrix Media. You have been licensed one copy of this document for personal use only. Any other reproduction or redistribution is strictly prohibited. All rights reserved.
This content is provided for test preparation purposes only and does not imply an endorsement by Mometrix of any particular political, scientific, or religious point of view.

time frame for his plan. He might want to add flexibility to his plan, and decide what to do if the first plan doesn't work out. Finally, he should implement his plan by creating his resume, applying for jobs, practicing interviewing, and making a cover letter.

Things for Prospective Employees to Consider When Creating Career Plans

There are many factors to consider when a prospective employee plans his or her career. First, he or she needs to consider his or her interests. Someone who likes to talk might want to venture into public relations, for instance. A person also has to consider what he or she is good at doing. Someone who is terrible at math would not want to go into accounting. In addition, an employee should decide what type of salary he desires as well as the working hours he is willing to work. He has to be realistic. He might have to put in long hours for a job that pays well. An employee should think about the environment he'd like to work in, as well as the opportunities available to him. He should not just think about now but also about the future and where he'd like his career to go. He should research potential opportunities, industries, and individual companies. He should map out his career and consider the timing.

Sources of Information About Potential Places of Employment

There are a wide variety of sources where an individual can learn about potential places of employment. Career centers at schools provide a great resource. They help students connect with businesses that are hiring. Sometimes they set up interviews and/or offer meetings with potential employers. Employment agencies and recruiters can be useful. These specialize in connecting employees with employers. The internet provides many ways to search for jobs. Individuals can search on one of the many job search websites such as Monster. These websites make it easy to upload resumes and apply. Job fairs provide another effective venue. Individuals can meet with potential employers. Many colleges and business schools offer these. Individuals can also look at classified advertisements in the newspapers or in trade publications. Personal networking is a very effective way as well. Individuals can "ask around" to people they know to see if they can connect with a potential employer.

Gaining Job Skills and Experience

A prospective employee can gain job skills and experience in many different ways, which can provide a valuable advantage when searching for a job. An internship is an excellent way to gain experience. A person can learn about a job as he (or she) works. Also, some jobs offer employment opportunities to their former interns. Job shadowing is another great way to attain experience. A person will follow and learn from a regular employee. An apprenticeship is another way to learn job skills. In apprenticeships, individuals learn from someone who is skilled at the job and will typically get to practice it. Some people might get a part-time job in which they can get applicable experience. Volunteering is another way to gain experience. This can be especially useful in a field in which it is difficult to get a paying job with no experience at all. It is typically far easier to get volunteer work. Another choice is a school-to-work program, where students train for the jobs as they transition from an educational environment to a work one.

Resume

A resume may be the first thing a potential employer sees; thus, it is vital for it to be professional and comprehensive. First, a resume should contain all pertinent contact information including name, phone number, address, email, and website. It should contain an objective such as the type of position for which the employee is searching. It should contain information about an individual's education, including areas of study and potentially her GPA, if it is impressive. The resume should also list experience, especially the recent experience and that specifically related to the desired job. It should include pertinent information, such as dates of work, responsibilities, and

Copyright © Mometrix Media. You have been licensed one copy of this document for personal use only. Any other reproduction or redistribution is strictly prohibited. All rights reserved.
This content is provided for test preparation purposes only and does not imply an endorsement by Mometrix of any particular political, scientific, or religious point of view.

accomplishments. It should list the individual's skills as well as accomplishments. A potential employee can list his (or her) activities and any awards or honors he received. Resumes should be thorough and contain information to validate claims. An impressive sales number is more powerful than simply saying the candidate is a good salesperson. All of the information should be pertinent and the document shouldn't be too long. It should be edited carefully so there are no errors.

Strong Cover Letter

A strong cover letter can make all the difference in attaining a job. It is best to create a customized cover letter for each job; companies will appreciate the effort. It is important to address the letter to a specific person instead of "To Whom It May Concern." Potential employees should do research to find the correct recipient. Next, the letter should focus on how the employee can help the company and the skills, abilities, and experience that she will use to do so. It should show impressive and substantiated information. For instance, someone who is hoping for a sales job may give impressive sales numbers from a previous job. A person should tailor this information to the details of the company and position. The cover letter should explain how the candidate meets the qualifications. It should not be just a generic letter. It should contain all pertinent information, including full contact information. It should be succinct and not too long—generally no more than one page—because employers are not going to spend a long time reading them. It should be professionally written and free of grammatical errors.

Filling out Strong Job Applications

A job application is one of the first documents a potential employer will see. When filling it out, a potential employee should use a black or blue pen or type it. An erasable pen can be useful. If printed, it should be extremely neat and large enough to be read. It is important to follow all directions on the job application. Everything should be filled out thoroughly, and there shouldn't be any blanks. If something doesn't apply, that should be indicated with "N/A" or a similar comment. Potential employees should explain any obvious issues such as if there was a long break between jobs. They should accentuate extremely pertinent information such as useful skills or statistics that highlight an advantage. Individuals should create a personal fact sheet they can bring with them to ensure all the information is accurate. They should check it over for accuracy and typographical errors.

Job Interview

An important step in preparing for a job interview is to practice interviewing. He or she should consider the most commonly asked questions and formulate and practice answers, preferably in front of someone who can evaluate him. He should research the company so he shows initiative and understanding of the company. He should prepare a resume, portfolio, business cards and other professional materials. A candidate should show up early to an interview, wearing professional clothing. He should be friendly and enthusiastic. He should show good body language, maintain eye contact, sit up straight, and not fidget. He should listen to the interviewers and answer the questions fully, putting the best light on his traits and highlighting how he can help the company. He should give valid data to support his points when possible. After the interview, he should follow up with a thank you card.

CTSO

Career and technical student organizations (CTSO) are organizations dedicated to helping students learn and prepare for careers. There are many CTSOs dedicated to business students. Many offer local, regional, and/or national meetings and conferences where business students come together to network and to learn about trends in the business world. They help prepare students for careers and will sometimes offer mentoring and other opportunities. Many of the

Copyright © Mometrix Media. You have been licensed one copy of this document for personal use only. Any other reproduction or redistribution is strictly prohibited. All rights reserved.
This content is provided for test preparation purposes only and does not imply an endorsement by Mometrix of any particular political, scientific, or religious point of view.

business CTSOs also offer competitions where students can compete in business-related events. These provide prizes and help students learn about business, in addition to looking good on a resume. Students in these organizations also benefit from the knowledge and experience of the faculty advisors. Some of the organizations offer scholarships as well. They can be a great way for students to learn about business and the ways to embark on a business career.

Benefits

Business students can learn about business careers and business in general through career and technical student organizations. It can be a great way to get pertinent experience. A CTSO also offers networking opportunities. Students mingle with those in the business world, which may help them gain an internship, a job, or other benefits that could lead to employment. A CTSO looks good on a resume because it shows initiative. In addition, many CTSOs offer competitive events. Doing well in these also looks good and exposes the student to more people in the business world. Some of them provide opportunities to be mentored. They can also be a resource when a business student is looking for a job. Students can meet other students, share information, and create relationships that may be useful in the future.

Roles of Faculty Advisors

Faculty advisors provide information and guidance to business students in student organizations. They may provide information about business in general. Many of the organizations have competitions, and they help the students study and prepare for the competitions. They also help the students with their career goals and aspirations and help facilitate the meetings. Many faculty advisors will accompany the groups when attending local, regional, or national conferences. They provide information about the groups and help the students make the most of their membership. They might introduce the students to others in the business world and help with networking. In addition, many advisors will mentor business students. They provide a valuable function to their students.

NBEA

The **National Business Education Association (NBEA)** is a professional organization for those involved in business education. It works to help members grow professionally and develop their skills in business education. It offers numerous publications; an informative national convention; networking opportunities at the local, regional, and national levels; advocacy in legislative issues; opportunities to develop professionally; and information regarding international business. It offers numerous webinars to provide information and allows members to interact both in person and online in places such as Facebook, Twitter, and NBEAconnect. It also offers awards and scholarships. Meetings and conferences offer numerous workshops, educational sessions, and exhibitors.

DECA

DECA started in 1946 as **Distributive Education Clubs of America** with the goal of helping high school and college students prepare for business jobs in the fields of management, marketing, finance, and hospitality. With over 200,000 members, it provides a number of opportunities for those interested in the business field. One opportunity is chance to participate in numerous competitions. Students can learn about business and show off their skills, as well as gain something useful for their resumes. Another opportunity is to learn from one of over 5,000 advisors. Students get the chance to attend conferences and network. DECA also offers leadership conferences and career development conferences, which provide workshops and other opportunities to help students embark on their business careers.

Copyright © Mometrix Media. You have been licensed one copy of this document for personal use only. Any other reproduction or redistribution is strictly prohibited. All rights reserved.
This content is provided for test preparation purposes only and does not imply an endorsement by Mometrix of any particular political, scientific, or religious point of view.

FBLA

The **Future Business Leaders of America (FBLA)** boasts over 200,000 members, making it the largest career organization for business students. It aspires to ready students for business and related jobs. It offers competitions, in which students can show off their business knowledge. It also offers informative literature, including *Tomorrow's Business Leader.* Conferences and seminars help students work on their leadership skills through workshops and exhibits. They can learn about current trends and ways to make their career goals come true. They can learn from each other and advisors, networking with those already in the business field. It has both local conferences and a national conference. It also offers leadership events and other special events for general members, as well as officers of the local chapters.

BPA

With 43,000 members, **Business Professionals of America (BPA)** is one of the largest career and technical student organizations for students interested in management, information technology, office administration, and similar careers. It seeks to prepare students for these careers through conferences, competitive events, and other resources, allowing students to hone their leadership, technological, citizenship, and academic skills. Conferences are organized at local, state, and national levels and offer the Workplace Skills Assessment Program (WSAP), which has 72 events in which students can learn and compete. It also offers scholarships, opportunities for officer positions, and a national Leadership Academy. BPA membership also allows for networking, both at a local and national level, and students can also learn from advisors. There are many advantages for students to join BPA.

Area Chambers of Commerce

Area chambers of commerce are organizations that allow local businesses to band together to work for the benefit of the business community as a whole. They range greatly in size, which is largely dependent on how large an area they represent. Business professionals can network and find ways to work with each other to benefit their businesses. Sometimes they work together to get favorable regulation or laws passed, although they do not have the ability to pass laws themselves. They may work with politicians to get initiatives that will benefit business. They may be non-profit, or the money may be provided by the government. They will generally have an executive council or a board of directors, as well as a CEO or similar individual to lead. It is advantageous for a business to join.

Benefits of Belonging to Professional Organizations

Many organizations offer workshops where teachers can learn about the latest trends in the business world. This can help them professionally, as well as give them information to disseminate to their students. In addition, business organizations provide opportunities to network at local, regional, and national conferences, as well as during meetings. Networking in the business world can be very positive and may help the business teacher move to a better position. Membership in a professional organization is also a good thing to have on a resume. It can look very prestigious. Many business education professional organizations also work to promote the interests of business education professionals, thus members can enjoy the benefits that come from these efforts. Many teachers may also enjoy interacting with others in the same field and with sharing and receiving information. It is very worthwhile for business education teachers to join professional organizations.

Copyright © Mometrix Media. You have been licensed one copy of this document for personal use only. Any other reproduction or redistribution is strictly prohibited. All rights reserved.
This content is provided for test preparation purposes only and does not imply an endorsement by Mometrix of any particular political, scientific, or religious point of view.

Chapter Quiz

Ready to see how well you retained what you just read? Scan the QR code to go directly to the chapter quiz interface for this study guide. If you're using a computer, simply visit the online resources page at **mometrix.com/resources719/mttcbusmmt** and click the Chapter Quizzes link.

Copyright © Mometrix Media. You have been licensed one copy of this document for personal use only. Any other reproduction or redistribution is strictly prohibited. All rights reserved.
This content is provided for test preparation purposes only and does not imply an endorsement by Mometrix of any particular political, scientific, or religious point of view.

Technology

E-Commerce

B2B and B2C E-Commerce

Business-to-business (B2B) e-commerce is very different from **business-to-consumer (B2C)** e-commerce and must be handled differently. When selling to a customer, websites are often very flashy, relying on sparking the customers' emotions with great deals and features that stand out. They let the customer check out quickly and easily, often without even registering to make it feel easier and more secure. They usually offer a lot of different options to try to find something that will interest the consumer. A B2B website is often more streamlined, simpler, and focused. B2B customers are less likely to be moved by emotion, so companies focus on showing how they can meet customers' goals. The goal is to build a relationship with the consumer. There needs to be extensive contact information and there may be numerous ways for the business to get more personal help. They may have an account set up and may pay right away or receive an invoice at a later time. Generally, B2B websites offer a lot more information to entice the customer to make the logical decision of choosing the product.

Internet Businesses

A **virtual business** is a business that operates on the internet instead of in a **brick-and-mortar store**. One of the best examples of this is Amazon.com. There may not be a lot of physical structure with a virtual business, lowering the startup, overhead costs, and required investment. Many conventional companies also have internet divisions. For instance, Target has many brick-and-mortar stores, but they also have a website where customers can purchase many of the items in stores as well as a wide variety of additional items. Most of the large companies offer online buying. Market creators such as eBay bring together buyers and sellers and make money by taking a share of the transactions. Many entrepreneurs start online businesses right from their homes For instance, a seamstress may make clothing at home and sell it online. Many businesses are started this way because of the low startup costs.

Effects of Online Business on the Economy

Online business has a major effect on the economy. It has accounted for a great deal of the GDP growth and has become one of its largest influencers. Many states have enjoyed additional taxes from these sales, which have increased since new laws have passed making more items taxable. It has also given great opportunities for smaller businesses as well as entrepreneurs to start a business without a lot of overhead and capital. Entrepreneurs can now sell to people around the world, whereas before they had been severely limited by location and financial constraints. It has also empowered consumers by giving them more buying choices and the opportunity to easily and quickly comparison shop. Consumers can also write and read reviews to find out what products are really like. In many ways, the internet has had many positive economic effects.

Benefits and Drawbacks to Consumers of Buying on the Internet

There are a wide variety of advantages and disadvantages to buying on the internet. One advantage is increased selection. Consumers can buy a vast variety of products on the internet, far more than they can purchase at any single store. Many consumers like the convenience of buying from home. They can make purchases at any time, day or night. This is especially convenient for people who have difficulty going to stores such as a mother with young children. A lot of people find it easier to search for items online. It can take less time, and people can easily comparison shop to save money.

Copyright © Mometrix Media. You have been licensed one copy of this document for personal use only. Any other reproduction or redistribution is strictly prohibited. All rights reserved.
This content is provided for test preparation purposes only and does not imply an endorsement by Mometrix of any particular political, scientific, or religious point of view.

Buying online also has drawbacks. Security issues like the theft of personal information are a common concern. It can also be difficult to evaluate an item without actually seeing it. For instance, a consumer cannot try on an outfit. The consumer may have to pay shipping costs and will have to wait for the item to be shipped. Returns can be more of a hassle and involve the extra cost of return shipping. Also, some consumers do not have internet access.

Methods Marketers Use to Collect Information Online

Marketers can find a wealth of information online. First, many companies put out online quizzes or surveys, which can explain a lot about consumers' preferences and behaviors. Marketers use cookies installed on web browsers to track users. They can see where users go, which helps them target people more effectively with advertising. They will also often get demographic and other personal information. Much of the information is then shared or sold to other companies, spreading it quickly in a big money business. Marketers can also attain a lot of information from social media websites such as Facebook. With data mining, marketers look for patterns in collected data. They can use a simple database program to analyze the data. There are different techniques such as association (connecting two items), classification of customers, clustering, prediction, sequential patterns, decision trees, and combinations. Many consumers do not realize how much information is collected.

Digital Marketing

There are various types of digital marketing, which can be effective in garnering customers and increasing sales. Many businesses possess websites where they share information about their company and advertise their products. Consumers can often purchase either directly from the website or follow a link to make a purchase. Email is another common form of internet marketing. Companies send out email blasts to potential and prior customers. This is a relatively cheap way to reach many people, although a lot of people discard the emails. Viral marketing involves using social media to spread information about the company or products. For instance, companies send out pictures, videos, games, memes, or posts on Facebook and encourage people to spread them around so that they go "viral." Social media in general is an efficient and effective way to market, and companies use websites like Facebook, Twitter, Instagram, and more. Companies also send out web videos to give a dynamic view of their offerings. Many companies use a variety of internet marketing techniques.

Privacy and Security Issues Related to Online Business

The increase in online business has also increased privacy and security issues. When intellectual property is put online, some people will take it and use it illegally. In addition, hackers will steal and illegally use personal information. There is a great deal of identity theft as well. There have been certain measures to try to combat privacy and security issues. Measures like firewalls and virus software can help. Passed in 1998, the **Digital Millennium Copyright Act (DMCA)** makes it illegal to produce and disseminate technology to try to get past processes that stop illegal viewing of protected information. It also increases copyright infringement penalties and lowers the liability of service providers from users' misdeeds in this area. The two parts of the DMCA are the **WIPO Copyright and Performances and Phonograms Treaties Implementation Act** and the **Online Copyright Infringement Liability Limitation Act.**

Branding and Product Placement Over the Internet

Companies can strengthen their brand over the internet. Many register **domain names** that are related to their brands and products so that people will instinctually know where to go. It can also help people remember websites. Companies can attract people to their website by using **search engine optimization**. This is the process of making a website in a way that will increase its rank on

Copyright © Mometrix Media. You have been licensed one copy of this document for personal use only. Any other reproduction or redistribution is strictly prohibited. All rights reserved.
This content is provided for test preparation purposes only and does not imply an endorsement by Mometrix of any particular political, scientific, or religious point of view.

Google and other search engines. There are various strategies that can help achieve this such as using the right keywords, updating often, and getting others to link to the site. It is important for companies to pay careful attention to website design. The website should be easy to read and navigate and should match their branding. It should include easy contact information and a call to action. Many companies hire professional website designers to best promote their brand.

Distribution Channels and Strategies

Distribution for internet businesses may be different than traditional businesses. One reason is that, because the items are shown and advertised online, the party selling them does not actually have to have them in stock. One popular method of Internet business is through drop shipping. With drop shipping, a seller does not physically have the products, but advertises and sells them. When a sale is made, the item goes from the wholesaler or retailer directly to the buyer. The seller will then get the difference in cost and price. This is commonly seen in auction websites like eBay. The company does not have to purchase the products in advance and risk losing the money if no one buys it. Internet companies may not need to keep as much in stock because they do not need to worry about 10 customers coming in at once and wanting the same product that they won't buy if it isn't physically there. If sellers can get more of the product easily, then they can keep none or very few on hand, reducing inventory costs.

Features of Traditional and Online Business

There are many differences between traditional and online businesses. One is the cost of entry. It can be very expensive to enter a traditional business. Entrepreneurs typically need a lot of capital to secure a physical building and get the products and labor and everything associated with a brick-and-mortar business. Alternatively, an online business can be started easily from someone's home with very little commitment and monetary output. Many entrepreneurs start their business while working another job. There are far fewer costs to entry. The customer service will be different for an online business than a traditional business. With a traditional business, someone will be there for face-to-face contact, but with an online business, the customer service is done by phone or through avenues such as email, forums, and live chat. The number of potential customers is far higher for an online business than for a traditional one. Online businesses can reach people all over the world, whereas traditional businesses usually attract more local people. Security can be an issue for both traditional and online businesses, but there are some additional issues for those online. They have to worry about identity theft, online fraud, and hacking.

Benefits and Drawbacks to Selling Online

There are both benefits and drawbacks to selling online. One advantage is businesses can reach a lot of people. A business might be able to sell to a person across the globe that they never would have otherwise been able to target. They can sell to people around the clock. Another advantage is cost. Someone can work from home and not have to incur the cost of a showroom or sales professionals. This can open up entrepreneurship to someone who doesn't have the resources to start a traditional business. It can also allow people to test the market. For instance, a person can sell a few things online to see if there is a market before committing to a brick-and-mortat store. Businesses must consider the drawbacks of online selling. Some people do not have online access. With some products, online selling makes less sense. For instance, someone selling shoes who gets a lot of returns might find it easier to have a brick-and-mortar store. Also, there is fraud online. It can be easy for hackers to perform identity theft or access sensitive data. Companies have to spend the time, effort, and resources to create a website and web presence.

Copyright © Mometrix Media. You have been licensed one copy of this document for personal use only. Any other reproduction or redistribution is strictly prohibited. All rights reserved.
This content is provided for test preparation purposes only and does not imply an endorsement by Mometrix of any particular political, scientific, or religious point of view.

Conventional vs. Online Businesses

Differing Strategies

The processes of selling online and in person are very different, thus so are the strategies. For instance, in a conventional setting, the business is very limited in the product mix it can offer because there is only so much shelf space. It must choose the products for the limited amount of space. Online, it is easy to simply add another product to be offered. An online store has fewer costs, thus they may be able to offer the same products for less. Also, it is very easy to comparison shop online and go for the lowest price, thus sellers will fight to have the lowest price. Online businesses use a variety of promotion strategies. They might make a strong presence on a social media website. They could focus on excellent website design and search engine optimization content to drive people to their websites. They may use blogs and social media like Pinterest and Twitter to promote their products.

Differences in Behavior and Decisions of Consumers

There are large differences in the behavior and decisions of consumers shopping at a conventional business versus an online one. One difference is that consumers online generally have access to more information. They can read reviews and comparison shop very quickly and easily. They can travel from store to store in an instant, which they obviously cannot do in a brick-and-mortar environment. They may make more informed decisions because of it. Someone in a store may be enjoying themselves and spend more time there as compared to someone online who is specifically looking for something. While at a store, a salesperson can pressure consumers into buying something more expensive or making an impulse buy.

Differences in Selling

People online are often more knowledgeable and need to be treated as such. They will often read reviews and do more research. People who go into a store may be looking for advice, so sellers need to be prepared to offer this. Consumers look at many different aspects of a product when they are in stores. They can actually see and feel it. Because they can only see pictures online, it is important to make sure the pictures are very flattering and show off the product in its best light. They need to provide information the consumer may not be able to perceive, such as dimensions. When selling online, customers have many choices and can easily leave. It's easier to switch to another website than go from one store to the next. Therefore, websites need to capture and keep customers' attention to make the sale.

Steps in Launching an Internet Business

First, the entrepreneur should decide on the business and write his or her business plan. He needs to make all the decisions about the product, such as pricing and how customer service will work. Next, he should consider how much and what type of funding to get. He might look for a loan or a capital investment, for instance. He should look at how he will generate revenue from the business and the expected profits. He needs to choose a domain name. A domain name is important because it can give consumers a preconceived notion of the business. He needs to make sure people will go to his website. He can formulate ways to promote it at places like Facebook and Twitter. He also needs to create a professional website. He can code it himself, use a template, or pay a designer. It needs to look professional and convey the right message. The entrepreneur also needs to consider how the product will be distributed. Once he launches the website, he should constantly evaluate the business and look for areas of improvement.

Copyright © Mometrix Media. You have been licensed one copy of this document for personal use only. Any other reproduction or redistribution is strictly prohibited. All rights reserved.
This content is provided for test preparation purposes only and does not imply an endorsement by Mometrix of any particular political, scientific, or religious point of view.

Strategies for Getting into Online Business

Offering goods and services at an online auction site or another marketplace site is a good way to try online business. It is very easy and inexpensive to list and sell products on these websites as much of the work is already done. In addition, the popular websites already garner many customers, and customers will see the product when they search for similar products. People may also use a social media website, such as Facebook, to promote their services. Once the entrepreneur is ready, he can create a website to sell his products. He may use blogs as well. There are many online tools that make creating a website easy, or one can hire a professional to set one up. It can be very inexpensive and easy to get into online business.

Obstacles That Internet Entrepreneurs Face

The internet business environment allows for many competitors. It can be difficult for a new company to establish itself and attract customers with all the different options available. It can be hard to gain credibility and customers' trust. There are many different legal and ethical issues that must be considered as well. Companies need to be careful about how they get data as well as how they use and share it. There are many steps in starting an online business, such as designing a website, which can be difficult. Entrepreneurs need to find a way to make their companies and websites are unique but also accessible and easy to use. There are many technological aspects to running an online business, and entrepreneurs need to make sure that everything runs smoothly. The more detailed and well-prepared the business is, the better its chances of success becomes.

Factors That Affect Success of Internet Businesses

Competition is a huge factor that determines whether an internet business will succeed. If the company has come up with something truly differentiated, it can help, but if there is a lot of competition from companies with similar offerings, it can be difficult to succeed, especially if they come from established companies. How well the business attracts investors makes a large difference. A business needs capital to start and needs to be able to attract investors. It also needs to attract customers and show that it has something special to offer above and beyond the competition. Sometimes this is a matter of being able to successfully promote the business. Even startups can do this successfully with inexpensive options such as promotions via social media. The company needs to have decent profit margins that allow for the continuation of the business. A solid business plan can help the business get off the ground.

Computers and Information Systems

Basic Computer Parts

The system unit is where the main computing parts are located. It is often shaped as a tower and contains the central processing unit, which processes the information; and the random access memory, which temporarily houses information. It will typically contain drives such as a CD/DVD drive, a floppy disk drive, and a hard disk drive. Cables connect the other components to the main unit. A mouse allows the user to point to and select items. Some people use a track ball instead. A keyboard allows users to input information like letters, numbers, and characters. It has function keys, a numeric keyboard, and navigation keys. Users control the computer with its many functions. A monitor displays information in text and graphic form. A printer allows users to print documents as well as information from the screen. Speakers allow users to hear music, dialogue, and other sounds. A modem gives the user access to the internet.

Copyright © Mometrix Media. You have been licensed one copy of this document for personal use only. Any other reproduction or redistribution is strictly prohibited. All rights reserved.
This content is provided for test preparation purposes only and does not imply an endorsement by Mometrix of any particular political, scientific, or religious point of view.

Networks and Networking

Many businesses possess computer networks that provide a wide variety of functions. A **local area network (LAN)** gives a group of nearby computers networking capability. For instance, they can share files, games, printers, and so forth. This can be inexpensive and easy to set up. They can be wired or wireless and can be connected to each other when networking needs grow. When it grows so large that it might go across cities or even countries, the company can make a **wide area network (WAN)** to connect their systems. The Internet itself is a WAN. The employees can usually go on the Internet from the network. A **virtual private network (VPN)** gives employees remote access to the network. The business can also have an **intranet** with internal web servers that let employees distribute confidential information to each other. This may include an internal email system as well as instant messaging and other forms of communication. To access this information, employees must be logged into the network. Many companies have a wide variety of computer systems.

Basic Troubleshooting of Computer Problems

Not every computer problem requires a call to the IT department. Users can do some simple troubleshooting on their own first. They should write down everything they do, as well as any error messages they receive, in case the problem needs to be escalated. The first thing to do is make sure all the cables and cords are properly connected. They should make sure the outlet or surge protector has power and that the monitor and speakers are on. A simple closing and reopening of a program or restarting the computer in general is often enough to fix the problem. The company may have a source where they list updates and/or identified issues. If the computer or program is frozen, users should press Control/Alt/Delete (Option/Command/Esc on a Mac) to access the task manager where they can select and end the task that is giving them problems. A "non-system disk or disk error" message may mean the user needs to remove a CD, flash drive, DVD, or floppy disk before booting up. If the user can't get the computer to shut down, he can hold down the power button to do it. He can also run antivirus software to scan for problems.

Bits, URLs, Bytes, Browsers, USB Flash Drives, Bandwidth, and CD-ROM Drives

In computing, a **bit** signifies the basic unit of information. It is generally 0 or 1. When bits are combined in groups of eight they make a **byte**. A **URL** stands for uniform resource locator and is the web address of a website. This will bring users to their desired website. A **browser** is the program most people use to navigate the internet. Internet Explorer and Google Chrome are two common web browsers. **USB flash drives** are small portable drives that can be used to store information such as Word files. They can be connected to the USB ports on desktop computers, laptops, and other devices. **Bandwidth** is the bit-rate of resources of data communication. It describes the speed of the network. A **CD-ROM** drive can access, read, and play CDs.

Laptop Computers

Laptops are used very often in business. They are produced from companies such as Dell, Toshiba, and Acer. They are very useful and allow a business professional to take all the features of his computer wherever he goes, including on business trips. Business professionals commonly use them for communication. They will email people and also use them for video conferencing. They can use them for word processing such as writing business letters. They can use them to create and show presentations to clients, customers, or business partners. They can use them to store business information. Especially for someone who travels a lot, this can be very important. Smartphones can also do a lot, but they cannot compare to a full computer. Laptops provide this convenience for many in the business world.

Copyright © Mometrix Media. You have been licensed one copy of this document for personal use only. Any other reproduction or redistribution is strictly prohibited. All rights reserved.
This content is provided for test preparation purposes only and does not imply an endorsement by Mometrix of any particular political, scientific, or religious point of view.

PDAs

Personal digital assistants (PDAs) are like small computers, similar to smartphones without the phone capability. For the most part they have been replaced with smartphones. They provide a wealth of information and give the user connection to the internet. They typically contain a calendar, schedule, listing of contact information, notes program, and calculator. They made it easy for business professionals to carry information and access the internet before smartphone became widely available. They range greatly in features, brands, and price. Most also allow for a form of portable memory to carry information. Some people still use them.

Smartphones

Smartphones are very commonly used in business. First, they allow people to make and receive phone calls while on the go, which is especially valuable for someone who is rarely at his or her desk. Business professionals can also contact others through a wide variety of functions such as texting, email, and video calls. They can conduct videoconferencing while on the go. Smartphones also allow business professionals to access information online. They can show off their websites to clients, for instance. They can access social media where they can post things about the business. There are many apps that may be useful for business professionals. They can access the GPS while on a business trip, or check the weather when planning an outdoor event. They can use it to set reminders and alarms or manage their schedules. They can use it to carry presentations. There are many smartphones, including the popular iPhone series, and Android-based phones.

Hardware and Computer Peripherals Utilized in Business

Memory storage devices allow users to store data. These come in many different sizes and connect in different ways. Some companies may get an external hard drive to provide more space. Flash drives make it easy to share information between people or carry files on the go. There are a number of devices used to connect to the Internet. Modems allow this. Routers create networks that pass and direct data. Scanners create digital copies from physical ones. For instance, companies can scan in receipts to cut back on paper and have a secure digital file. Printers are used to print documents. Other common peripherals include the keyboard, which is used to input data; the mouse, which allows people to select items; and the microphone and camera, which allow for video conferencing.

Computer Viruses

Computer viruses are programs that "infect" computers and spread from one to another. They will interfere with the computer, sometimes allowing hackers to steal information or damaging the computer or its programs. They are often spread without the user realizing it in ways such as email attachments, instant messaging, or internet downloads. It is important for users to protect themselves against computer viruses. Programs like AVG and Norton Antivirus can scan and protect computers against viruses and should be updated regularly. It is important for users not to download files unless they are certain the source is secure. Some viruses will send out emails to a user's address book with the virus, so even if something is from a trusted source, it still might not be safe. Users should keep up to date on the most recent viruses and remove any as soon as they can.

Security Measures When Using Technology

With the prevalence of identity theft, scams, and online fraud, it is important for businesses to protect themselves when using technology. One measure is to use **password protection**. Access to sensitive information should be protected by passwords. These passwords should not be easy to crack and should never be shared. In some cases, there should be multiple passwords. Businesses

Copyright © Mometrix Media. You have been licensed one copy of this document for personal use only. Any other reproduction or redistribution is strictly prohibited. All rights reserved.
This content is provided for test preparation purposes only and does not imply an endorsement by Mometrix of any particular political, scientific, or religious point of view.

also encrypt their information. This is where the messages are encoded or changed so they can only be read by the correct users. Even if someone intercepts the message, he or she will not be able to interpret it. Another strategy is the use of **firewalls**. These control the traffic in and out of a network. These can protect against threats online, blocking harmful programs and also blocking others from looking at sensitive data. Most businesses have a firewall to protect them. Businesses also use **antivirus software** to protect against viruses.

Software Often Utilized in Business

Word processing programs allow users to create, read, edit, and manipulate documents. Database management software allows companies to manage their databases. It both manages and analyzes data. There are a lot of specialized programs that allow users to forecast sales and get other data. Spreadsheet software allows users to make spreadsheets and tables and calculate information. Excel is a popular one. Companies also use presentation programs to create, edit, and view presentations. There are a number of software programs related to communication. These allow for email as well as video conferencing and other forms of communication. Many companies have specific programs for accounting and operations. These can help a company manage its business more effectively. Within each of these categories are a wide range of software choices.

Word Processing Software

Word processing software allows users to create, read, edit, save, and format documents. These are often based in text, but may have images as well. They may have tables and other features. They are used very frequently in business for everything from business letters to resumes to company reports and more. The formatting options in the modern programs are vast and allow for great customization of documents. They also allow a lot of shortcuts to make it quick and easy to create a document as well as tools to make a quality document, such as a spelling and grammar checker. There are a number of word processing programs, and Microsoft Word (from Microsoft Office) is one of the most widely used. Other popular programs include WordPerfect (Corel Corporation), Writer (OpenOffice by Apache), and Pages (Apple Inc.).

Database Management Software

Decision support systems are popular. These computerized information systems help managers make decisions. They are interactive and take data, business models, and other information such as sales data to calculate valuable information. They might compare sales numbers, project revenue, or project the consequences of different moves, for instance. A database management system (DBMS) is another system that lets users create, store, change, and view information from a database. They range greatly in size as well as technical specifications and may be organized in a relational, flat, network, or hierarchical manner, with relational being the most common. They preserve the data's integrity. Structured Query Language (SQL) is the standard interface.

Spreadsheet Software

Spreadsheet software allows users to create spreadsheets, making it easy to view information. These programs allow for calculations and manipulations of the data. For instance, a business professional can calculate payroll deductions or average sales results. Microsoft Excel is one of the most common spreadsheet software programs used today. It has columns (denoted by letters) and rows (denoted by numbers), and the current cell is called the Active Cell, which is denoted by the letter of the column and number of the row. It is useful to know the basic Excel formulas for calculations. First, a user starts with the equal sign and then the formula. For instance, if he wanted the D4 cell to be the sum of C1 and C2, then he would put in the formula =C1+C2. Users can also make a similar formula with subtraction (-), multiplication (*) and division (/). They can put more

Copyright © Mometrix Media. You have been licensed one copy of this document for personal use only. Any other reproduction or redistribution is strictly prohibited. All rights reserved.
This content is provided for test preparation purposes only and does not imply an endorsement by Mometrix of any particular political, scientific, or religious point of view.

than one of these in a formula. Also, to add a range of values, users can use the SUM function. For instance, SUM(B1:B3) adds the values of B1, B2, and B3.

Traditional Software

With traditional, or **closed-source software**, the software owners do not allow others to see or modify their code. This is the case with many of the large programs like Microsoft Office. Companies may prefer it because they do not want anyone changing or stealing their code. Users might like knowing exactly what a program will contain when they get it and not worry about changes to the code. There are disadvantages for users, however. Users cannot go into the code to add or disable features. When the code is open-source, people can look through and fix bugs, but this is not possible with closed-source.

Open-Source Software

Open-source software is software that has the source code available to people for viewing, modification, and enhancement. Individuals can go in to the source code and take out things they do not like or add code to create additional features. It is advantageous because people can make improvements or disable parts of the code they do not wish to utilize. People can also spot errors in the code. They can adapt it for their own needs and then pass it on, so others can take advantage of the new features and altered programming. It also helps teach individuals how to program and understand code. Many companies choose not to do open-source code because they do not wish others to change their programs.

Common Computer Operations Utilized in Business

One very useful computer operation is **file management**. Companies typically have a lot of files, and they need to be able to manage, sort, store, and access them efficiently. For instance, an insurance company will have a wide range of files for its different clients. There are many file management programs that allow companies to easily manage their files. **Network operations** involve the management and maintenance of a telecommunications network. Computers allow users to communicate with each other in various ways such as email. Companies also use computers for **data backup**. They can send information offsite so that even if something catastrophic happens to the first source of data, the data will remain secure in another location. There are also specific **shutdown procedures** that make everything easy and logical. It is important to close all programs and then use the Shut Down button located on the Start menu.

Techniques to Input Data on Computers

There are many special function keys and shortcuts that allow users to perform a myriad of functions on the computer. The Tab key moves the cursor to the following tab stop. The Insert key changes the inputting between the overtype mode, in which it overtypes existing text; and insert mode, in which the existing characters are forced one forward to make room for the new character. The Home key moves the cursor to the start of the line or to the start of the document if the text cannot be edited. There are a number of key combinations that make it easy to perform tasks. Many of these use the Control (Ctrl) key (or the Command key on a Mac), which is combined with another key to perform a function. Some of the popular ones are Copy (Ctrl and C), Undo (Ctrl and Z), Cut (Ctrl and X), Paste (Ctrl and V), Select all (Ctrl and A), New browser window (Ctrl and N), Terminate application or restart computer (Ctrl and Alt and Delete), Find (Ctrl and F), and Save document (Ctrl and S). Users can also access special features on the computer such as the spell checker through the Review tab, Proofing group, and Spelling & Grammar option.

Copyright © Mometrix Media. You have been licensed one copy of this document for personal use only. Any other reproduction or redistribution is strictly prohibited. All rights reserved.
This content is provided for test preparation purposes only and does not imply an endorsement by Mometrix of any particular political, scientific, or religious point of view.

Find and Replace Functions on Computers

The Find and Replace functions allow a user to find one or more characters in a document and then (if the user chooses) replace it with a different characters or characters. The user can go through the document to view every time the characters appear, or just replace them all. To access it, users can either click on the Find icon (the word or magnifying glass) or press down Control (Ctrl) and the letter F. The user will then type in the characters to be searched for and can choose options such as matching case and whole words only. They can click on Find or Enter. They can then go to Replace (which might show up right away or be in its own tab, depending on the computer program) and type what is to replace the item. The user can specify whether to replace one or all of them at the same time.

Techniques to Format Documents

There are many options to format a document in popular word processing programs such as Microsoft Word. A user can change the font style and size in the drop-down box in the Home tab. He or she can go to the paragraph option to justify text, change line spacing and change indentation. He can click the appropriate icon to create a numbered or bulleted list. The page layout page has a number of options. In the page setup section, a person can click on the columns tab to make columns. He can change the margins and orientation from the tabs of the same name. In the page background section, he can add a watermark or change page colors or page borders. When he clicks on the icon, he will be taken to an easy-to-understand menu that provides options such as type and thickness of border. The Insert tab allows users to insert a variety of elements such as tables, pictures, and clip art. They can insert a page break, blank page, or cover page in the pages section. There is also a header and footer section where these can be inserted and formatted.

Making, Formatting, and Modifying Tables on Computers

It is simple to make, format, and modify a table in Microsoft Word. Users should go to the Insert tab and click on the Table icon, where they can specify the size of the table. It has some built-in templates for tables such as a calendar, a matrix, and a tabular list. Users can also draw a table to customize it to their exact specifications by using the Draw Table option. Once the table is created, the user can go to the table tools design tab to specify things like banded rows, banded columns, table style, shading, and borders. Users can type in the tables. They can go to the layout section under table tools to make further formatting changes such as changing cell margins and text direction, managing properties of tables, inserting rows and columns, specifying height and width, and more. It is very flexible and allows users to modify the text and format to whatever they want.

Information Processing and Computer Technology Applications

Effects of Computers and Technology on Business

One major way computers and technology have affected business is through communication. The internet has made sending communication easy, inexpensive, and convenient, even if the recipient is on the other side of the world. People can send messages instantaneously and have conference calls and video chats with people in all areas, eliminating the need for business trips in some cases. It is also easy to send and access data from different areas, saving a great deal of money and time. Data can also be recorded, edited, and evaluated in many different ways, providing a wealth of information to businesses. Companies have new ways to promote and advertise their products; many of these, such as social media, are relatively inexpensive and powerful. Through the ease of the internet, many smaller businesses can now compete with large businesses. Streaming video lets consumers get information immediately, and wireless technology makes it easier and more convenient. Computers and technology have benefited businesses tremendously.

Copyright © Mometrix Media. You have been licensed one copy of this document for personal use only. Any other reproduction or redistribution is strictly prohibited. All rights reserved.
This content is provided for test preparation purposes only and does not imply an endorsement by Mometrix of any particular political, scientific, or religious point of view.

Effects of Internet on Traditional Media Industries

The internet has impacted traditional media industries in a number of ways. First, many people wish to view their news on the internet as it happens, and many news companies have opened extensive websites that are updated throughout the day as a response. They've had to keep up with the new speed of information. Some of them have found new ways to earn money such as by requiring subscriptions to read online coverage. Many traditional newspapers have seen their readership decrease because of the information available online. They also have to compete with many more sources of information such as social media. Thus, the internet has provided both negatives, such as increased competition, and positives, such as new ways to reach people.

Effects of Computer Technology on Society

People can connect with each other across societies, cultures, and even oceans. It is easy and inexpensive to communicate with someone across the world with email or video. Some cultures have adopted new things from other cultures as a result. People can also express themselves in new ways. They can use it for art, make blogs, or create social media presences to share their views. Businesses have a much greater market to sell to and can also more easily reach their target markets. It can also be less expensive to reach people through social media and other online options. Social networking in general is much easier. People can keep connected and share information very quickly. If a person or company can cause something to "go viral," it will reach many people. Businesses should take advantage of the new opportunities technology has provided.

Effects of Computer Technology on Politics

Political information can be quickly spread. A news headline does not have to wait for the evening news or tomorrow's newspaper to reach the public. Also, with social media, people can share political information, either positive or negative. They can try to influence their friends. If there is a major happening, it may go "viral" on social media, spreading the information within a matter of minutes. Political blogs have also popped up all over the Internet, where people can give their political opinions and try to inform (or sway) followers. Many politicians keep websites that they use to promote themselves. Computer technology has opened up a new door for political fundraising. It makes it easy for people to donate, even if it's just a few dollars. Those small contributions add up. The internet has made quite a difference in the world of politics.

Information Technology Needs of Businesses

Companies should consider all the types of information technology that can help their company. First, they need a good system of data management. They need to maintain data on products, customers, and other business needs in a neat and organized fashion. There also should be a way to analyze the data. There are many programs that can accomplish this. Companies need technology for communications such as email capability. Many businesses do videoconferencing as well. Companies that perform e-commerce will need systems for that. Most large companies have a website, and many sell or promote their products on it. They need to have a system to take the orders efficiently and effectively. Some use technology for production. There are various other technology needs a company may have based on their industry.

Steps in Planning Information Technology

Companies should follow clear steps to plan their information technology to make sure they obtain the most effective, efficient, and cost-effective system. First, they need to evaluate their technology needs. They need to understand exactly what they need as far as technology in communication, production, accounting, and other functions. They should not just consider what they currently need, but what they might need as they grow. They should spend the time to research the trends in

Copyright © Mometrix Media. You have been licensed one copy of this document for personal use only. Any other reproduction or redistribution is strictly prohibited. All rights reserved.
This content is provided for test preparation purposes only and does not imply an endorsement by Mometrix of any particular political, scientific, or religious point of view.

technology. There are always new things coming out in the technological field, and they want to take advantage of everything that is offered. Then they can choose to get ready-made systems or get something personalized. There are many companies that put together customized systems that address all of their needs. The more they plan, the better system they will get.

Strategies When Acquiring Information Technologies

Companies need to be careful and logical when acquiring information technologies to ensure they receive the right products at the right prices. First, they need to evaluate both their current and future needs. They should consider the products they want and the functions provided. It is important for companies to look at competing products and services, evaluating them for features, quality, and support. They should research the different vendors and what they provide. Businesses will often purchase a great deal of equipment at one time and may get special deals or incentives. Some companies offer a bidding process in which they allow companies to bid for the contract. They will look at what each company offers at the price and choose the one that most aligns with their needs. By taking their time in this process, they will increase the chances of securing the best technology solutions.

Obtaining and Evaluating Internet Information

Those in business should be careful when obtaining and online evaluating information. There is a great deal of false information. Users should search for reputable websites such as websites of reliable news agencies, websites affiliated with schools, and well-known and trusted websites. Search engines are a powerful tool for finding information. Users should choose their keywords carefully. They may want to make use of quotation marks if searching for a particular phrase or use "+" or "-" if there is a word they want included or excluded from their search results. There are a number of other advanced search features such as a site search. Once a website is reached, users should determine its credibility by factors such as its author (although people will lie about their credentials), who it is affiliated with, if the information is up to date, and whether there are any biases, such as if the person is trying to sell something. They can also confirm the information by checking several websites.

Utilization of Internet by Businesses

One of the ways businesses use the internet is it to communicate, both with business associates and with their customers. Many of them have an email system that facilitates that. Companies also communicate with their customers in other ways such as through live chat or through social media websites like Facebook and Twitter. Many customers prefer to reach customer service online. The internet is also very commonly used for promotion. It can be a very cost-effective way to reach many customers. For instance, many companies try to have a strong social media presence that allows them to reach a lot of people while only spending a small amount of time, effort, and money. The internet can also be used in research. For instance, a company can learn about their competition or perform market research. Of course, many companies actually sell online giving the convenience of anytime shopping from home to their customers. Companies should take advantage of all the internet has to offer.

Business Uses of the Web

Most companies offer websites, where business partners, clients, and customers can learn about what they offer. Oftentimes, items are sold directly through these websites. Customer service is also offered through websites. This makes it available 24/7. Blogs are also often used to market products or brands. People in companies write regular articles about the company or other subjects to keep people interested in the company. Companies also get email mailing lists so they can send

Copyright © Mometrix Media. You have been licensed one copy of this document for personal use only. Any other reproduction or redistribution is strictly prohibited. All rights reserved.
This content is provided for test preparation purposes only and does not imply an endorsement by Mometrix of any particular political, scientific, or religious point of view.

out mass emails to customers. They can also take advantage of social media to promote their companies. Most companies use many of these strategies.

Security Threats Due to Use of Technology in Business

Technology provides many useful applications for business, but there are also substantial security risks. **Online fraud** is one common threat, and comes in many forms. Someone might pretend to be someone else and convince an individual or business to share financial information. They may sell a nonexistent or defective item. **Identity theft** is also very common. Someone will steal a person's personal information and make purchases using his or her credit. A major threat for companies is getting their personal or business information hacked. Several major issues have arisen when customers' credit card information was stolen from major store chains. These numbers were then utilized in identity theft. There are a number of ways companies can lower this risk through the use of firewalls and other security measures, but they will always exist to some extent.

Issues Regarding Privacy and Online Marketing

There are many issues surrounding privacy and online marketing. Marketers use cookies to collect information about people without their knowledge. Many people do not realize how much information marketers have on them; information that is then sold and shared with others. Everything that someone enters into a website or social media site could be saved, shared, and used. There is also a great deal of spam that is sent to people, including mass unsolicited emails that fill up email inboxes. Sometimes these are scams and do not represent real opportunities or offers. It can be hard to distinguish between ethical and unethical marketing practices and people need to protect themselves as best they can by being careful with what they share and reading the privacy policies of companies.

Legal Issues Regarding Intellectual Property with Use of Technology

Intellectual property refers to intangible things people have created with their minds. This includes written copy, artwork, phrases, designs, symbols, logos, and more. Protection comes in many forms, including copyrights, patents, and trademarks. With technology in business, these items may become less secure. For instance, an art company may put protected art on their website and then others may copy that artwork. Some companies may use copyrighted material (purposely or inadvertently) on websites such as a song by a famous singer. The laws protecting their use cover a range based on the type of property and other details, but there have been many court cases over improper use of protected material online. It can be more difficult for a company to protect its material if it is being sent to the entire internet because it is easy to copy others' materials. These court cases will continue to define the laws.

Use of Technology in Production Systems

Robotics are often utilized to piece together products or perform other production duties. They may move quicker or be more precise than humans. **Computer-aided design** lets people utilize computers when creating or modifying designs. They may use it to optimize a design or evaluate it. For instance, it may be used to create electronics. It can provide a great deal of information and different views of the design. **Computer-aided manufacturing** is the use of computers to control the devices that manufacture workpieces. It seeks to accelerate the production process with improved material consistency and more accurate dimensions.

Benefits and Drawbacks

One benefit of utilizing technology with production systems is the cost savings. Companies may be able to save a lot of money in the long run by having computerized systems and lowering the need for paid employees. It can also make production more efficient and save time. The computerized

Copyright © Mometrix Media. You have been licensed one copy of this document for personal use only. Any other reproduction or redistribution is strictly prohibited. All rights reserved.
This content is provided for test preparation purposes only and does not imply an endorsement by Mometrix of any particular political, scientific, or religious point of view.

system may be able to produce many more items at a quicker rate. It may also do a better job at making the items exactly as the company desires and exactly the same, helping with quality control. One drawback of a computerized production system is that there can be a high initial cost for the initial system. Although cost savings may be realized later, it can take a large output to get it set up. The system may allow for less flexibility than if people were doing it. Also, if there is a problem, it can stop the entire line. Some companies are resistant to making changes, and technology could result in job losses.

Social and Economic Impact

As companies use technology, they become more efficient and can save money, becoming more competitive. This can have a positive effect on an economy because the company will have an advantage over other companies and produce positive change. In some areas, however, this increased technology can mean a loss of jobs, which can be negative for the economy. When technology has allowed business to become more efficient, society can benefit. For instance, if it is less expensive to make products like cars, then more people can enjoy them. As technology improvements make production cheaper, more people will be able to enjoy these products.

Educating Employees in Computers and Technology

Many businesses require employees to be educated in computers and technology. It is important to have efficient and effective procedures for doing so. First, employees should be evaluated for their current skills. Some employees may need little or no training, while others will need significant training. The students may be placed into groups based on abilities. Training sessions should be planned in advance so employees can learn before they are expected to perform the activities. Sometimes training will be on the job by another employee. Other times the business will get a computer program that will train new employees or it might be done through live lectures or a video. Students should be evaluated after the training to ensure that it was effective. Training should be ongoing as necessary.

Tailoring Training to Meet Needs

Technology training is not one size fits all. Businesses need to tailor training to the needs of their business. For instance, training just a few employees is very different than training a large group of employees. A business that has just a few employees to train might have one employee train another. If a big group needs to be trained, however, then it may invest in customized computer training or videos that can handle a lot of people. Also, companies need to evaluate the employees before training because the training will very much depend on how skilled they already are. They may invest in computer training that can be tailored to the level the person is at. Companies should not waste time and resources training employees on knowledge they already have. These employees may be trained more in the specifics of the job than common computer knowledge.

Evaluating Employees on Computer Knowledge Before and After Training

It is important for a company to ensure that its computer training program is effective by evaluating employees both before and after training. There are various methods to accomplish this. Many computer-based training programs come with a pre-training and post-training evaluation. The employee will take a test on the computer that will evaluate his or her computer competency. This might be in general computer use, in something specific to the job position, or both. Sometimes it is a simulation of the job the employee will be performing. After the training, the employee will receive the same or a similar test to ascertain whether the training was effective. This test could also be given on paper. Another way to evaluate an employee is to have the employee try to do computer functions in front of someone knowledgeable. The person can evaluate the employee on his or her computer skills before and after training.

Copyright © Mometrix Media. You have been licensed one copy of this document for personal use only. Any other reproduction or redistribution is strictly prohibited. All rights reserved.
This content is provided for test preparation purposes only and does not imply an endorsement by Mometrix of any particular political, scientific, or religious point of view.

Developing and Implementing Technological Support for Employees

A company must determine its needs, which will largely be determined by the complexity of computer systems as well as the size of the company. Many larger companies have an information technology (IT) department, which is responsible for making sure the technology is running smoothly and provides a contact point for employees who are having difficulty. Some companies that are smaller may instead contract with another company that can provide IT support. Of course, one can sometimes contact the vendor of the computer product. Some very small companies may have employees who are not specifically assigned to IT, but who are computer literate and help with problems. Companies may also provide support on websites. They may provide a list of common complaints, for instance, or provide other information. Many companies combine various forms of IT support.

Chapter Quiz

Ready to see how well you retained what you just read? Scan the QR code to go directly to the chapter quiz interface for this study guide. If you're using a computer, simply visit the online resources page at **mometrix.com/resources719/mttcbusmmt** and click the Chapter Quizzes link.

Copyright © Mometrix Media. You have been licensed one copy of this document for personal use only. Any other reproduction or redistribution is strictly prohibited. All rights reserved.
This content is provided for test preparation purposes only and does not imply an endorsement by Mometrix of any particular political, scientific, or religious point of view.

MTTC Practice Test #1

Want to take this practice test in an online interactive format?
Check out the online resources page, which includes interactive practice questions and much more: **mometrix.com/resources719/mttcbusmmt**

Multiple Choice Questions

1. Which of the following is MOST directly related to a weaker US dollar?

a. Foreign exports increase
b. US exports increase
c. Foreign exports decrease
d. US exports decrease

2. Which business discipline is defined as the practice that includes researching, identifying, and satisfying consumer needs and wants?

a. Marketing
b. Organizational behavior
c. Communication
d. Sales management

3. David is an office administrator for a large corporation. He receives hundreds of automated emails throughout the day with various requests. He has folders set up for the different types of requests he receives, but he still finds that it takes time to sort through them. It would be more efficient if the automated emails would automatically sort into the various folders he has set up. Using Microsoft Outlook, which feature could David use to improve efficiency?

a. Categorize
b. AutoArchive
c. Rules
d. Folder Permissions

4. When on the Internet, which of the following is the LEAST common use for links.

links are used in all but which of the following ways?

a. They direct Internet users to other websites that have additional relevant information
b. They are used for marketing purposes, to entice Internet users to navigate away from one website to view another one
c. They allow Internet users to open additional windows that explain a webpage's content or provide technical assistance
d. They directly open and operate software programs on the local PC

Copyright © Mometrix Media. You have been licensed one copy of this document for personal use only. Any other reproduction or redistribution is strictly prohibited. All rights reserved.
This content is provided for test preparation purposes only and does not imply an endorsement by Mometrix of any particular political, scientific, or religious point of view.

5. Which choice below is NOT a characteristic of the sole proprietorship form of business ownership?

a. The owner has flexibility with how the business is operated.
b. It is the most common form of business ownership.
c. Establishing a sole proprietorship is costly and complex.
d. The owner is personally liable for all business obligations.

Refer to the following for question 6:

	Cost	Franchise fee	Average gross monthly revenue	Average monthly expenses
Business A	$500,000	5% of gross revenue	$20,000	$15,000
Business B	$440,000	4% of gross revenue	$16,000	$10,000
Business C	$320,000	None	$10,000	$5,000
Business D	$175,000	None	$8,000	$5,000

6. If Sarah wanted to get her initial investment back as quickly as possible, which of the following options would you advise her to choose, based upon the information in the table?

a. Business A
b. Business B
c. Business C
d. Business D

7. A manager gives a floor worker free reign to implement a new organization system that helps to cycle out old stock right before new stock arrives. She notices over the next few weeks that the employee's performance in other areas improves as well. What is the motivational theory that suggests the employee will be more successful when they are challenged to grow professionally based on their skills and abilities?

a. Piaget's cognitive stages
b. Locke's goal-setting theory
c. McClelland's achievement motivation theory
d. Maslow's hierarchy of needs

8. If a country is a net exporter, this means that:

a. The value of the goods that it imports exceeds the value of the goods that it exports
b. The value of the goods that it exports exceeds the value of the goods that it imports
c. The value of the goods that it exports exceeds the value of the products it consumes.
d. The value of the products it exports exceeds the value of the goods it produces.

9. Which part of a contract is the promise of something of value in exchange for something of value?

a. Offer
b. Acceptance
c. Capacity
d. Consideration

Copyright © Mometrix Media. You have been licensed one copy of this document for personal use only. Any other reproduction or redistribution is strictly prohibited. All rights reserved.
This content is provided for test preparation purposes only and does not imply an endorsement by Mometrix of any particular political, scientific, or religious point of view.

10. A potential business owner projects that she will need to invest $100,000 in equipment to start a dry cleaning business, and the business' monthly expenses on rent, insurance, labor costs, and other incidentals are $5,000 Which of the following options best represents how many months it will take for her to earn back her initial investment if the average monthly gross revenue is $8,000.

a. Less than 9 months
b. Less than 20 months
c. Less than 34 months
d. None of the above

11. Organizations should have a policy specifying which communication ____ will be used by employees, clients and vendors in order to prevent confusion or frustration due to a breakdown in communication.

a. Channels
b. Formats
c. Systems
d. Schemes

12. Upon which organization does the international community primarily rely to deal with claims of unfair protectionism by one country against another?

a. North Atlantic Treaty Organization (NATO)
b. World Trade Organization (WTO)
c. Organization of Petroleum Exporting Countries (OPEC)
d. International Committee of the Red Cross (ICRC)

13. What is the biggest challenge or risk associated with conducting an employee satisfaction survey?

a. Skewed results because only the most satisfied employees respond
b. The potential for employees to not be truthful in their responses
c. The potential for the responses to not be anonymous
d. No employer follow-through on the results gathered from employees

14. What term refers to an organization's administration and includes these five general functions: planning, organizing, staffing, leading, and controlling?

a. Leadership
b. Board of directors
c. Corporate authority
d. Management

15. According to standard economic theories, countries that have a comparative advantage in the production of cotton should:

a. Export another product, and import cotton
b. Export cotton, and import other products
c. Implement tariffs to protect their domestic cotton industry
d. Work hard to reduce their comparative advantage and diversify their economy

Copyright © Mometrix Media. You have been licensed one copy of this document for personal use only. Any other reproduction or redistribution is strictly prohibited. All rights reserved.
This content is provided for test preparation purposes only and does not imply an endorsement by Mometrix of any particular political, scientific, or religious point of view.

16. Anna is interested in purchasing a computer for her small landscaping business. She wants to be able to compose simple fliers and advertising materials, communicate with clients via email, and order supplies online. Which of the following lists best describes the hardware and software components that Anna's computer should look for?

a. An internet connection, Quickbooks, and at least 16 GB of memory
b. An internet connection, word processing software, and Quickbooks
c. An internet connection, word processing software, and 8 GB of memory
d. An internet connection, Quickbooks, and 8 GB of memory

17. An external hard drive is an example of what type of computer hardware?

a. Device memory
b. Peripheral device
c. Random-access memory (RAM)
d. Core memory

18. Using Boolean operators, what is the best phrase to type into an academic database when conducting research on teaching strategies for students with attention deficit disorder?

a. "Teaching strategies, attention deficit disorder"
b. Teaching strategies "attention deficit disorder" not hyperactive
c. "Teaching strategies" and "attention deficit disorder" not "hyperactive"
d. Attention deficit disorder; teaching strategies

19. Each of the following are sentences from a job description. Select the sentence that clearly and correctly communicates its intended meaning.

a. The employee, will have excellent oral communication skills.
b. The employees oral communication skills will be excellent.
c. The employee will communicate orally and in writing well.
d. The employee will have excellent writing skills.

20. Which of the following file types would be best for exporting a document containing text, that is not intended to be changed or copied from in the future?

a. PDF
b. XLSM
c. DOCX
d. JPEG

21. What is true about an effective instructional strategy that improves teaching effectiveness and student performance

a. Teachers' telling students success stories will not help them see cause and effect.
b. Teachers should have students keep logs to help them connect efforts to results.
c. Teachers' tangible rewards to students are more effective than symbolic rewards.
d. Teachers should ensure equitable treatment by making student rewards uniform.

22. What is the common name of employment websites where employers post jobs, and individuals can research companies and apply to openings?

a. Job boards
b. Job fairs
c. Hiring events
d. Online career searches

Copyright © Mometrix Media. You have been licensed one copy of this document for personal use only. Any other reproduction or redistribution is strictly prohibited. All rights reserved.
This content is provided for test preparation purposes only and does not imply an endorsement by Mometrix of any particular political, scientific, or religious point of view.

23. In preparation for a class project, the teacher is discussing computer databases. Which statement should be excluded?

a. Research databases offer collections of related information.
b. Databases include references and citations.
c. Databases are specific in nature.
d. Publishers check the content of databases so the information is more accurate and reliable than general internet searches.

Refer to the following for questions 24–25:

Businesses often partner with local schools to offer support in many ways. They may assist with fundraising efforts or may work with individual students with job shadowing or work study programs. This week, the owner of a local business is coming into a business education classroom to conduct mock job interviews with students. She wants to help students learn how to discuss non-technical skills that include flexibility, teamwork, and time management.

24. What is the common term used to describe a business's involvement in its community?

a. Social responsibility
b. Corporate citizenship
c. Public relations
d. Due diligence

25. What are the skills that the business owner wants to teach students called?

a. Hard skills
b. Requisite skills
c. Personality skills
d. Soft skills

26. When itemizing deductions on a federal tax return, an individual taxpayer may be able to deduct all but which of the following?

a. Interest paid on a mortgage
b. Charitable donations
c. Losses from theft
d. Life insurance premiums

27. Dividing a broad customer base into different subgroups is referred to as

a. Differentiation
b. Targeting
c. Market segmentation
d. Profiling

28. Which of these statements accurately reflects recommended practices for giving students learning goals and feedback?

a. Learning goals for students should be unrelated to their personal goals.
b. Contracts are good ways to define goals and grades for reaching them.
c. Teachers should give students general, delayed, and positive feedback.
d. Teachers should be the only ones who lead student feedback sessions.

Copyright © Mometrix Media. You have been licensed one copy of this document for personal use only. Any other reproduction or redistribution is strictly prohibited. All rights reserved.
This content is provided for test preparation purposes only and does not imply an endorsement by Mometrix of any particular political, scientific, or religious point of view.

29. What is one advantage of using "styles" in a word processor document for the formatting of repeated elements such as headers?

a. A document using styles has a significantly smaller file size.
b. Styles ensure that no two types of element have the same formatting.
c. You can change all the formatting of all the corresponding elements throughout the document by just changing the style.
d. It ensures consistency between computers; if you edit your file on a different computer, the formatting will still be the same.

30. Which of these practices contributes the least to internet data security?

a. Checking web pages for HTTPS or TLS
b. Requiring authentication
c. Giving responsibility for privacy to cloud providers
d. Deleting cookies

31. When manually proofreading a business document for a colleague, which of the following answers describes the correct way one would indicate that a section of text should be removed?

a. An X should be drawn through the text
b. A caret should be drawn at the beginning and end of the text
c. A diagonal line should be drawn through the text from bottom left to top right
d. A horizontal line should be drawn through the text with a loop at the right end of the line

32. What is the term for the correct or acceptable way to communicate on the internet?

a. Netiquette
b. Grammarly
c. Common Courtesy
d. Online Protocol

33. Which of the following terms describes communication between individuals in different units and at different levels in a company?

a. Vertical
b. Horizontal
c. Top-down
d. Diagonal

34. Federal courts have three main levels. Which one is NOT part of this court system?

a. District courts
b. Circuit courts
c. County courts
d. The Supreme Court of the US

35. Which term refers to the buying and selling of goods and services via the internet?

a. B2B
b. E-commerce
c. Online promotion
d. Mobile shopping

Copyright © Mometrix Media. You have been licensed one copy of this document for personal use only. Any other reproduction or redistribution is strictly prohibited. All rights reserved.
This content is provided for test preparation purposes only and does not imply an endorsement by Mometrix of any particular political, scientific, or religious point of view.

36. Which of the following examples demonstrates a conflict between verbal and nonverbal communication?

a. A sales representative does a presentation to a potential client, making eye contact, speaking in a clear and even tone, and using hand gestures occasionally to accentuate an important point.
b. A candidate for an open position arrives to an interview dressed in a business suit, makes eye contact with the hiring manager, shakes hands with the interviewer, and speaks confidently.
c. A vendor arrives at a business to negotiate a contract. The vendor representative smiles often, speaks clearly and confidently, and maintains good posture, even during tense moments.
d. An employee meets with her manager to discuss a rumor she heard about layoffs. As he looks down at his computer, the manager says in a high-pitched voice not to be concerned because the rumors are false.

37. Which of the following list contains ONLY examples of soft skills?

a. Adaptable, mathematical, problem-solver
b. Bilingual, creative, intelligent
c. Cooperative, persuasive, musical ability
d. Strong work ethic, time management skills, communication skills

38. Which of the following is not true of stock dividends?

a. They are not usually directly taxable
b. They are offered voluntarily by companies in order to make their stock more attractive
c. Their amount and frequency are determined directly by shareholders at large
d. They may be discontinued or reduced at any time

39. Henry owns and operates a business. He pays a licensing fee to a parent company to cover the cost of marketing, use of the brand name, turn-key set up, a proven success rate, and other pre-determined benefits. Henry also pays a royalty fee on profits. What type of business is Henry running?

a. Sole proprietorship
b. Limited liability company
c. Franchise
d. S corporation

40. If a file has the extension htm, what kind of file is it likely to be?

a. A web page
b. A text document
c. An image
d. A Microsoft Word file

41. According to the National Environmental Policy Act of 1969, a business is required to prepare an environmental impact statement (EIS) when it:

a. Hires a new worker
b. Makes a charitable contribution
c. Develops a new marketing initiative
d. Builds a new factory

Copyright © Mometrix Media. You have been licensed one copy of this document for personal use only. Any other reproduction or redistribution is strictly prohibited. All rights reserved.
This content is provided for test preparation purposes only and does not imply an endorsement by Mometrix of any particular political, scientific, or religious point of view.

42. How does effective marketing benefit society?

a. It utilizes technology, increases product support, and decreases consumer waste.
b. It eliminates unnecessary products, increases customer value, and improves sales.
c. It decreases competition, improves customer service, and increases product choices.
d. It increases competition, improves product quality, and lowers product prices.

43. Which of the following activities that are conducted by high school student leadership organizations would be the MOST effective tool for teaching applied business skills?

a. Raising money by selling concessions at athletic events
b. Performing community service by painting a local elementary school
c. Holding an awards ceremony to honor scholarship winners
d. Tutoring middle school students in math and reading

44. Ben is a database administrator at the local school district. One of the teachers in the district has recently been promoted to assistant principal. In this new position, she will need to be able to access more secure student information that she was not privy to as a teacher. What settings does Ben need to change for her?

a. Elevate security clearances
b. Increase user permissions
c. Modify role-based access controls
d. Change from user to administrator

45. If the exchange rate between the Euro (€) and the US dollar ($) is $2.5 to € 1, how many dollars would it take to purchase a plane ticket that costs € 1580.00?

a. $39,500.00
b. $3,950.00
c. $395.00
d. $632.00

46. Focus groups are an effective means to gather employee feedback. For what are they best suited?

a. Employees in the same division or department
b. Specific subjects of discussion
c. Fewer than five participants
d. Unstructured brainstorming sessions

47. ABC Toys is a small, independently owned toy store. They are selling the newest doll house on the market for $150. Five miles down the road, Walmart sells the exact same doll house for $120. What is the economic term used to explain why Walmart sells the toy for less than the small toy store?

a. Economies of scale
b. Cost of capital
c. Opportunity cost
d. Price discrimination

Copyright © Mometrix Media. You have been licensed one copy of this document for personal use only. Any other reproduction or redistribution is strictly prohibited. All rights reserved.
This content is provided for test preparation purposes only and does not imply an endorsement by Mometrix of any particular political, scientific, or religious point of view.

48. On her 13th birthday, Mary received a gift of $500 from her aunt. Mary wants to save this money for college, and she is not willing to assume any risk on her investment. Which form of savings will likely yield the highest rate of return with little to no risk?

a. A savings account
b. Purchase of stock
c. Certificate of deposit
d. Mutual fund

49. Effective strategies to recruit students for business education extracurricular activities include the following EXCEPT

a. Giving students extra class credit for participating in these activities
b. Keeping guidance counselors up to date on events, guest speakers, and off-campus activities
c. Using social media for reminders and to post viral videos
d. Offering freebies to new members

50. Which federal agency collects consumer complaints about business practices, investigates them, and files suit against perpetrators?

a. Better Business Bureau
b. Consumer Product Safety Commission
c. Financial Consumer Agency
d. Federal Trade Commission's Bureau of Consumer Protection

51. Which of the following is NOT considered a domestic economic advantage of global trade?

a. Global trade provides raw materials to countries that otherwise would not have access.
b. Global trade reduces costs of production, therefore also reducing prices for consumers.
c. Global trade creates mutual economic growth between trading nations.
d. Global trade allows for imports on some goods, such as agriculture, much cheaper than buying domestically.

52. The cluster of shared values, practices, and beliefs of a company is referred to as its

a. Job environment
b. Company culture
c. Selection process
d. Transformation

53. Which federal agency is available to help start-up entities write their business plans?

a. Small Business Administration
b. Internal Revenue Service
c. US Export-Import Bank
d. US Department of Commerce

54. A company is considering manufacturing a product in several different emerging markets. Which of the following is LEAST likely to influence the company's decision?

a. Likelihood of political instability
b. Labor costs and regulations
c. Cost of shipping goods from that country to the destination country
d. Housing markets in the local area

Copyright © Mometrix Media. You have been licensed one copy of this document for personal use only. Any other reproduction or redistribution is strictly prohibited. All rights reserved.
This content is provided for test preparation purposes only and does not imply an endorsement by Mometrix of any particular political, scientific, or religious point of view.

55. If you click on a file in the operating system, and then click again on its name, the filename is highlighted. What does this allow you to do?

a. Rename the file
b. Set the file to Read Only
c. View the extension of the file
d. Find other files with the same name

56. What happens when the money supply is increasing faster than the economy?

a. Commercial banks are able to increase lending
b. Money loses value, resulting in a recession
c. The Federal Reserve will increase rates
d. The value of the dollar decreases and inflation will occur

57. If a stock has a high P/E ratio, this means that:

a. The stock's price is low considering the value of the company's earnings
b. The stock pays a high dividend based on its earnings per share
c. The stock's price is high considering the value of its earnings per share
d. The company's earnings per share are high

58. Each year, early in the flu season, the Centers for Disease Control and Prevention (CDC) uses data collected on patients throughout the United States to determine the most prevalent strands of the flu and the rate of infection to compute projections for the rest of the season. This data analysis is an example of what type of data processing?

a. Data mining
b. Data projections
c. Forecasting
d. Probability

59. Which of the following is an example of an IP address?

a. http://en.wikipedia.org
b. /wiki/wikipedia
c. <html class= "client-nojs" lang="en" dir="ltr">
d. 208.80.154.224

60. A business education teacher wants to evaluate her program in terms of how well graduates are prepared for the workforce. Which of the following strategies would be most likely to provide the best data to answer this question?

a. Setting up an advisory committee of local employers to gather feedback on graduates' performance in the workplace
b. Asking students to complete internships with local employers
c. Conducting a survey of recent graduates to see if they were able to find jobs with local employers
d. Asking the business professors at a local community college to provide feedback

Refer to the following for questions 61–62:

Mrs. Jacobs teaches a careers class. She wants her students to be more engaged in their learning, so she decides to break them into groups and have each team research and present a lesson on a career of the group's choosing. Each member of the team is assigned a task and will be graded on their individual and group efforts. One group decides to focus on a career in the environmental

Copyright © Mometrix Media. You have been licensed one copy of this document for personal use only. Any other reproduction or redistribution is strictly prohibited. All rights reserved.
This content is provided for test preparation purposes only and does not imply an endorsement by Mometrix of any particular political, scientific, or religious point of view.

field. Matt is a student in this group, and after doing the initial research, he seems very interested in considering it as a future career. He wants to study this topic in greater depth, develop specific expertise in sustainable practices, and research other environmental jobs to consider as future career paths.

61. The project Mrs. Jacobs assigned is an example of which type of instruction?

a. Ability grouping
b. Kinesthetic learning
c. Cooperative learning
d. Flipped classroom

62. Which type of classroom learning center would best help Matt accomplish all of his goals?

a. Any or all of these
b. An enrichment center
c. A skill development center
d. An interest/exploratory center

63. What should a marketing teacher advise a student to do first in the job search process?

a. Analyze growing sectors in the job market
b. Write a resume and general cover letter
c. Assess personal strengths and weaknesses
d. Prepare for interviews by gathering industry facts

64. Which of these tasks would NOT be a primary function of an organization's human resources department?

a. Recruiting, screening, and training new employees
b. Managing employee benefits
c. Managing client accounts
d. Coordinating payroll activities

65. What is the copyright status of images you find on the web?

a. Any images found on the web can be freely used and redistributed.
b. Any images found through Google Images can be freely used and redistributed, but not necessarily images found elsewhere on the web.
c. Any images found on the web can be freely used and redistributed unless they bear an explicit copyright notice.
d. Any images found on the web should be assumed to be under copyright unless their owners explicitly release them into the public domain.

66. What key or key combination is most commonly used to obtain help with a computer application?

a. F1
b. F2
c. F3
d. Ctrl-H

Copyright © Mometrix Media. You have been licensed one copy of this document for personal use only. Any other reproduction or redistribution is strictly prohibited. All rights reserved.
This content is provided for test preparation purposes only and does not imply an endorsement by Mometrix of any particular political, scientific, or religious point of view.

67. What is the statistical method used to determine the range of acceptable outcomes, based on observable data, to determine the reliability of an estimate? For example, a company needs to create a budget based on the highest and lowest possible revenues and expenses, as they cannot forecast exact numbers with 100% accuracy. Using this method, a business can determine an acceptable range to make financial decisions, knowing their highest and lowest limits.

a. Confidence intervals
b. Probability
c. Coefficient of correlation
d. Standard error of estimate

68. What does the refresh button do on a web browser?

a. Reloads the current webpage
b. Closes and reopens the browser
c. Takes the user back to the default homepage
d. Clears all saved data from the current browsing session

69. The Equal Employment Opportunity Commission (EEOC) is responsible for enforcing all but which of the following laws?

a. Civil Rights Act of 1964
b. Equal Pay Act
c. Clean Air Act
d. Americans with Disabilities Act

70. Which of the following types of assets is LEAST subject to depreciation?

a. Heavy equipment
b. Computers
c. Real estate
d. Company vehicles

71. Which program focuses on understanding the economic behavior of groups of families, individuals, or consumers?

a. Consumer economics
b. Home economics
c. Consumer science
d. Financial science

72. SWOT analysis is often used to understand the international business climate for a company looking to expand. SWOT is an acronym for

a. Strengths, weaknesses, opportunities, threats
b. Strategies, work, operations, tactics
c. Strategies, wages, outsource, tendencies
d. Service, work, opportunities, tactics

Copyright © Mometrix Media. You have been licensed one copy of this document for personal use only. Any other reproduction or redistribution is strictly prohibited. All rights reserved.
This content is provided for test preparation purposes only and does not imply an endorsement by Mometrix of any particular political, scientific, or religious point of view.

73. Which of the following correctly summarizes the accounting equation for a sole proprietorship?

a. Assets = Liabilities + Owners' equity
b. Liabilities = Assets + Owners' equity
c. Owners' equity = Assets + Liabilities
d. Revenue = Assets – Liabilities

74. What is the use of the field called CC in emails?

a. Store a hidden record of the email
b. Request a read receipt of the email
c. Send a copy of the email to an indirect recipient
d. Send a hidden version of the email to another recipient

75. Andrew works in the warehouse of a big box store. As he is stocking shelves, a bolt comes loose, and one of the massive shelving units collapses. Andrew sustains injuries as a result. What form of commercial insurance will cover Andrew's medical expenses and lost wages?

a. Liability insurance
b. Workers' compensation insurance
c. Unemployment compensation insurance
d. Property insurance

76. Which financial report is considered a "snapshot" of one moment in time?

a. Income statement
b. Cash flow statement
c. Balance sheet
d. Statement of changes in owner's equity

77. Which pact is a regional trade agreement including the United States of America?

a. EU-UK
b. OPEC
c. ASEAN
d. USMCA

78. Which of the following is true of a Wide Area Network (WAN)?

a. A WAN is equivalent to a LAN
b. Businesses usually have their own WAN
c. The Internet is an example of a WAN
d. Businesses prefer WANs to LANs because their data transfer speed is higher

79. An increasingly popular piece of presentation hardware is the interactive digital whiteboard. Which of the following accurately describes an advantage of these whiteboards over conventional, non-digital whiteboards?

a. They take up less space than conventional whiteboards.
b. They allow the presenter to project images from a computer.
c. They allow the presenter to easily write on and erase the screen.
d. Unlike conventional whiteboards, they work even without electronic power.

Copyright © Mometrix Media. You have been licensed one copy of this document for personal use only. Any other reproduction or redistribution is strictly prohibited. All rights reserved.
This content is provided for test preparation purposes only and does not imply an endorsement by Mometrix of any particular political, scientific, or religious point of view.

80. Which one of these actions is NOT included in consumer protection laws?

a. Checking an organization's reputation
b. Enforcing antitrust regulations
c. Regulating bill collectors
d. Preventing sellers from fraudulent tactics

81. A business class is discussing the sort of person who might want to be an entrepreneur, and many characteristics are suggested. Which one should be removed from the list of typical traits?

a. Does not want a boss
b. Has a curious and ambitious nature
c. Fits into the corporate environment
d. Likes to work flexible hours

82. Which of the following best describes Congress' purpose in setting up Freddie Mac in 1970?

a. Expanding opportunities for home ownership
b. Deregulating the credit market
c. Improving regulation of the Internet
d. Creating a place for small businesses to get loans

83. When a consumer purchases a new mattress from a manufacturer, they have the right to expect that mattress to meet safety standards and to have the features the manufacturer claims it has, even if there is no explicit promise made. What form of contract does this represent?

a. Express contract
b. Written contract
c. Implied in-law contract
d. Implied in-fact contract

84. The company that Scott Smith works for provides full time employees with a 100% 401k match after one year on the job if they contribute 4% of their paycheck. If Scott becomes a full time employee after a year, makes $2,000 per paycheck, and contributes 4% to his 401k each pay period, how much would the company have to contribute to his 401k during each pay period?

a. $160
b. $80
c. $40
d. Cannot be determined

85. The biggest factor that leads American companies to manufacture their products overseas in developing countries like China and India is:

a. Higher quality of craftsmanship
b. Lower labor costs
c. Decreased transportation costs
d. Effective legal systems

Copyright © Mometrix Media. You have been licensed one copy of this document for personal use only. Any other reproduction or redistribution is strictly prohibited. All rights reserved.
This content is provided for test preparation purposes only and does not imply an endorsement by Mometrix of any particular political, scientific, or religious point of view.

86. What is a popular tool used by lenders to evaluate the likelihood of loan repayment?

a. VantageScore
b. Credit bureau reports
c. Debt-to-income ratio
d. FICO score

87. Accounts receivable are:

a. Fixed assets
b. Fixed liabilities
c. Current assets
d. Current liabilities

88. Which of the following is NOT an effective approach for a supervisor delivering feedback to a struggling employee?

a. The supervisor should list every area of deficiency and how it impacts the team and/or organization.
b. The supervisor should provide specific examples of instances in which the employee had a misstep.
c. The supervisor should make performance expectations clear.
d. The supervisor should provide some praise around the things the employee is performing well.

89. Which entrepreneurial opportunity describes someone who just bought and intends to operate a single local Subway restaurant?

a. Network marketing
b. Franchise
c. Distributorship
d. Dealership

90. Which type of correspondence is used for cover letters, thank you notes, and letters of recommendation?

a. Memorandum
b. Formal business letter
c. Personal note
d. Email

91. According to Fayol's Administrative Theory of Management, which of the following is a correct list of the five essential functions of management?

a. Controlling, composing, planning, organizing, implementing
b. Containing, controlling, implementing, planning, organizing
c. Composing, coordinating, controlling, planning, organizing
d. Controlling, commanding, coordinating, planning, organizing

92. An advantage of protectionism for countries that implement it is that it:

a. Improves the country's global competitiveness
b. Ensures that domestic jobs will be retained in the short term
c. Encourages economic growth
d. Prevents corruption

Copyright © Mometrix Media. You have been licensed one copy of this document for personal use only. Any other reproduction or redistribution is strictly prohibited. All rights reserved.
This content is provided for test preparation purposes only and does not imply an endorsement by Mometrix of any particular political, scientific, or religious point of view.

93. In 1994, a war began between Adidas America and Payless Shoesource over the use of the famous three stripes. After several years of lawsuits, Payless was ordered to pay several million dollars to Adidas. What type of intellectual property did Payless violate?

a. Trademark
b. Copyright
c. Patent
d. Trade secrets

94. Which of the following would be a violation of the Occupational Safety and Health Act (OSHA)?

a. An employee becoming injured while commuting to work
b. An employee becoming injured because an employer did not provide equipment in good working order
c. An employer requiring employees to work with toxic chemicals
d. An employer failing to accompany an OSHA compliance officer on an inspection

95. Banks require ____ when issuing a secured loan, giving them more security should the customer default on their payments.

a. Insurance
b. Cosigners
c. Tier 1 credit scores
d. Collateral

96. When researching a presentation about a national shipping business, the most detailed and comprehensive source of information about the top management of the company and its competitors would most likely be:

a. The company's investor-relations website
b. Hoovers.com
c. LexisNexis.com
d. The catalogue at your local library

97. Which of the following is an example of a peripheral device?

a. The central processing unit of a computer
b. A computer keyboard
c. An image file in .jpg format
d. A web browser

98. Joe is a highly skilled baker working for a large bakery in the city. Joe does not believe his skills are being recognized and he doesn't like reporting to anyone else. Joe has decided to open a bakery in his town. However, he does not have enough initial capital to start a business on his own. His brother, Steve, has offered to lend enough cash to get Joe started up, but has no interest in running a bakery. What is the most likely type of business structure for the bakery?

a. Partnership
b. Sole proprietorship
c. Joint venture
d. Limited liability company

Copyright © Mometrix Media. You have been licensed one copy of this document for personal use only. Any other reproduction or redistribution is strictly prohibited. All rights reserved.
This content is provided for test preparation purposes only and does not imply an endorsement by Mometrix of any particular political, scientific, or religious point of view.

99. Referring to the graph below, what does the point at the intersection of the total expenses line and the total sales revenue represent?

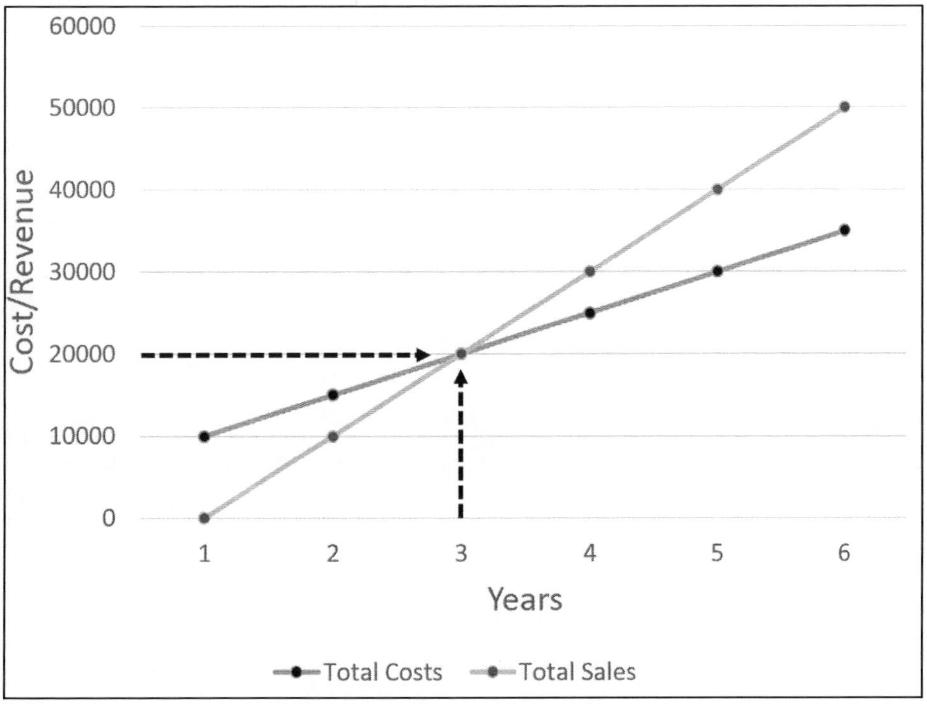

a. Net revenue
b. Gross profit margin
c. Breakeven point
d. Unit sales

100. Which step in the accounting cycle transfers original entries to the accounts?

a. Calculate a trial balance
b. Record entries in the general ledger
c. Prepare journal entries
d. Produce financial statements

Constructed Response

1. You have purchased a business that sells prescription eyeglasses. Sales have recently decreased, although demand for these products appears to be high, and competitors have maintained the same level of sales. The highest-selling product, which has been on the market for three years and is targeted to consumers between the ages of 20 to 29, has experienced the most significant decrease in sales. Currently, all advertising is done via direct mail and radio broadcast. Customers often complain about the slow processing of orders. Frequently, items must be placed on back order because they are not in stock.

Using your knowledge of marketing strategies and inventory control, prepare a response in which you use the information above to propose strategies to:

- Improve advertising campaigns, especially those for products popular with younger audiences
- Achieve general customer satisfaction

Copyright © Mometrix Media. You have been licensed one copy of this document for personal use only. Any other reproduction or redistribution is strictly prohibited. All rights reserved.
This content is provided for test preparation purposes only and does not imply an endorsement by Mometrix of any particular political, scientific, or religious point of view.

- Increase overall sales and brand recognition

Copyright © Mometrix Media. You have been licensed one copy of this document for personal use only. Any other reproduction or redistribution is strictly prohibited. All rights reserved.
This content is provided for test preparation purposes only and does not imply an endorsement by Mometrix of any particular political, scientific, or religious point of view.

Answer Key and Explanations for Test #1

Multiple Choice Questions

1. B: When US dollar or products are less expensive for foreign customers, then US firms will export more products. If US products are more expensive for foreign customers, then US firms will export fewer products. The amount of exporting done by foreign nations is not necessarily affected by the US exchange rate.

2. A: Marketing refers to all business activities that promote consumer purchases of a business's goods or services. This generally includes researching, identifying, and satisfying consumer needs and wants to the end of making a sale. Organizational behavior is a business discipline that studies how people behave in groups. Other business disciplines include finance, management, and information technology. Communication and sales management are business activities.

3. C: David would benefit from using the Rules feature in Microsoft Outlook. Rules allow the user to automatically move, flag, or reply to email messages. By using Rules to separate the automated emails into their appropriate folders, David can focus on one set of tasks at a time, making more efficient use of his workday.

4. D: Links are used in all of the ways described here, except that they usually do not allow computer users to open software programs on their PC. In order to do that, one would typically click on an icon on one's own PC. Links, on the other hand, are inserted into a website's source code in such a way that clicking on them leads the Internet user to another website or webpage within the same site. Most safety protocols would prevent a webapp from directly controlling a local computer.

5. C: Sole proprietorships—the most common form of business ownership—are easy to form, and there is typically very little regulation. Start-up requirements often involve simply securing a business license. The owner has flexibility with how the business is operated and is personally liable for all business obligations.

6. D: If Sarah wanted to get her initial investment back as quickly as possible, she would be best advised to choose Business D, which would allow her to recoup her initial investment of $175,000 in just over 58 months. One can estimate how long it will take to recoup the initial investment for a business by dividing the cost of buying the business by the average monthly profit.

7. B: Locke's goal-setting theory is a theory that was developed in the 1960s that insists that specific and difficult, but reasonable, goals lead to improved performance when compared to more general, easy goals. Not only is performance expected to improve, but the motivation of affected employees also often improve as a result.

8. B: If a country is a net exporter, this means that the value of the goods that it exports exceeds the value of the goods that it imports. Net exporters have positive trade balances, meaning that the value of the goods that they sell to other countries exceeds the value of the goods that they buy from other countries.

9. D: Consideration is the exchange of items of value. (e.g., the seller's consideration in a contract to sell a home would be the house, and the buyer's consideration would be the amount being paid.) An

Copyright © Mometrix Media. You have been licensed one copy of this document for personal use only. Any other reproduction or redistribution is strictly prohibited. All rights reserved.
This content is provided for test preparation purposes only and does not imply an endorsement by Mometrix of any particular political, scientific, or religious point of view.

offer is what someone is going to do, and acceptance is the agreement to the offer. Capacity refers to all parties being able to enter the contract (both in terms of age or maturity and mental ability).

10. C: If the business owner has invested $100,000 into the business, and makes an average monthly profit of $3,000 ($8,000 average gross revenue minus the $5,000 monthly costs of running the business), it will take approximately 33.3 months for her to make back her initial $100,000 investment.

11. A: Communication channels include oral, written, and electronic communication. When an organization develops a communications policy, careful consideration needs to be made regarding the information senders and recipients. In some instances, face-to-face communication is required. In other instances, email or text may be most efficient. Another option is distributing information via social media.

12. B: The primary organization upon which the international community relies to deal with claims of unfair protectionism by one country against another is the World Trade Organization (WTO). NATO is a military alliance among many North American and European countries, OPEC is an organization of oil-producing countries that regulates supply and prices, and the Red Cross is an international humanitarian organization.

13. D: The biggest organizational risk when conducting an employee satisfaction survey is the potential for not taking any action based on the findings of the survey. This may backfire and create ill will among employees instead of the intended result of boosting morale or making people feel heard.

14. D: Management is an administrative area and is usually organized as a hierarchy with senior, middle, and lower management levels. In smaller businesses, fewer managers may assume more expansive roles. Leadership refers to the people who direct others. The board of directors is elected by the shareholders to set policy for the corporation and for general oversight. Corporate authority is the power appropriately exercised by corporate officers.

15. B: Economic theory states that countries with a comparative advantage in producing a particular product should produce and export that product, and use the proceeds to import the other products that they need from other countries.

16. C: Anna would need word processing software, an Internet connection, and a minimum of 8 GB of memory to keep up with basic computing standards. Word processing software would allow Anna to compose simple fliers and advertising materials, and an Internet connection would allow Anna to communicate with clients via email and order supplies online. 8 GB of memory is what standard home and small business computers need, and Quickbooks is a type of accounting software that may be useful for Anna, but would not be necessary for the tasks listed in this question.

17. B: An external hard drive is an example of a peripheral device. Peripheral devices are connected to a main unit, either wired or wirelessly. These devices are connected to a main unit through hardware and may require software drivers or interfaces to work as intended.

18. C: The best search phrase in this situation would be to use the Boolean operators "and" and "not." This narrows the search from approximately 8 million results to around 19,000 results. Narrowing the search will return results that are more aligned to what you are searching for.

Copyright © Mometrix Media. You have been licensed one copy of this document for personal use only. Any other reproduction or redistribution is strictly prohibited. All rights reserved.
This content is provided for test preparation purposes only and does not imply an endorsement by Mometrix of any particular political, scientific, or religious point of view.

19. D: "The employee will have excellent writing skills" states the desired qualification clearly and correctly. "The employee, will have excellent oral communication skills" is incorrect because the comma is unnecessary. In the second sentence, "employees" is meant to be possessive, and should have an apostrophe ("employee's"). The second sentence is also written in passive language, which is not technically incorrect, but may convey a lack of clarity. In the third sentence, the word "well" is misplaced and would be best placed next to the verb which it modifies ("communicate well" would be correct).

20. A: Portable Document Format (PDF) is commonly used for displaying different types of content, and can be used to encrypt and lock elements to deter change or theft. The format .docx could be used to prevent alteration, but it does not prevent readers from copying and pasting content into new documents.

21. B: As educator expert Robert Marzano has noted, effective instructional strategies include relating success stories to students, which reinforces their efforts in school and helps them see the causal relationship between effort and achievement. Another strategy that promotes this connection is having students keep logs and analyze them (B). Marzano advises teachers to give symbolic, not tangible, rewards to students (C) to recognize their efforts and achievements more effectively, and to personalize or individualize those rewards for each student to make them more meaningful and relevant than uniform rewards (D).

22. A: In addition to viewing employment opportunities, job boards allow individuals to apply for jobs and/or submit resumes, read company reviews, and research salary ranges. Popular US job boards include Indeed, CareerBuilder, Glassdoor, and Simply Hired.

23. C: In addition to offering collections of related information with bibliographies and citations, databases are checked by publishers to ensure their content is accurate and reliable. Databases can be specific or general in nature.

24. B: Corporate citizenship means that businesses need to participate in the communities in which they reside, beyond just paying their local taxes. Partnerships with local school districts are one way they can maintain a good image and relationship in their communities. This is mutually beneficial to the school and the business. Many contributions are tax deductible, reducing or eliminating the expense to the business and improving the school's benefit with the added financial support.

25. D: Soft skills are personal attributes that enable employees to interact. Because of the importance of these skills in the workplace, educators are expected to include lessons on them. Job applicants should include these personality traits in their cover letters and discuss them in job interviews.

26. D: When itemizing deductions on a federal tax return, a taxpayer may be able to deduct all of the things listed here except for life insurance premiums. Mortgage interest, losses from theft, and charitable donations are all tax-deductible under certain circumstances.

27. C: Market segmentation allows companies to personalize marketing campaigns, which leads to a more efficient use of marketing resources. These target markets allow businesses to focus on common demographics (e.g., hurricane-reinforced windows might be marketed to those who live in areas prone to tropical storms).

28. B: One recommended way for defining student learning goals and what grades they will receive for meeting those goals is for teachers and students to write and sign contracts agreeing to goal and

Copyright © Mometrix Media. You have been licensed one copy of this document for personal use only. Any other reproduction or redistribution is strictly prohibited. All rights reserved.
This content is provided for test preparation purposes only and does not imply an endorsement by Mometrix of any particular political, scientific, or religious point of view.

grade terms. Experts say student learning goals should be compatible with student personal goals, not unrelated (a). They note it is important for teachers to give students specific, timely, and corrective feedback (c). They also recommend that teachers invite students to lead feedback sessions (d).

29. C: The main advantage of styles is that they allow the user to change the formatting of many elements at once. For example, if you use a header style for all the headers in your document, then if you change the formatting of that style the formatting of all the headers will change accordingly. Without styles, you'd have to go through and change the style of each header individually. For a complex document with many elements, this can mean a huge saving in time and effort.

The formatting of a document should be consistent between computers with or without styles (unless you use a font not available on the other computer), and the effect of styles on file size is generally negligible. Nothing prevents two styles from having the same formatting, nor is there necessarily any reason why this would be undesirable.

30. C: Personal information being accessed without permission is referred to as an internet data breach. Giving responsibility for privacy to cloud providers can lead to unsafe security, so you should review the controls that are in place. Checking for HTTPS, TLS, or SSL on a web page before submitting personal data, keeping anti-virus software up to date, deleting cookies, requiring authentication so that credentials submitted match stored data, and using trusted websites are ways to protect internet privacy.

31. D: When manually proofreading documents, the correct way to indicate that a section of text should be removed is to draw a horizontal line through the text with a loop at the right end. Carets are used to indicate that something should be inserted into the text, and diagonal lines are used to indicate that a letter should be lower case instead of capitalized. Xs are not standard proofreading marks.

32. A: Netiquette refers to the common rules of etiquette that apply while communicating over the internet. Without facial expressions or nonverbal cues, misunderstandings can happen. Netiquette attempts to discourage unwanted behavior with established social conventions. Grammarly is a software that checks grammar, spelling, and potential plagiarism. It also offers writing suggestions.

33. D: *Vertical communication* refers to information sharing between staff in the same unit but at different levels; e.g., Top-Down or Down-Top. *Horizontal communication* refers to information sharing between staff in the same unit and at the same level. *Diagonal communication* refers to the sharing of information between people in a company who are neither in the same unit nor at the same level.

34. C: District courts are the general trial courts for both civil and criminal proceedings. Circuit courts are also known as courts of appeals. Any decision of a district court can be appealed to a circuit court. Finally, the Supreme Court of the United States (also referred to as the "court of last resort") is the highest court in the federal judicial system. Appeals can be made to the Supreme Court for any circuit court cases and for state cases that involve federal law.

35. B: E-commerce is the recognizable term referring to online buying and selling. Consumers look for sites that are easy to navigate (including the checkout function), have recognizable security features, offer mobile device functionality, and feature promotions or other discounts. Mobile shopping and online promotion refer to e-commerce activities. B2B (business-to-business) is one type of e-commerce.

Copyright © Mometrix Media. You have been licensed one copy of this document for personal use only. Any other reproduction or redistribution is strictly prohibited. All rights reserved.
This content is provided for test preparation purposes only and does not imply an endorsement by Mometrix of any particular political, scientific, or religious point of view.

36. D: Nonverbal communication is often a more accurate portrayal of communication than spoken words. Making eye contact, using hand gestures appropriate to the conversation, and having good posture are all examples of positive nonverbal communication. Avoiding eye contact and speaking with a nervous or high-pitched voice communicate nervousness or dishonesty, even if the words that are spoken seem to indicate otherwise.

37. D: Soft skills are the personal aptitudes that demonstrate a person's ability to work with others or generally adapt to situations in a job. Hard skills are measurable and are usually learned with education or training. For example, hard skills mixed into the other choices include mathematics, bilingualism, and musical ability. These are considered hard-skills because they involve some sort of specific, technical skill that may apply to the job directly in a technical way. Soft skills are usually tied to a person's character or work habits and influence the way they can approach any job or situation.

38. C: Stock dividends are not usually directly taxable, unless they are traded for cash dividends. They may be discontinued or reduced at any time, and they are offered voluntarily by companies to make their stock more attractive. However, the amount and frequency of dividend payments are determined by the company's board of directors, not by shareholders at large.

39. C: Henry is running a franchise. The licensing fee is paid to cover the costs of the brand name, marketing, etc. that the parent company provides. There are many pros associated with franchising, such as the benefit of an established brand, an existing customer base, business support, advertising and marketing, and sometimes financial assistance. Conversely, one of the major downsides of franchises is royalty payments. The more successful and profitable your franchise business is, the more you pay to the parent company. Some other cons of owning a franchise are the initial investment, limited creative authority, and other fees established by the parent company.

40. A: The *extension* of a file is a sequence of characters at the end of the filename that specifies the type of file it is. The extension comes after a period, and is often, though not always, three letters long. The extension "htm" or "html" corresponds to a web page—the "htm(l)" stands for HyperText Markup Language, the format in which web pages are written. Text files usually have the extension "txt", and Microsoft Word files have the extension "doc" or "docx". There are many different formats for image files, each with their own extensions, but none of these extensions is "htm"; common extensions for image files include "gif", "jpg", and "png".

41. D: According to the National Environmental Policy Act of 1969, a business is required to prepare an environmental impact statement (EIS) when it builds a new factory, but not when it hires a new worker, makes a charitable contribution, or develops a new marketing initiative. Environmental impact statements assess the possible environmental concerns and damage that could result from a proposed action. Hiring new workers, making charitable contributions, and even developing marketing initiatives may be important decisions from a business perspective, but they are unlikely to have any major negative impact on the environment, and thus are exempted from the EIS requirement.

42. D: The best answer is choice D because marketing forces firms to compete for business, which in turn forces improvements in quality and lowers product prices. Choice A is incorrect because marketing does not necessarily use technology or relate to consumer waste. Choice B is wrong because improved sales are not necessarily beneficial to society. Choice C is incorrect because competition increases with marketing.

Copyright © Mometrix Media. You have been licensed one copy of this document for personal use only. Any other reproduction or redistribution is strictly prohibited. All rights reserved.
This content is provided for test preparation purposes only and does not imply an endorsement by Mometrix of any particular political, scientific, or religious point of view.

43. A: Of the activities listed here, the most effective tool for teaching business skills would be raising funds by selling concessions at athletic events. This would teach students how to attain permits and licenses, purchase and price inventory, develop a supply process, schedule employees, provide customer service, and account for sales, among many other functions that are necessary for running a small business. The other activities listed here would teach important skills, but fundraisers teach skills most directly relevant to business.

44. B: Ben would need to change her user permissions to allow access to more secure fields or pages of the database. User permissions protect personal information from those who may not need to view all details. This also protects the user in the event of an information leak; those without access to the more secure information are excluded from an investigation of a data leak.

45. B: If the exchange rate between the Euro (€) and the US dollar ($) is $2.5 to € 1, it would take $3,950.00 to purchase a plane ticket that costs € 1580.00. This is calculated by multiplying the number of dollars to one Euro (2.5) by the cost of the plane ticket in Euros (1580).

46. B: Focus groups with employees are optimal when they pertain to specific topics, such as feedback on the benefit plan or succession planning. Around eight to 10 participants are best, and they should be a diverse group of employees to more accurately represent opinions across the organization. Although employees should feel free to voice their opinions openly, the facilitator should bring some semblance of structure to the focus group. He or she should give an introduction, ask open-ended questions to participants, and be prepared to summarize the discussion at the conclusion.

47. A: Walmart can purchase a very large quantity of doll houses which will be sold by their stores nationwide. This gives them leverage to negotiate a better price with the manufacturer. ABC Toys will only order a few doll houses, so the manufacturer does not have incentive to offer them the same deal they offered to Walmart. In this example, Walmart is benefiting from the economic concept of economies of scale.

48. C: Mary will be saving her money for approximately 5 years. A standard savings account assumes almost no risk, but also will also return a low amount of interest. Stock and mutual funds come with varying rates of risk and return, so this would not be a good option given Mary's unwillingness to assume risk. The best choice would be the certificate of deposit (CD). Mary can decide the length of the term, she will receive a higher interest rate than a standard savings account, and there is very little risk associated with a CD. The risks that are involved in a CD primarily revolve around inflation and early-withdrawal penalties.

49. A: Sharing information online about the value of these activities, having sign-up areas during lunch and before school, using social media, keeping guidance counselors up to date on events, and offering freebies to new members are all effective strategies to educate students about the benefits of business education. Most school districts prohibit extra credit for assignments that are not directly connected to the curriculum or state standards.

50. D: In addition to responding to potentially unscrupulous business activity, the Federal Trade Commission's Bureau of Consumer Protection provides services to educate the public about consumer law. The Better Business Bureau is a nonprofit member organization that rates businesses on its consumer friendliness and works with members to resolve marketplace issues. The Consumer Product Safety Commission is an independent US government agency that works to promote the safety of consumer products. The Financial Consumer Agency enforces consumer protection laws in Canada.

Copyright © Mometrix Media. You have been licensed one copy of this document for personal use only. Any other reproduction or redistribution is strictly prohibited. All rights reserved.
This content is provided for test preparation purposes only and does not imply an endorsement by Mometrix of any particular political, scientific, or religious point of view.

51. D: While it is true that importing certain goods, such as agriculture, can be cost effective, the result of these transactions is often detrimental to domestic producers. US farmers often cannot compete with the lost costs of imported produce. Closing domestic farms has a negative impact on the economy and GDP.

52. B: Company culture is a set of shared values and goals that is reflected in decision-making, conflict resolution, and employee interactions. It is also present in hiring practices, so prospective employees should seek to determine if they will be comfortable in the established company culture.

53. A: The Small Business Administration supports small businesses across the country and often helps match start-ups to lenders. The Internal Revenue Service is responsible for taxation matters, and the Department of Commerce is concerned with promoting economic growth. The US Export-Import Bank exists to help American businesses with exporting goods by providing loans and insurance.

54. D: Housing markets may play some role in establishing new businesses and looking for factors that directly influence employee stability, but it is less likely to influence whether or not to manufacture a product for specific markets. Political instability could put the company's investment at risk, and the labor and shipping costs associated with a given country can be a decisive factor in investment decisions.

55. A: Clicking on the filename of the selected file will highlight the filename, allowing you to rename it by simply typing in the new name. You can also rename a file by right-clicking on it and selecting "Rename" from the pop-up menu. In macOS, you can also hit Return to rename a highlighted file; in Windows, you can rename it by selecting the Rename icon in the Home menu.

Setting a file to Read Only is a slightly more complicated process that involves going to the file's Properties (Windows) or Info (macOS) window. Whether the file extensions are visible depends on the preferences you have set, and is not changed by clicking on the filename. Finally, finding files is done through a separate command, and not simply by clicking on a file.

56. D: If the money supply increases at a rate that is faster than the economy, the value of money drops. When money has less value, the cost of goods and services increases, which is inflation. As money begins to lose value, consumers and businesses tend to spend more now, out of the fear of another drop in the value of the dollar. This means the money supply goes even higher, causing inflation to continue to rise.

57. C: If a stock has a high P/E ratio, this means that the stock's price is high considering the value of its earnings per share (EPS). The P/E ratio is calculated by dividing the share price by the company's EPS. The closer the result is to zero, the cheaper the stock is in relation to the amount of money the company is earning.

58. C: The analysis of existing information to detect patterns and relationships is called data mining, but using it to project into the future is called forecasting. In the example of the CDC, information collected on patients early into the flu season can help scientists and doctors determine which strands are most common, how quickly it is spreading, and which geographic locations are likely to have the highest number of cases.

59. D: An **IP address** is a numerical code used by internet processes to identify a particular device on the network. It generally consists of four numbers between 0 and 255, separated by periods. Normally, users do not refer to websites and other internet addresses by the IP address directly, but by URLs (an acronym for Uniform Resource Locator), a sequence that specifies first the domain

Copyright © Mometrix Media. You have been licensed one copy of this document for personal use only. Any other reproduction or redistribution is strictly prohibited. All rights reserved.
This content is provided for test preparation purposes only and does not imply an endorsement by Mometrix of any particular political, scientific, or religious point of view.

of the site in question, and then optionally a directory within that domain. Choice A is an example of a URL without a directory; the "http://" at the beginning specifies the kind of protocol to use for the resource—the http protocol is used for web pages—and the rest specifies the domain. Choice B is an example of how a directory is specified; these two choices put together, "http://en.wikipedia.org/wiki/wikipedia", in fact make up the full URL for the Wikipedia page about Wikipedia itself. Choice C is a snippet of HTML, the language in which web pages are written.

60. A: The best way for a business education teacher to evaluate her program in terms of how well graduates are prepared for the workforce would be to consult with local business leaders to find out where graduates have room for improvement. Asking students to complete internships would help prepare students for the workforce, but it would not provide the necessary feedback on students' preparedness. Surveying recent graduates would be useful, but it would provide less direct and detailed information about their performance in the workforce. Last, community college professors would be more familiar with students' performance in college courses than their performance in the workplace.

61. C: Mrs. Jacobs' class is participating in cooperative learning. This is an instructional method that requires students to work together in teams to learn about their assigned topic mostly independent of the teacher. Ability grouping is when a teacher arranges students in groups according to their strengths and needs. Kinesthetic learning is based on hands-on learning using tactile activities. The flipped classroom method is when teachers have students learn content outside of the classroom, usually using pre-recorded videos, using in-person classroom time for discussion and deeper learning.

62. A: Self-contained classroom learning centers supply varied, easily accessed learning materials for self-directed student learning activity. Students can independently study class topics in greater depth in enrichment centers (b), learn specific expertise related to such topics in skill development centers (c), and find out more information, like researching various careers related to these topics, in interest and/or exploratory centers (d).

63. C: The first step in the job process is performing a self-assessment. A student should consider his or her interests, strengths, and weaknesses before embarking on a random job search. Identifying job opportunities, writing a resume, and preparing for interviews are important, but should not occur until a student has a strong understanding of his or her own abilities. If a student lacks the skills, personality, or education for a particular job path, then the student should reconsider their job objectives.

64. C: Recruiting, screening, and training job applicants; managing employee benefits; and coordinating payroll activities are functions of the human resources department. Staffing and development as well as employee and labor relations also fall under the human resources umbrella.

65. D: While many people mistakenly assume that text and images on the web are free to use, in fact copyright applies to online material just the same as it does to text and images printed in physical books. The creators of online content may choose to release their content into the public domain, or they may choose to release it under other licenses, such as the "Creative Commons Attribution-ShareAlike" license that allows the user to reuse the content as long as proper credit is given and any derivative work is released under a similar license. (This is the license under which Wikipedia articles are released.) However, the content is copyrighted by default, unless explicitly released by its owner.

Copyright © Mometrix Media. You have been licensed one copy of this document for personal use only. Any other reproduction or redistribution is strictly prohibited. All rights reserved.
This content is provided for test preparation purposes only and does not imply an endorsement by Mometrix of any particular political, scientific, or religious point of view.

The fact that an image is found on Google Images has no effect on its copyright status. Google Images is not a repository of free-to-use images; it is just a search engine that finds images elsewhere on the web. If you want to find out the copyright status of an image you find on Google Images (or by any other means), check the site where the image is hosted. If there is no licensing notice on the site, assume the content is under copyright by the site owner or the page's creator. If you really want to reuse the content, it may be possible to contact the copyright owner and ask for permission.

66. A: F1. This is a standard that dates to the 1987 IBM Common User Access documentation. This documentation outlined standards that were to be used by programs to make things more common and more usable across programs. It was quickly adopted by Windows, and all Microsoft programs will allow a user to press F1 to obtain help. When developing a program, an application programmer can write the program so that any key can have any action, but most users will expect the F1 key to lead them to help in some manner. The F2 does not have a clear, common standard for its use. The F3 key is often used to activate a search function, but still is not as much a standard as the F1 key leading to help. Ctrl-H is not a standard key combination for any use.

67. A: The confidence interval helps businesses assess the reliability of an estimate based on data gathered from previous sales, historical expenses, customer information, etc. Because an estimate may not be 100% accurate, the confidence interval provides a range of acceptable outcomes, allowing for a small margin of error or adjustment.

68. A: The refresh button (or the corresponding hotkey, typically F5 or Ctrl-R in Windows, Command-R in macOS) reloads the webpage that the user is currently viewing, downloading the data anew from the remote site. This is useful if the user is looking at a dynamic page that changes over time, and the user wants to see what has changed on the page since it was originally loaded—for instance, if the user is looking at a comment thread that may have accumulated new posts. It may also be useful if the page initially failed to load completely; refreshing the page may (or may not) cause it to load successfully on the second try, especially if the connection status has changed.

69. C: The Equal Employment Opportunity Commission (EEOC) is responsible for enforcing Civil Rights Act of 1964, the Equal Pay Act, and the Americans with Disabilities Act, but not the Environmental Protection Act. The EEOC is primarily responsible for enforcing civil rights, while the Environmental Protection Agency (EPA) is responsible for enforcing environmental protection statutes, such as the Clean Air Act or Clean Water Act.

70. C: Of the given options, real estate is the least subject to depreciation. Real estate can be subdivided into depreciating structures, sucha s buildings, and land, which does not depreciate at all. While real estate often appreciates (increases) in value, assets like vehicles and computer equipment inevitably depreciate (decline in value) due to normal wear and tear. Note that in economic terms, while an assett can appreciate in net, it does not technically negate the idea of a depreciation expense.

71. A: Traditional branches of economics focus on governments and businesses. Consumer economics looks at the buying choices made in a particular economy. These economists observe consumer patterns and then identify the needs and problems of the observed groups.

72. A: Strategic planning using SWOT involves looking at: strengths: the company's internal characteristics in which it excels, including brand recognition; weaknesses: internal characteristics that present challenges; opportunities: external issues, including the developing markets; and threats: external issues, including factors impacting international business.

Copyright © Mometrix Media. You have been licensed one copy of this document for personal use only. Any other reproduction or redistribution is strictly prohibited. All rights reserved.
This content is provided for test preparation purposes only and does not imply an endorsement by Mometrix of any particular political, scientific, or religious point of view.

73. A: The accounting equation for a sole proprietorship is correctly stated as Assets = Liabilities + Owners' equity. In the accounting equation for a corporation, owners' equity is replaced by shareholders' equity.

74. C: CC stands for carbon copy, which sends a copy to an indirect recipient, who is not the primary intended recipient. Another feature, blind carbon copy (BCC) is also available, which does the same thing, except that the secondary recipients are hidden and inaccessible to other recipients.

75. B: Workers' compensation insurance is required in most states. It covers employees who may have a work-related illness or injury. Workers' compensation covers medical expenses, lost wages, and even covers the company if the employee files a lawsuit in some instances.

76. C: The balance sheet reports the entity's assets, liabilities, and owner's equity at a specific moment. A balance sheet's title includes the date and may include the phrase "as of _____." The other three reports present information covering a period of time that is also specified in the report's title.

77. D: Free trade agreements are treaties between two or more countries that seek to reduce the burdens of taxes, tariffs, quotas, and other trade restrictions. NAFTA (North American Free Trade Agreement) went into effect in 1994 between the US, Canada, and Mexico. This was superseded in 2020 by the United States–Mexico–Canada Agreement (USMCA). EU-UK (European Union and United Kingdom) includes the European Union's 27 member states representing 450 million people. OPEC (Organization of the Petroleum Exporting Countries) is not a free trade agreement. ASEAN is the Association of Southeast Asian Nations.

78. C: The Internet is an example of a Wide Area Network (WAN). WANs are networks that cover an extremely large area. LANs (local area networks) cover smaller areas, like offices. LANs usually have faster data transfer speeds than WANs.

79. B: One advantage of digital whiteboards is that they allow the user to easily project images from a computer to the whiteboard screen. This is not limited to still images; the content of the computer display can be dynamically projected on the screen, allowing the presenter to show videos, presentations, and animations and demonstrate the use of applications. Conventional whiteboards and digital whiteboards both come in a variety of sizes; it is not accurate to say that digital whiteboards take up less space. Choice C is true of both digital whiteboards and conventional whiteboards; digital whiteboards may allow the presenter to write on and erase the screen with digital tools, but this is not a clear advantage that digital whiteboards have over conventional ones. Choice D reverses the facts of the comparison; digital whiteboards do require electronic power, while conventional whiteboards do not.

80. A: Consumer law topics include creating a fair marketplace by enforcing regulations, regulating bill collectors, preventing sellers from fraudulent or deceptive tactics, product liability, bill collector regulation, and utility shutoffs.

81. C: In addition to not wanting a boss, being curious and ambitious, and liking to work flexible hours from any location, entrepreneurs usually want to change the world and do not fit into a corporate environment. Entrepreneurs are typically described as passionate, open-minded, and determined. They are also characterized as innovators, problem solvers, job creators, and contributors to society. Entrepreneurs do not have to have these characteristics, however, as anyone can decide to pursue a business opportunity and can succeed.

Copyright © Mometrix Media. You have been licensed one copy of this document for personal use only. Any other reproduction or redistribution is strictly prohibited. All rights reserved.
This content is provided for test preparation purposes only and does not imply an endorsement by Mometrix of any particular political, scientific, or religious point of view.

82. A: Expanding opportunities for home ownership was Congress' primary purpose in setting up Freddie Mac. This organization was charged with increasing the availability of money for home loans by pooling mortgages together to create mortgage-backed securities.

83. D: An implied in-fact contract exists when two parties enter into an agreement, such as the purchase of a mattress. The manufacturer is expected to produce a mattress that meets all advertised expectations, and the customer is expected to pay the price the manufacturer charges and to use the product as it is intended to be used.

84. B: If Scott contributes 4% of his $2,000 paycheck to his 401k, this would total $80 per pay period, and the company would have to match 100% of this contribution, which would be $80.

85. B: The biggest factor that leads American companies to manufacture their products in developing countries is lower labor cost. Labor costs in developing countries (countries with a comparatively low GDP per capita) are lower than in the US because unemployment is higher and labor regulations are less stringent.

86. D: FICO scores were developed by the Fair Isaac Corporation to evaluate an individual's credit worthiness and are used by approximately 90 percent of lenders. An individual's score estimates the level of future credit risk and is calculated by information collected by the three major credit reporting agencies (Experian, Equifax, and TransUnion). Important considerations include payment history, amounts owed, length of credit history, and credit mix.

87. C: Accounts receivable are current assets, also known as short-term assets. This term refers to open accounts that are not yet due and those that are already due or overdue but which have not yet been paid. For example, if a landscaping company mows Anna's lawn today and the company sends her a bill for the service that is due one month later, then Anna's account would be in "account receivable" status until the due date.

88. A: When providing feedback, a supervisor should limit the focus to one or two areas of deficiency. Otherwise, it tends to make the employee feel defensive.

89. B: Many entrepreneurial opportunities do not require starting from scratch. Franchises allow a local entity to purchase and operate a local branch under the name of a larger brand, such as Subway or Chick-fil-A. Network marketing is the practice of a business model in which individuals sell to others with the opportunity to benefit as a network is built (e.g., Avon or Amway). Distributorships allow a business to sell its products at the wholesale level (e.g., soda distributors). Dealerships are agencies that have the right to sell goods to the public (e.g., car dealerships).

90. B: A formal business letter is used for correspondence between two companies and also between a company and employees, vendors, media, and other stakeholders. A memorandum (commonly called a memo) is a written message that is typically used within a business office. Email is a method of exchanging messages via computer.

91. D: According to Fayol's Administrative Theory of Management, the five essential functions of management are controlling, commanding, coordinating, planning, and organizing. Henri Fayol, a French engineer, pioneered the Classical Theory of Management. He argued that any individual who performed these five functions could be considered a manager, regardless of his or her actual job title.

92. B: An advantage of protectionism for countries that implement it is that it helps ensure that domestic jobs will be retained in the short term. By implementing protectionist measures that

Copyright © Mometrix Media. You have been licensed one copy of this document for personal use only. Any other reproduction or redistribution is strictly prohibited. All rights reserved.
This content is provided for test preparation purposes only and does not imply an endorsement by Mometrix of any particular political, scientific, or religious point of view.

decrease the competitiveness of otherwise cheaper foreign goods, governments can protect the domestic industries that produce those goods and preserve the jobs of the people who work in them.

93. A: Payless violated the trademark Adidas had on the three stripes. A symbol, such as the stripes, can be trademarked, as well as words, colors, names, and sounds. A copyright is a body of work that is protected from anyone else copying, distributing, reproducing, or even licensing that work. Patents are used for new inventions. Trade secrets can be a little more difficult to prove than the others in this category. A trade secret is confidential information about a company that offers any kind of an advantage over competitors.

94. B: If an employee becomes injured because an employer did not provide equipment in good working order, this would be an example of an OSHA violation by the employer. Employees are allowed to work in hazardous conditions, so long as the employer provides adequate safety protection. Employers have the right to accompany an OSHA compliance officer on an inspection, but they are not required to do so. Employees are not covered by the OSHA act during normal commutes to and from work.

95. D: Collateral is an asset owned by the borrower. With a secured loan, the borrower uses this asset to guarantee the lender that they will repay the loan. If they default on the loan, the bank will sell the asset to recover funds that were not repaid. For example, with a mortgage loan, the property is the collateral.

96. B: When researching a presentation about a national shipping business, the most detailed and comprehensive source of information about the top management of the company and its competitors would most likely be Hoovers.com. LexisNexis.com is also useful for business research, but it is a searchable database of academic and news articles, rather than a database of information about specific companies and industries, like Hoovers. The local newspaper or library would be unlikely to have detailed information about competitors across the country, although it may have specific information about those located in the immediate vicinity. The company's investor-relations website is unlikely to have the type of information publicly available for the person in question.

97. B: The term "peripheral" refers to any piece of computer hardware *aside* from the computer itself and its main processor. The central processing unit is a part of the computer itself, and is therefore not considered a peripheral. Neither a .jpg image nor a web browser are hardware; the former is a file and the latter a software application, and both reside on a disk drive or elsewhere in memory and are not physical objects. A computer keyboard is a piece of hardware that is not a part of the computer itself; it meets the definition of a peripheral.

98. B: The most likely form of business structure would be a sole proprietorship. Joe wants to run his own business and only be accountable to himself. Steve wants to help his brother but does not have any interest in running a bakery. In this situation, Joe would start a sole proprietorship and Steve would be an unofficial investor. Sole prorietorships cannot have investors in the traditional sense, but a sole proprietor may take a loan from an entity or a person. A partnership would exist if Steve wanted to help with the management and operating of the bakery. A joint venture is a newly formed enterprise by two or more separate businesses for a special project or a new business. A limited liability company (LLC) is a partnership that has gone through the steps of filing articles of organization, which separates the owners from personal liability.

Copyright © Mometrix Media. You have been licensed one copy of this document for personal use only. Any other reproduction or redistribution is strictly prohibited. All rights reserved.
This content is provided for test preparation purposes only and does not imply an endorsement by Mometrix of any particular political, scientific, or religious point of view.

99. C: The intersection of total expenses and total sales revenue is called the breakeven point. This is the point where the business is neither making a profit nor experiencing a loss. It is important for business decision-makers because it determines how much the business needs to earn in sales in order to cover their fixed and variable expenses.

100. B: The general ledger provides a record of each financial transaction and shows a running balance of each account after journal entries have been posted. Accounts and balances are then identified to create a trial balance.

Constructed Response

1. Essay question graders commonly look for the following elements in a strong response: strong content knowledge, clear organization, and effective arguments or examples. Language and usage are not usually strictly graded, but they can make a big impact on the clarity of your ideas.

Please use the provided rubric to make sure your response meets these common criteria. Try to have a friend or family member grade your response for you or take a break after writing your response and return to grade it with fresh eyes.

Constructed Response Rubric

Domain	Description
Content Knowledge	• The response directly addresses every part of the prompt. • The response demonstrates independent knowledge of the topic. • The response discusses the topic at an appropriate depth.
Organization	• The response introduces the topic, usually with a thesis statement or by restating the prompt. • The response directly addresses the prompt by providing a clear and concise answer or solution. • The answer or solution is supported by logical arguments or evidence. • The response restates the main idea in the conclusion.
Arguments and Examples	• The response provides a reasonable answer to the prompt. • The answer is supported by strong reasoning or evidence. • The response develops ideas logically and connects ideas to one another. • The reasoning and evidence provided act to support a unified main idea.
Language and Usage	• The response demonstrates effective use of grammar and uses varied sentence structure throughout the response. • The response demonstrates correct use of spelling, punctuation, and capitalization. • The response demonstrates strong and varied use of vocabulary relevant to the topic and appropriate for the intended audience.

Copyright © Mometrix Media. You have been licensed one copy of this document for personal use only. Any other reproduction or redistribution is strictly prohibited. All rights reserved.
This content is provided for test preparation purposes only and does not imply an endorsement by Mometrix of any particular political, scientific, or religious point of view.

MTTC Practice Tests #2 and #3

To take these additional MTTC practice tests, visit our online resources page:
mometrix.com/resources719/mttcbusmmt

Copyright © Mometrix Media. You have been licensed one copy of this document for personal use only. Any other reproduction or redistribution is strictly prohibited. All rights reserved.
This content is provided for test preparation purposes only and does not imply an endorsement by Mometrix of any particular political, scientific, or religious point of view.

How to Overcome Test Anxiety

Just the thought of taking a test is enough to make most people a little nervous. A test is an important event that can have a long-term impact on your future, so it's important to take it seriously and it's natural to feel anxious about performing well. But just because anxiety is normal, that doesn't mean that it's helpful in test taking, or that you should simply accept it as part of your life. Anxiety can have a variety of effects. These effects can be mild, like making you feel slightly nervous, or severe, like blocking your ability to focus or remember even a simple detail.

If you experience test anxiety—whether severe or mild—it's important to know how to beat it. To discover this, first you need to understand what causes test anxiety.

Causes of Test Anxiety

While we often think of anxiety as an uncontrollable emotional state, it can actually be caused by simple, practical things. One of the most common causes of test anxiety is that a person does not feel adequately prepared for their test. This feeling can be the result of many different issues such as poor study habits or lack of organization, but the most common culprit is time management. Starting to study too late, failing to organize your study time to cover all of the material, or being distracted while you study will mean that you're not well prepared for the test. This may lead to cramming the night before, which will cause you to be physically and mentally exhausted for the test. Poor time management also contributes to feelings of stress, fear, and hopelessness as you realize you are not well prepared but don't know what to do about it.

Other times, test anxiety is not related to your preparation for the test but comes from unresolved fear. This may be a past failure on a test, or poor performance on tests in general. It may come from comparing yourself to others who seem to be performing better or from the stress of living up to expectations. Anxiety may be driven by fears of the future—how failure on this test would affect your educational and career goals. These fears are often completely irrational, but they can still negatively impact your test performance.

Elements of Test Anxiety

As mentioned earlier, test anxiety is considered to be an emotional state, but it has physical and mental components as well. Sometimes you may not even realize that you are suffering from test anxiety until you notice the physical symptoms. These can include trembling hands, rapid heartbeat, sweating, nausea, and tense muscles. Extreme anxiety may lead to fainting or vomiting. Obviously, any of these symptoms can have a negative impact on testing. It is important to recognize them as soon as they begin to occur so that you can address the problem before it damages your performance.

The mental components of test anxiety include trouble focusing and inability to remember learned information. During a test, your mind is on high alert, which can help you recall information and stay focused for an extended period of time. However, anxiety interferes with your mind's natural processes, causing you to blank out, even on the questions you know well. The strain of testing during anxiety makes it difficult to stay focused, especially on a test that may take several hours. Extreme anxiety can take a huge mental toll, making it difficult not only to recall test information but even to understand the test questions or pull your thoughts together.

Copyright © Mometrix Media. You have been licensed one copy of this document for personal use only. Any other reproduction or redistribution is strictly prohibited. All rights reserved.
This content is provided for test preparation purposes only and does not imply an endorsement by Mometrix of any particular political, scientific, or religious point of view.

Effects of Test Anxiety

Test anxiety is like a disease—if left untreated, it will get progressively worse. Anxiety leads to poor performance, and this reinforces the feelings of fear and failure, which in turn lead to poor performances on subsequent tests. It can grow from a mild nervousness to a crippling condition. If allowed to progress, test anxiety can have a big impact on your schooling, and consequently on your future.

Test anxiety can spread to other parts of your life. Anxiety on tests can become anxiety in any stressful situation, and blanking on a test can turn into panicking in a job situation. But fortunately, you don't have to let anxiety rule your testing and determine your grades. There are a number of relatively simple steps you can take to move past anxiety and function normally on a test and in the rest of life.

Physical Steps for Beating Test Anxiety

While test anxiety is a serious problem, the good news is that it can be overcome. It doesn't have to control your ability to think and remember information. While it may take time, you can begin taking steps today to beat anxiety.

Just as your first hint that you may be struggling with anxiety comes from the physical symptoms, the first step to treating it is also physical. Rest is crucial for having a clear, strong mind. If you are tired, it is much easier to give in to anxiety. But if you establish good sleep habits, your body and mind will be ready to perform optimally, without the strain of exhaustion. Additionally, sleeping well helps you to retain information better, so you're more likely to recall the answers when you see the test questions.

Getting good sleep means more than going to bed on time. It's important to allow your brain time to relax. Take study breaks from time to time so it doesn't get overworked, and don't study right before bed. Take time to rest your mind before trying to rest your body, or you may find it difficult to fall asleep.

Along with sleep, other aspects of physical health are important in preparing for a test. Good nutrition is vital for good brain function. Sugary foods and drinks may give a burst of energy but this burst is followed by a crash, both physically and emotionally. Instead, fuel your body with protein and vitamin-rich foods.

Also, drink plenty of water. Dehydration can lead to headaches and exhaustion, especially if your brain is already under stress from the rigors of the test. Particularly if your test is a long one, drink water during the breaks. And if possible, take an energy-boosting snack to eat between sections.

Along with sleep and diet, a third important part of physical health is exercise. Maintaining a steady workout schedule is helpful, but even taking 5-minute study breaks to walk can help get your blood pumping faster and clear your head. Exercise also releases endorphins, which contribute to a positive feeling and can help combat test anxiety.

When you nurture your physical health, you are also contributing to your mental health. If your body is healthy, your mind is much more likely to be healthy as well. So take time to rest, nourish your body with healthy food and water, and get moving as much as possible. Taking these physical steps will make you stronger and more able to take the mental steps necessary to overcome test anxiety.

Copyright © Mometrix Media. You have been licensed one copy of this document for personal use only. Any other reproduction or redistribution is strictly prohibited. All rights reserved.
This content is provided for test preparation purposes only and does not imply an endorsement by Mometrix of any particular political, scientific, or religious point of view.

Mental Steps for Beating Test Anxiety

Working on the mental side of test anxiety can be more challenging, but as with the physical side, there are clear steps you can take to overcome it. As mentioned earlier, test anxiety often stems from lack of preparation, so the obvious solution is to prepare for the test. Effective studying may be the most important weapon you have for beating test anxiety, but you can and should employ several other mental tools to combat fear.

First, boost your confidence by reminding yourself of past success—tests or projects that you aced. If you're putting as much effort into preparing for this test as you did for those, there's no reason you should expect to fail here. Work hard to prepare; then trust your preparation.

Second, surround yourself with encouraging people. It can be helpful to find a study group, but be sure that the people you're around will encourage a positive attitude. If you spend time with others who are anxious or cynical, this will only contribute to your own anxiety. Look for others who are motivated to study hard from a desire to succeed, not from a fear of failure.

Third, reward yourself. A test is physically and mentally tiring, even without anxiety, and it can be helpful to have something to look forward to. Plan an activity following the test, regardless of the outcome, such as going to a movie or getting ice cream.

When you are taking the test, if you find yourself beginning to feel anxious, remind yourself that you know the material. Visualize successfully completing the test. Then take a few deep, relaxing breaths and return to it. Work through the questions carefully but with confidence, knowing that you are capable of succeeding.

Developing a healthy mental approach to test taking will also aid in other areas of life. Test anxiety affects more than just the actual test—it can be damaging to your mental health and even contribute to depression. It's important to beat test anxiety before it becomes a problem for more than testing.

Study Strategy

Being prepared for the test is necessary to combat anxiety, but what does being prepared look like? You may study for hours on end and still not feel prepared. What you need is a strategy for test prep. The next few pages outline our recommended steps to help you plan out and conquer the challenge of preparation.

Step 1: Scope Out the Test

Learn everything you can about the format (multiple choice, essay, etc.) and what will be on the test. Gather any study materials, course outlines, or sample exams that may be available. Not only will this help you to prepare, but knowing what to expect can help to alleviate test anxiety.

Step 2: Map Out the Material

Look through the textbook or study guide and make note of how many chapters or sections it has. Then divide these over the time you have. For example, if a book has 15 chapters and you have five days to study, you need to cover three chapters each day. Even better, if you have the time, leave an extra day at the end for overall review after you have gone through the material in depth.

If time is limited, you may need to prioritize the material. Look through it and make note of which sections you think you already have a good grasp on, and which need review. While you are studying, skim quickly through the familiar sections and take more time on the challenging parts.

Copyright © Mometrix Media. You have been licensed one copy of this document for personal use only. Any other reproduction or redistribution is strictly prohibited. All rights reserved.
This content is provided for test preparation purposes only and does not imply an endorsement by Mometrix of any particular political, scientific, or religious point of view.

Write out your plan so you don't get lost as you go. Having a written plan also helps you feel more in control of the study, so anxiety is less likely to arise from feeling overwhelmed at the amount to cover.

Step 3: Gather Your Tools

Decide what study method works best for you. Do you prefer to highlight in the book as you study and then go back over the highlighted portions? Or do you type out notes of the important information? Or is it helpful to make flashcards that you can carry with you? Assemble the pens, index cards, highlighters, post-it notes, and any other materials you may need so you won't be distracted by getting up to find things while you study.

If you're having a hard time retaining the information or organizing your notes, experiment with different methods. For example, try color-coding by subject with colored pens, highlighters, or post-it notes. If you learn better by hearing, try recording yourself reading your notes so you can listen while in the car, working out, or simply sitting at your desk. Ask a friend to quiz you from your flashcards, or try teaching someone the material to solidify it in your mind.

Step 4: Create Your Environment

It's important to avoid distractions while you study. This includes both the obvious distractions like visitors and the subtle distractions like an uncomfortable chair (or a too-comfortable couch that makes you want to fall asleep). Set up the best study environment possible: good lighting and a comfortable work area. If background music helps you focus, you may want to turn it on, but otherwise keep the room quiet. If you are using a computer to take notes, be sure you don't have any other windows open, especially applications like social media, games, or anything else that could distract you. Silence your phone and turn off notifications. Be sure to keep water close by so you stay hydrated while you study (but avoid unhealthy drinks and snacks).

Also, take into account the best time of day to study. Are you freshest first thing in the morning? Try to set aside some time then to work through the material. Is your mind clearer in the afternoon or evening? Schedule your study session then. Another method is to study at the same time of day that you will take the test, so that your brain gets used to working on the material at that time and will be ready to focus at test time.

Step 5: Study!

Once you have done all the study preparation, it's time to settle into the actual studying. Sit down, take a few moments to settle your mind so you can focus, and begin to follow your study plan. Don't give in to distractions or let yourself procrastinate. This is your time to prepare so you'll be ready to fearlessly approach the test. Make the most of the time and stay focused.

Of course, you don't want to burn out. If you study too long you may find that you're not retaining the information very well. Take regular study breaks. For example, taking five minutes out of every hour to walk briskly, breathing deeply and swinging your arms, can help your mind stay fresh.

As you get to the end of each chapter or section, it's a good idea to do a quick review. Remind yourself of what you learned and work on any difficult parts. When you feel that you've mastered the material, move on to the next part. At the end of your study session, briefly skim through your notes again.

But while review is helpful, cramming last minute is NOT. If at all possible, work ahead so that you won't need to fit all your study into the last day. Cramming overloads your brain with more information than it can process and retain, and your tired mind may struggle to recall even

Copyright © Mometrix Media. You have been licensed one copy of this document for personal use only. Any other reproduction or redistribution is strictly prohibited. All rights reserved.
This content is provided for test preparation purposes only and does not imply an endorsement by Mometrix of any particular political, scientific, or religious point of view.

previously learned information when it is overwhelmed with last-minute study. Also, the urgent nature of cramming and the stress placed on your brain contribute to anxiety. You'll be more likely to go to the test feeling unprepared and having trouble thinking clearly.

So don't cram, and don't stay up late before the test, even just to review your notes at a leisurely pace. Your brain needs rest more than it needs to go over the information again. In fact, plan to finish your studies by noon or early afternoon the day before the test. Give your brain the rest of the day to relax or focus on other things, and get a good night's sleep. Then you will be fresh for the test and better able to recall what you've studied.

Step 6: Take a Practice Test

Many courses offer sample tests, either online or in the study materials. This is an excellent resource to check whether you have mastered the material, as well as to prepare for the test format and environment.

Check the test format ahead of time: the number of questions, the type (multiple choice, free response, etc.), and the time limit. Then create a plan for working through them. For example, if you have 30 minutes to take a 60-question test, your limit is 30 seconds per question. Spend less time on the questions you know well so that you can take more time on the difficult ones.

If you have time to take several practice tests, take the first one open book, with no time limit. Work through the questions at your own pace and make sure you fully understand them. Gradually work up to taking a test under test conditions: sit at a desk with all study materials put away and set a timer. Pace yourself to make sure you finish the test with time to spare and go back to check your answers if you have time.

After each test, check your answers. On the questions you missed, be sure you understand why you missed them. Did you misread the question (tests can use tricky wording)? Did you forget the information? Or was it something you hadn't learned? Go back and study any shaky areas that the practice tests reveal.

Taking these tests not only helps with your grade, but also aids in combating test anxiety. If you're already used to the test conditions, you're less likely to worry about it, and working through tests until you're scoring well gives you a confidence boost. Go through the practice tests until you feel comfortable, and then you can go into the test knowing that you're ready for it.

Test Tips

On test day, you should be confident, knowing that you've prepared well and are ready to answer the questions. But aside from preparation, there are several test day strategies you can employ to maximize your performance.

First, as stated before, get a good night's sleep the night before the test (and for several nights before that, if possible). Go into the test with a fresh, alert mind rather than staying up late to study.

Try not to change too much about your normal routine on the day of the test. It's important to eat a nutritious breakfast, but if you normally don't eat breakfast at all, consider eating just a protein bar. If you're a coffee drinker, go ahead and have your normal coffee. Just make sure you time it so that the caffeine doesn't wear off right in the middle of your test. Avoid sugary beverages, and drink enough water to stay hydrated but not so much that you need a restroom break 10 minutes into the

Copyright © Mometrix Media. You have been licensed one copy of this document for personal use only. Any other reproduction or redistribution is strictly prohibited. All rights reserved.
This content is provided for test preparation purposes only and does not imply an endorsement by Mometrix of any particular political, scientific, or religious point of view.

test. If your test isn't first thing in the morning, consider going for a walk or doing a light workout before the test to get your blood flowing.

Allow yourself enough time to get ready, and leave for the test with plenty of time to spare so you won't have the anxiety of scrambling to arrive in time. Another reason to be early is to select a good seat. It's helpful to sit away from doors and windows, which can be distracting. Find a good seat, get out your supplies, and settle your mind before the test begins.

When the test begins, start by going over the instructions carefully, even if you already know what to expect. Make sure you avoid any careless mistakes by following the directions.

Then begin working through the questions, pacing yourself as you've practiced. If you're not sure on an answer, don't spend too much time on it, and don't let it shake your confidence. Either skip it and come back later, or eliminate as many wrong answers as possible and guess among the remaining ones. Don't dwell on these questions as you continue—put them out of your mind and focus on what lies ahead.

Be sure to read all of the answer choices, even if you're sure the first one is the right answer. Sometimes you'll find a better one if you keep reading. But don't second-guess yourself if you do immediately know the answer. Your gut instinct is usually right. Don't let test anxiety rob you of the information you know.

If you have time at the end of the test (and if the test format allows), go back and review your answers. Be cautious about changing any, since your first instinct tends to be correct, but make sure you didn't misread any of the questions or accidentally mark the wrong answer choice. Look over any you skipped and make an educated guess.

At the end, leave the test feeling confident. You've done your best, so don't waste time worrying about your performance or wishing you could change anything. Instead, celebrate the successful completion of this test. And finally, use this test to learn how to deal with anxiety even better next time.

Review Video: Test Anxiety
Visit mometrix.com/academy and enter code: 100340

Important Qualification

Not all anxiety is created equal. If your test anxiety is causing major issues in your life beyond the classroom or testing center, or if you are experiencing troubling physical symptoms related to your anxiety, it may be a sign of a serious physiological or psychological condition. If this sounds like your situation, we strongly encourage you to seek professional help.

Copyright © Mometrix Media. You have been licensed one copy of this document for personal use only. Any other reproduction or redistribution is strictly prohibited. All rights reserved.
This content is provided for test preparation purposes only and does not imply an endorsement by Mometrix of any particular political, scientific, or religious point of view.

Online Resources

Due to our efforts to try to keep this book to a manageable length, we've created a link that will give you access to all of your online resources:

mometrix.com/resources719/mttcbusmmt

It's Your Moment, Let's Celebrate It!

Share your story @mometrixtestpreparation

Copyright © Mometrix Media. You have been licensed one copy of this document for personal use only. Any other reproduction or redistribution is strictly prohibited. All rights reserved.
This content is provided for test preparation purposes only and does not imply an endorsement by Mometrix of any particular political, scientific, or religious point of view.